Ex Auditu

An International Journal of
Theological Interpretation of Scripture

Ex Auditu is published annually by Pickwick Publications, 4137 Timberlane Drive, Allison Park, Pennsylvania, 15101-2932, U.S.A.

Subscriptions:
Individuals:
U.S.A. - $15.00
Canada - $12.00 (in U.S. Funds)
All other countries - $15.00 (in U. S. Funds)
Students - $10.00

Institutions:
U.S.A. - $25.00
Canada - $20.00 (in U.S. Funds)
All other countries - $25.00 (in U. S. Funds)

Indexed in Religion Index One: Periodicals, published by the American Theological Library Association, Chicago, Illinois, available oneline in the ATLA Religion Database through BRS Information Technologies (Latham, New York); DIALOG Information Services (Palo Alto, California); Internationale Zeitschriftenschau für Bibelwissenschaft und Grenzgebeite; Religion and Theological Abstracts.

Please address all subscription correspondence and change of address information to Pickwick Publications.

ISSN 08883-0053

EX AUDITU

An International Journal of Theological Interpretation of Scripture

THE EDITORIAL CONSULTANTS represent various disciplines and denominations. Theological Interpretation of Scripture is a task to be taken seriously by scholars who are committed to the Christian faith and tradition. However, as one editorial consultant stated it: "let people gradually get used to the idea that a sane hermeneutics is both oriented in advance toward agreement/consent and is simultaneously exigent, discriminating, critical."

ISSN 08883-0053

EX AUDITU

Volume IV 1988

CONTENTS

Introduction

This year's theme, "The Church and Israel: Romans 9-11," looks at the one extended, explicit discussion in the New Testament of the socially and theologically complex relationship of the Church and Israel. The task is ambitious. Simply finding some consensus on Paul's thought in these three chapters might appear fortuitous, when their place within Romans itself, not to mention their place in Paul's thought, is under heavy dispute today. Indeed the very wording of the theme begins with certain aasumptions, not least being the meanings of "Church" and "Israel."

On the one hand, Paul never uses the word "church" in Romans 9-11. Rather he refers to Israel's counterpart, apparently the majority of his readers in Rome (cf. 11:13), as "Gentiles." Yet he does not mean Gentiles in general. He refers more specifically to the Gentiles who have heard and accepted the preaching about Christ, who believe that God raised him from the dead, and who have confessed Jesus to be Lord (Rom 10:9, 17). Therefore, one could accurately refer to the Gentiles of Romans 9-11 as non-Jewish "Christians."

On the other hand, Paul does use "Israel" on several occasions in these chapters. Yet there is "Israel" and there is "Israel" ("Not all who descend from Israel belong to Israel," 9:6). He distinguishes between "children of the flesh" and "children of the promise" (9:8), suggesting a distinction between an ethnic and a spiritual Israel, a "remnant" (11:5-6), with the latter physically related to the former (cf. "I myself am an Israelite, a descendant of Abraham, " 11:1) but sharing the faith of the "Gentiles" (cf. 11:5-6).

Once one clarifies the terminology, a less than certain achievement, one is still left with the fundamental question of why Paul raises the issue of "Israel's" response or lack of response to his message at the heart of his Letter to the Romans. This question reaches to the very heart of contemporary Pauline studies about his view of the law, justification by faith, the nature of his call/conversion, in short, his view of the gospel.

Our theme is further complicated by contemporary concerns. Apart from the "ecclesiological" questions of the Church and Israel, old and new covenant, continuity and discontinuity, the "soteriological" questions emerge regarding the nature and means of salvation. What does Paul's concluding statement that "all Israel will be *saved*" really mean? To this concern belongs the basic "missiological" issue of defining and sharing the Christian "gospel" and whether or not Romans 9-11 encourages even a dialogue with Israel. The "sociological" reality of a Church that has lost credibility by its use of "theological" grounds for discriminating against and even seeking to destroy a people raises its ugly head. Certainly, the Jewish holocoast stands as Exhibit A, but even a cursory review of church as well as secular history will show that it is but one, heinous to be sure, of many such exhibits.

Finally, one confronts the difficulty of defining "Israel" today. For some it refers ethnically to a people. For some it is a political state with its citizens. For some it refers to a religious group. Even within the state of Israel one finds competing views about who is a Jew today. Nevertheless, despite the lack of precise definition of "Israel," the many dialogues between Christians and Jews, liberal and conservative on each side, indicate that the theme, "The Church and Israel," remains a prime concern.

The articles that follow focus both on understanding Paul's thought in Romans 9-11 and on the relevance of his thought for the Church today. The concern of EX AUDITU from the outset has been to combine historical and theological exegesis through the integration of the various theological disciplines with a view to the Church today. What follows is a collection of hermeneutical, exegetical, historical, theological and homiletical reflections on Romans 9-11.

The opening article by Ben Meyer sets Paul's argument within its historical and theological framework ("election-historical") and challenges the current distorting attempts to read Paul apart from that framework. Markus Barth, in a reprint of chapter two from his book, **The People of God** (Sheffield: JSOT Press, 1983) discusses the Church and Israel in terms of who are the "people of God" and finds a Christological center to be the key to Paul's thought. Bruce Chilton then looks more closely at how Paul's rhetorical argument in Romans 9-11 within a "protreptic letter" takes its complex shape by developing from and making use of the Hebrew Scriptures, an interaction that summons us no less to a dialogue with Judaism. Then Scott Hafemann walks us through Paul's intricate argument for the salvation of Israel in Romans 9-11 and the integrity of God's word against the backdrop of Krister Stendahl's work that has proven so influential in both a restructuring of Pauline thought and in Jewish/Christian dialogue.

I. John Hesselink adds a historical note by examining Calvin's work, especially his commentary fraught with the familiar tensions of this passage. Then Stephen R. Haynes examines the contemporary historical (e.g. K. Stendahl) and theological (e.g. K. Barth) reading of Romans 9-11 in the light of the new attempts to "recover the real Paul" and the necessity of wedding theology and exegesis is no less critical an issue than the current question of the Church and Israel. H. Martin Rumscheidt explores the thought of Georg Eichholz, a German New Testament scholar and theologian relatively unknown in the States, whose passion for the Church was not only seen in his role as a member and leader in the Confessing Church but in his writings that combined his dual theological and exegetical appointment at Wuppertal School of Theology. His work reflects what has come to be known at times as "Jewish holocaust exegesis," i.e., exegesis informed by the tragedy of the Jewish holocaust.

Finally, two essays focus on the homiletical use of Romans 9-11. Donald G. Miller raises the question of whether or not one can preach from these chapters, since his survey through the centuries demonstrates how rare it is to find sermons that deal with the issue of these chapters. He concludes his survey by raising anew the implications not only of Paul's hope for Israel but of a mission to Jews in an age concerned with anything that might smack of anti-Judaism. David G. Buttrick concludes the series with a provocative essay on developing a sermon from Romans 9-11 in a cultural setting where the topic of the Church and Israel as well as Romans 9-11 have been selectively handled at the expense of the social and theological issues implicit in each.

Papers from the Frederick Neumann Symposium on Theological Interpretation of Scripture hosted by Princeton Theological Seminary have provided the theme and content of EX AUDITU for the past two years with the Reverend Thomas W. Gillespie, President of Princeton Theological Seminary, as editor. This year's theme, "The

Church and Israel, Romans 9-11" was suggested by our publisher and Peter Stuhlmacher. The theme for the coming year has emerged from a motif found in this year's topic, "all Israel will be saved" (Rom 11:26). What does it mean "to be saved?" Facets of the theme--such as what is the meaning of "eternal life" in the New Testament? and what is the meaning of the resurrection of Christ?--will be handled from the various perspectives of Old and New Testament studies, church history, systematics and practical theology.

The Editorial Board is also pleased to announce that North Park Theological Seminary of Chicago, Illinois, will host the future Symposiums beginning in the Fall of 1990 (October 12-15, 1990), which will serve as the forum for future themes.

We of the Editorial Board are most grateful to Puzant and Angèle Gulesserian of San Jose, California, for their most generous financial support for the publication of this issue of EX AUDITU. Angèle Gulesserian is the sister of Dikran Y. Hadidian of Pickwick Publications.

Easter, 1989

Robert A. Guelich
Editor

ELECTION-HISTORICAL THINKING IN ROMANS 9-11, AND OURSELVES

BEN F. MEYER

From the patristic era, East and West, to the nineteenth century, the classical exegesis of Romans 9-11 and especially of Romans 9 failed to find the real question shaping the Pauline text. That real question asked how finally to make religious sense of Israel's refusal to enter into messianic salvation. Had the word of God--the word promising Israel salvation--failed?

Paul rejected the notion that the word of God had failed. Romans 9 says: no, for the word of God was addressed not to the physical but to the election-historical children of Abraham. Romans 10 says: no, it was Israel that failed, namely by preferring a righteousness of its own devising to "the righteousness of God." Romans 11 says: no, for he saved a remnant; moreover, just as God turned the refusal of Israel into the salvation of the Gentiles, so he will turn the salvation of the "full number" of Gentiles into the salvation of "all Israel" (Rom 11:25-26).

Classical exegesis took the key question to be: why are some people saved and others damned? That the original Pauline point of a text might be missed is understandable, but how did it happen that readers installed themselves in this misconstrual, mounting and sustaining for centuries a dedicated exploration of issues that Paul himself had not raised? Whatever the worth of the inquiry into the predestination of the individual to glory, that question was not Paul's question and none of the answers given to it over more than a thousand years can be attributed to Paul. (Indeed, many if not most of the answers, from the Greek Church Fathers to the Reformers, would have to be adjudged incompatible with Paul's own theology.)

It is clear that the Pauline text was in several respects opaque to the gentile Church. Without elaboration or insistence Paul had supposed a certain set of questions vital to the earliest Christian thinking, such as the primary question in these chapters: how to make coherent sense of Israel's unbelief in Jesus? Paul furthermore had proceeded to deal with his questions and sub-questions in a way intelligible, no doubt, in his own time and milieu, but profoundly perplexing in a new time and new milieu. Paul's style included a way of drawing on biblical resources and notably on the biblical writers' election-historical schemes of thought. In Paul questions and answers alike belonged to the horizons and perspectives--to the "code"--of biblical thoughtforms. But among gentile Christians a generation or two later, there was no longer the sheer wonder that even Gentiles could be saved. Having lost interest in Israel as the primary rightful heir to messianic salvation, and hence incurious respecting the intricate and remote resources that Paul had deployed in his passionate pondering of the destiny of Israel, gentile Christians could no longer lock easily onto Paul's level and line of discourse. As the burden of his meditation became progressively foreign to them, they had to find a different meaning in the text. It was not until the latter-nineteenth century that a philologically instructed historical exegesis in Germany finally broke through the constraint of classical theology and recovered the structural lines of the thought of the historical Paul.

We are now aware that Paul was not bent on a theology of the predestination of the individual to glory. This, however, does not mean that we have managed to measure up to the Pauline text. The text, it seems, continues to be alien to us. It is little preached. The Church at large seems to have relegated these chapters to "time-conditioned material," that is, what Austin Farrar once called "period trash."[1] It is not that concern for Israel or for Jewish-Christian relations is of little interest among interpreters and thinkers today. On the contrary, this concern has never been more intense. But so far from promoting a sober and solid recovery of Paul's own thinking, it has led to the most well-intentioned but extraordinarily misleading efforts of inter-faith ecumenism.[2] Whether disposed of as time-conditioned or spectacularly misconstrued, chapters nine to eleven of the Letter to the Romans have attested a striking disparity between Paul's world and ours. Is this all our fault? Or can the fault be said to lie on both sides?

In Romans 9-11 Paul offers a "totalizing" view of history. It is not identical with earlier biblical views, but it has more in common with them than with the totalizing views of history that have arisen among us over the past two hundred years. Paul knew that the world was very old, but from our vantage point his time-scale was minuscule. He had little notion of how wide the world was. He did not know that there had existed in his time civilizations and cultures older and in some respects richer than his own. He did not expect the world to last much, if at all, beyond his lifetime. His totalizing view of history bears the mark of these limits. Concentrated on a narrow apocalyptic line, it leaves out of consideration vast fields of historical causation, their complexities and discontinuities. In the end it is up to the biblical theologian to say why Paul's thought ought not to be dismissed as simplistic and reductionist. But first there should be some effort to retrieve and understand the mode of thought that permeates these pages of the Letter.

We may begin abruptly by asking: what is election? In biblical tradition it is divine love sovereignly choosing its instruments for the realization of a divine plan. Out of the human mass, this love chooses the patriarchs and the people (Josh 24:3-13) to be in some special sense God's own (Exod 19:5-6). In the "primary history" from Genesis to 2 Kings, election of individuals--Abraham, Isaac, Jacob and his sons, Moses and Aaron, David and Solomon--are elements or moments in a plan of divine blessings on Israel and the world. The builders of "a city and a tower with its top in heaven" (Gen 11:4a) were a classic paradigm of the autonomous world, blindly misconstruing its own projects and arriving at results diametrically opposed to its intentions (Gen 11:4b, 8).

What were the biblical writers doing in interpreting persons, places, and events in terms of election? At bottom, they were affirming God's lordship over the course of history. This accords with what Gregory Dix called Syriac (=biblical) culture's conception of the "living God."[3] In Greece the intelligible sphere of the divine (*to theon)* was part of the ordered whole of reality. The bright Olympians had their place in the scheme of things. Beyond this sphere, however, stood a power that transcended the gods. This power, impersonal, implacable, and oppressive, was fate. Dix interpreted fate as the Greek conception of God "in himself."

Among the Hebrews, on the other hand, reality was not a presupposed given. It was, first, the living God; second, the product of God's free act of creation. The creature was without independent claims. That the creator should be reduced in status to a privileged part in an eternal whole was unthinkable. Without the living God, creation would lapse into nothingness. The reverse side of this utter dependence, however, was the minute reliability of God's loving care: "Are not sparrows sold two for a penny? And yet not one of them can fall to the ground against the Father's will (Matt 10:29-Luke 12:6).

The traits of the living God's lordship over events correlate with this conception of God as at once independent of creation and freely committed to creation. The first commandment affirmed the status of YHWH: Israel would worship him alone (Exod 20:3; Deut 5:7). The (original) second commandment (cf. Exod 20:4; Deut 5:8a) cut off all access to the manipulation of YHWH by means of a graven image of him. Not only the laws, but the stories and celebrations, the meditations and entreaties of Israel reflect the twofoldness of God's sovereign lordship--free, unmanipulable, beyond all bargaining or blackmail--and God's presence, commitment, and compassion. God could be counted on (*ʾĕmet; ʾĕmûnâ*). God was ready to pour out on Israel his covenant-love (*ḥesed*) and spontaneous graciousness (also *ḥesed*). The one thing that might loosen God's bond with Israel was Israel's own sin, but God's compassion (*raḥămîm*) more than met this problem, for it took special account of the sinners overwhelmed by their sins (Pss 25:6-7; 51:3; 79:7-8; cf. Ps 40:11-12).

The conception of God yielded by biblical tradition focused on both facets of YHWH's love: no human effort could secure it; sovereignly bestowed, however, it could be absolutely relied upon. Each of these sides qualified the other. YHWH was "our God" (*ʾĕlōhênû*), but it was beyond us to force God's hand. We could only cry to God. If we did, God's "benefits" were forgiveness, healing, redemption from the pit, loving-kindness (*hesed*), tender mercy (*raḥămîm*) (Ps 103:2-4). In the dynamic tension of these traits the factor of divine commitment somehow won out in the end over the factor of divine freedom. Still, the freedom factor made itself known in YHWH's "way" (*derek*). It was an ever-surprising way, flawless, facile, uncanny. Without being capricious, God's "way" constantly upset expectations and calculations. Those who played God's game were left dazzled, defeated winners.

> *My thoughts are not your thoughts*
> *neither are your ways my ways, says YHWH.*
> *For as the heavens are higher than the earth*
> *so are my ways higher than your ways*
> *and my thoughts than your thoughts* (*Isa 55:8*).

Hence the long and varied tradition of reversals that marked biblical narrative from the sagas of Abraham to the Gospel stories of Jesus.YHWH, the promiser himself, repeatedly put at risk his promise to Abraham, but the risks were run without loss. Through a series of divine shifts and dodges, YHWH schooled Abraham in his "way." Again and again the unlikely and implausible found realization. Such was YHWH's good pleasure. Abraham's son and heir (Ishmael) lost out, for Sarah, Abraham's sterile wife, conceived and gave birth. This unlikely realization of a promise was immediately put in jeopardy, and with it YHWH's promises of a people was immediately put in jeopardy, and with it YHWH's promises of a people and of land. No matter; nothing blocked his will. The pattern continued as elective love regularly set aside the regular order of things. Esau, Isaac's first-born, lost primogeniture (*bĕkōrâ*) and blessing (*bĕrākâ*) to Jacob. Jacob lost Joseph. But no; Joseph saved his father Jacob and all his brothers in Egypt. . . .

Paul drew on exactly these paradigmatic stories from Genesis to make his point on God's sovereignly free election (Rom 9:7-13). The pattern continued through the whole of biblical history, notably featured in the Exodus (Exodus 1-18), in the rise of David (1 Samuel 16-2 Samuel 8), and in Solomon's succession to David's throne (2 Sam 6-1 Kings 2). As the prophets turned the popular notion of the day of YHWH inside out, they also undercut false assurance presumptuously founded on election. When Hosea's daughter was born, YHWH ordered: "Call her name Lo-ruhamah" (= "Not-pitied"). As for the son that followed, "Call his name Lo-ammi" (= "Not my people").

Election could be lost. It was neither democtratic nor inalienable. What counted was the success of the divine plan. Nevertheless, this plan would reveal itself as divine love for all.

Such was the legacy on which Paul drew: the traditional conception of God as simultaneously transcendent and committed, rebelled against and infinitely resourceful. The nexus between the grand exposition of Romans 1-8 and the treatment of Israel in Romans 9-11 lay in the theme of " the righteousness of God." Research in the past generation (Stanislas Lyonnet,[4] Ernst Käsemann, [5] and others[6]) has allowed us better to understand and appreciate the righteousness of God as God's power to save and will to save in accord with God's commitment to creation and, more particularly, to God's chosen ones, Abraham, Isaac, and Jacob and their heirs. The righteousness of God (Rom 1:17), like the truthfulness of God (Rom 3:7), was at once a quality and an act, the quality of God's being himself righteous (Rom 3:5, 26b) and the act of rectifying, making right, making righteous (Rom 3:26c, 30; 4:5 [cf 4:25]; 8:30, 33). God showed his righteousnness by his climactic and definitive saving act in the death (Rom 3:25; 4:25; 5:8-10a; 6:3; 8:3) and resurrection (Rom 4:25; 5:10b; 6:4; 8:3, 10, 11) of his Son.

The argument of Romans 9 and 10 might seem faultless, but it was incomplete. True, the word of God to Israel had not failed , for God's word had not envisaged merely physical descendants of Abraham (Romans 9); besides, failure was all on Israel's side (Romans 10). This vindicated the state of affairs in the present, but it did not meet the requisite of the righteousness of God. Hence Romans 11, where, first, there is a reprise of the theme of the remnant. As in biblical tradition, the remnant theme included the motif of the restored people. "Remnant" and "nation" were paralled in Micah 4:7, under the aegis of the reign of God:

> *I will make of the lame a remnant*
> *and of the outcast a strong nation,*
> *and YHWH shall reign over them on Mount Zion*
> *from thenceforth and forever.*

The saved remnant would be made up of forgiven sinners (Micah 7:18-19), whose restoration accorded with God's promise to the patriarchs (Micah 7:20). The survivors would "increase and multiply" (Jer 23:3).

> *The remnant of the house of Judah*
> *shall again strike root downward*
> *and bear fruit upward* (Isa 37:31).

Hence Israel's destiny according to the Isaian apocalypse: a rich vine covering the world.

> *In days to come Jacob shall take root;*
> *Israel shall sprout and blossom*
> *covering all the world with fruit* (Isa 27:6).

Resonant with these overtones, the remnant theme leads Paul to contemplate a great reversal (Rom 11:11): out of Israel's transgression (refusal of faith) has come salvation for the Gentiles (see Rom 9:22-23). This reversal is followed by a *qal wāhōmer* argument (Rom 11:12): if their diminished number (*hēttēma*) has meant wealth for the Gentiles, what will their full number (*plēroma*) mean?

Now, having barely evoked the salvation of the "full number" of Israel, Paul breaks off to address the Gentiles among the Christians of Rome. Their own "full number" (Rom 11:25) would be the divinely appointed harvest of the world mission, but the temptation to presumption on the part of gentile Christians called for a pregnant warning. If Israel could turn away from the call of God as in fact it had, how much more easily could these newly saved Gentiles do the same?

This said, Paul returns to the theme of the full number of Israel, disclosing an eschatological secret (*musterion*): once the Gentiles in "full number" have "come in," then--at the parousia--God will save "all Israel" (Rom 11:26):

> *The Deliverer will come from Zion,*
> *he will banish ungodliness from Jacob;*
> *and this will be my covenant with them*
> *when I take away their sins.*

The call of God and the blessings of God are irrevocable (Rom 11:29). More: when the infinitely resourceful Lord of history sends his exalted Son to bring time and history to completion, he will win the long-withheld assent of Israel: "Blessed is he who comes in the name of the Lord."

Such is Paul's prophetic vindication of the righteousness of God in the fulness of its meaning and in full scope of its reference. Through most of OT literature "election" bore on God's choice of persons or places or institutions to realize historical tasks in the service of his plan of salvation. In late OT texts and in the NT the horizons of "election" comprehended eternity under rubrics like "the age to come." Paul's treatment of Israel and the Gentiles (Romans 9-11) was concentrated, laser-like, on the election-historical plan of God. He made no effort to deal with history in any other terms. This, surely, is the reason why we may not dismiss his text as simplistic and reductionist. His rudimentary suppositions about the historical past are irrellevant to the thrust of his affirmations. His suppositions about the imminent consummation merely attest the disparity between the symbolic terms of prophecy and the real terms of its realization.[7] Whereas we can and ought to affirm in faith the truth of this prophecy, we cannot specify in advance the "how" of its realization at the parousia, nor for that matter any of the particularities of the referent of "parousia."

It is not these limits, however, that disclose the real reason for our misunderstanding or neglect of Romans 9-11. Gregory Dix put his finger on the real reason. If we have lost our hold on election-historical thinking, it is because we have lost our hold on the biblical understanding of the living God.

We have reverted to the Greeks. The dull Greek dread of the far side of the divine, an "ultimate" that was impersonal, implacable, and oppressive, has resurfaced in our world, diminishing and poisoning the Western imagination. We are not alone, says science fiction, so long as there are others--as good as us or maybe even better--somewhere out in space. Otherwise, it is implied, we are indeed alone. In this version the ultimate is neither benevolent nor malevolent, just empty. The near side of the Greek conception of the divine, that of the Olympians, has become one more affirmation of ourselves and our choices. Whether this near side of the divine is harmful or harmless is unsettled. Hitler's *der Allmächtige* was not harmless. The "living doll" affirmed by the born-again actress was harmless. Karl Barth's word for this modern god was No-God.[8] No-God did not rectify and redeem his creation. He was rather "the complete affirmation of the course of the world. . . as it is."[9]

The intense unhappiness and immense distractedness of our time derive from a Western reversion to being Greeks in part but not all of our thinking, particularly in our thinking about the cosmos.

> But Western man is still haunted in that deeper part of his thinking which concerns himself and the meaning of his own life by. . . (1 John 5:19): "We *know* that we are of God"--the Syriac God, with all its consequence for man. Western man is trying confusedly to save many of these consequences in his own soul, while thinking like a Greek, and is facing spiritual schizophrenia in the process.[10]

It would be a dreadful mistake stoically to accept this schizophrenia as our destined lot. But we cannot heal it merely by the cultivation of technically excellent NT interpretation. Without deep cultural changes neither we nor even perhaps the interpreter himself will be quite up to a full encounter with the interpreted text. Exegetical excellence will perforce remain a sterile and isolate achievement.

But for the schizophrenia that Dix has diagnosed there is a promising therapy. It consists in the discovery that, as the question of God is implicit in all our questioning, so the love of God is the basic fulfillment of all our intending.[11] The actualization of this love is religious conversion and it sows the seeds of moral and intellectual conversion. The human subject in whom these conversions take place is ready to profit from technically excellent NT interpretation, to transpose it into encounter with the living God and with the election history that attests God's lordship and love.

NOTES

1. Austin Farrer, **Finite and Infinite** (Westminster: Dacre Press, 1943; reprinted 1964) ix.

2. An example: Krister Stendahl, "Paul Among Jews and Gentiles," in **Paul Among Jews and Gentiles and Other Essays** (Philadelphia: Fortress Press, 1976) 1-77.

3. Gregory Dix, **Jew and Greek** (Westminster: Dacre Press, 1953) 9-14.

4. Stanislas Lyonnet, "Pauline Soteriology," in **Introduction to the New Testament**, ed. A. Robert and A. Feullet (New York/Tournai: Desclee, 1965) 820-865, at 832-836.

5. Ernst Käsemann, "'The righteousness of God' in Paul," in **New Testament Questions of Today** (London: SCM Press, 1969) 242-249.

6. An excellent, more recent treatment: Peter Stuhlmacher, "The Apostle Paul's View of Righteousness," in **Reconciliation, Law, and Righteousness** (Philadelphia: Fortress Press, 1986) 68-93, at 77-82.

7. B. F. Meyer, **The Aims of Jesus** (London: SCM Press, 1979) 242-249.

8. Karl Barlth, **The Epistle to the Romans** (Oxford: Oxford University Press, 1922; reprinted 1976) 40.

9. Barth, ibid.

10. Dix, **Jew and Greek,** 14.

11. Bernard Lonergan, **Method in Theology** (London: Darton, Longman & Todd, 1972) 101-105.

One God, One Christ, One People*

Markus Barth

The core of the Pauline arguments about the essence and identity of God's people is found in Romans 9-11 and Ephesians 2. Although Romans 2-4, Galatians 3-5, 2 Corinthians 3, and Philippians 3 also make important contributions to our topic, Protestant theologians tend to concentrate their attention on Romans 9-11 when they discuss the Israel/Church relationship. Although the whole of Ephesians 2, and 2:11-22; 3:6 in particular, are devoted to the same theme, the witness of Ephesians is pushed into the background, in part because this Letter has been declared spurious and "early catholic." Roman Catholic research and documents, however, attribute to Ephesians at least the same importance as to Romans. In turn, the churches in the Middle East and in Russia react bitterly against both Western churches, for they discover in them too much eagerness to speak in favour of Jews and of the state of Israel. All Western theology has been accused of being "geo-political theology."[1] What does Paul actually teach?

We begin with four observations concerning the whole of Roman 9-11; we continue with an outline of the structure and the highlights of these three chapters; and we conclude with a brief glance at some other Pauline texts. A detailed and complete interpretation cannot be presented here; in fact, not even all main questions and topics emerging in Romans 9-11 and in the other texts mentioned can be discussed.[2] Instead, we search for an answer to one question only: What do these chapters say about the people of God?

I. TRAJECTORIES THROUGH ROMANS 9-11

1. The Faithfulness of God

The whole passage Romans 9-11 intends to glorify the faithfulness of God. The summation of the three chapters is indicated as early as Rom 3:3: the unfaithfulness, *viz.* the unbelief, of "some" (Israelites) does not cancel out the faithfulness of God toward this people. God's faithfulness is unilateral, free, sovereign, and it calls for faith and attestation. According to biblical reasoning, the free and irresistible will of God does not exclude human decision; on the contrary, it destines and equips the chosen people for responsible action. God's election and call create and sustain, endure and judge, pardon and build a community which invokes and proclaims in one spirit the name of the one God.

Before Gentiles were granted participation in this worship, the "Israelites" alone were made God's sons; only among them did the *shekinah* dwell; since the time of Abraham, it was with them that the covenants were made, to them the law, worship, and the promises were entrusted; theirs are the partriarchs, and the descent of Christ is from them (Rom 9:4-5). These declarations are not restricted to events of the past. God's word, once spoken, does not crumble under the impact of time, or of rebellion (3:2-3; 9:6); God has not rejected Israel (11:1-2); the whole of Israel will be saved (11:26a); the godlessness will be removed from Jacob, their sins will be forgiven (11:26b-27); the members of this people remain "God's beloved" for the sake of the elected patriarchs, because God revokes neither his gracious gifts nor his calling (11:28-29).

What is the Apostles's reason for impressing these points upon the Roman congregation whose members were mainly gentile Christians? The answer must be: Only because God is faithful to Israel do the gentile Christians have good reason to rely on him. Or, to say the same thing in negative terms: unless God proves faithful to the people he has chosen a long time ago, gentile Christians now implanted into the same people have no reason to believe that their election by God is free from arbitrariness and capricious changes. A God who would be unreliable in his relation to Israel could not be trusted to be faithful to any nation or person. Therefore, God's mercy over the whole of Israel is the basis and essence of the faith which confesses that there is nothing in the heights or depths which can separate those called by the divine love manifested in the Messiah (cf. Rom 8:35-39).

2. The Loyalty of the Apostle

The references made in Romans 9-11 to *God's* faithfulness find a surprising correspondence in expressions of the *Apostle's* faithfulness to God and to Israel. Utterances of Paul about himself, and personal confessions introduce Romans 9-11, interrrupt them twice, and conclude them (see 9:1-5; 10:1-2; 11:1-3, 13-14, 33-36). Nearly all of these personal statements express a hope or have the form of a prayer. Paul is far from viewing God's actions as a mere spectator; nor does he indulge in abstract speculation. Were he to speak of God's faithfulness without giving any sign of his own faith, he would not be trustworthy. Only the faithful can speak convincingly of faithfulness.

Sincere and great emotion is apparent in the Apostle's complaint about the hardening of his physical brothers and his wish to be able to save them, be it even at the price of his own life, which Paul like Moses (Exod 32:32) would readily offer to God in exchange for theirs. The admiration he has for the zeal of the Jews is far from ironical; indeed, he himself has been a very zealous Jew (Gal 1:13-14; Phil 3:4-5). Paul is conscious of his descent from the Israelite tribe of Benjamin and grateful for it, because this fact has for him specific meaning:[3] it predisposes him for his missionary work among Gentiles.

The personal statements conclude with the adoration of the mysterious wisdom of God. Far from any arbitrariness, there is a liturgical order in the sequence of all of these pronouncements: they begin with lamentation, proceed to thanksgiving (related to the function entrusted to Paul), and conclude with adoration.

The faithfulness of God drives the Apostle to recognise his responsibility and to work very hard. Even his activism, however, is characterised by his suffering for Israel and by his hope for the strength which God alone can provide. To recognize God's will is an existential act for Paul, including knowledge of the essence and value of his life. At the same time, knowledge of God also includes awareness of the origin, essence, and purpose of the church in Rome. Paul would not write about his relation to Israel unless he wanted all members of the congregation to share his insights and follow his way.

3. Jesus Christ in the Center

One single person (rather than an idea of his own, a general principle, or a blind fate) makes Paul an imitator of God's faithfulness: This person is Jesus Christ alone. In Romans 9-11 Paul quotes texts from the Pentateuch, the Prophets, and the Psalms which long before Jesus Christ's birth had announced a time when the dominion and the worship of God would be extended over the nations (Rom 10:18-20; cf. 15:7-12). The advent, revelation, and work of the Messiah prompted the apostle to refer to those texts and to act accordingly. Because of his coming Paul knows that "all men" are consigned to disobedience in order that God may pour out mercy upon all (cf. 11:28-32). Though in the concluding verses of Romans 9-11 (that is, after 11:27), Jesus Christ is not explicitly mentioned, the substance of Romans 1-8, as well as the first verse and many other sentences in Romans 9-11, points to Christ as the center of Paul's argument.

The occurrence of the formula "in Christ" in Rom 9:1 means more than support for an oath; it signals clearly that the following discourse cannot be understood except on the basis of its Christological affirmations. To be "outcast from Christ" would be, according to 9:3, the worst fate Paul can imagine. The advent of Israel's Messiah and the significance of this event is noted in various ways: "his natural descent" is from Israelites (9:5); he has come to reveal the sense, the unity, the purpose, and above all, the fulfillment of the law (10:4); he is the "stone of stumbling" which was rejected in Zion (9:33); he is the life-giving word, the substance of faith and confession, the invoked Lord who is present wherever his people assemble (10:5-18); allusions to his crucifixion are made in 9:33 and 11:3; his resurrection is explicitly mentioned in 10:9; finally, he is the deliverer of Jacob who will come from Zion (11:26b). Perhaps Jesus Christ is called "God" in 9:5; certainly in 10:9 he is designated by the divine title "Lord." All of these sentences proclaim Christ who is the same yesterday, today and forever (Heb 13:8); the one who is, was, and is to come (Rev 1:8, 17-18; 22:13). His past, present, and future cannot be separated from one another when his work is described.

We observe further that in Romans 9-11 each one of the Christological statements depict Jesus Christ in a special relation not only to the Church but also to Israel. The functions which are here attributed to Jesus Christ, especially the emphasis set on his original, present and future relation to Israel (Jacob, or Zion), deserve special attention. They forbid the notion that the "problem of Israel" is discussed by Paul incidentally and for no purpose other than to exemplify "man's" justification by grace, or to illustrate God's judgment over the "pious" in general.[4] In Romans 9-11, God's chosen people--including the historical Israel which takes offence at the Messiah Jesus --serves not only as a *model* but also as an *instrument* of God's mercy upon all humankind. While in 1 Thess 2:14-16 the Jews were depicted as murderers of Jesus Christ, in Romans 9-11 they are denoted as the womb of the Saviour of the world and as the last recipients of redemption (9:5; 11:26f.). In the time between Jesus' birth and the parousia, it is precisely the hardening of Jews which brings about the preaching of the gospel to Gentiles (10:19; 11:7-22, 25, 28-32). Jesus Christ who has become the Saviour of the nations cannot be separated from the Jews.

4. The use of the Old Testament

In Romans 9-11 the Old Testament is frequently quoted, and once, perhaps, an apocryphal dictum. As long as such quotations are viewed merely as a scholarly, poetic, or fanciful collection of "proof texts" or "parallel texts," their substance and function are misjudged. In fact, the allusions to Israel's history and to the promises, threats, and commissions given to this people serve a much higher purpose. They are intended to show that the history of Jesus Christ and of the nations is embedded in the history of Israel, continues that history, and leads to its fulfillment. Large groups of Protestant and Catholic scholars label this history "saving history" (*Heilsgeschichte*). However, since this concept is linked to the notion of a "new" people of God which takes the place of the "old"--an idea which is completely foreign to Romans 9-11--we will not mention it again.

In these chapters, the Old Testament quotations are meant to demonstrate that election by pure and free grace is neither novel nor provisional in God's will and action. They show that God's purpose stands fast although it is counteracted by rebellion and unbelief. They indicate that, even by reduction of the chosen people to a mere remnant, unexpected multitudes are led to adoration. Finally, they reveal that both the law and the promises given by God to Israel are perfectly fulfilled in Jesus Christ so that under no circumstances can the nations be saved without Israel or at her expense.[5] The indestructible co-inherence of the salvation of the Jews with the salvation of the newcomers from the gentile nations is most strikingly formulated in Rom 11:25-26: "A hardening has come upon part of Israel until the full number of the Gentiles come in (to Zion), and so the whole of Israel will be saved." The weight and the phrasing of this statement are so exceptional that it can be considered a pre-Pauline dictum cited by the apostle from a source he considered authoritative.[6]

After this perusal of four elements common to the whole literary unit Romans 9-11, we turn now to the structure and some special traits of the individual parts of chapter 9-11.

II. THE STRUCTURE OF ROMANS 9-11

Leaving aside the introduction and conclusion (Rom 9:1-5 and 11:33-36), the structure of Romans 9-11 is usually presented as follows:

Part 1 (9:6-29): The Freedom, the Right, and the Power of God who Elects
Part 2 (9:30-10:21): Israel's Guilt and Fall
Part 3 (11:1-32): The Mystery of God's Actions[7]

In view of our quest for the essence and destiny of the people of God, we propose, however, different titles for the three main sections:

1. God's free election and sovereign faithfulness pertain to a people in revolt and keep it together.
2. The Jew Jesus Christ performs and consummates the worship which Israel failed to offer.
3. The good Lord made the unbelief of some serve the salvation of many.

These three parts and their subsections bristle with quite astonishing details:

1. A People in Contradiction

In Rom 9:6-29 Paul refers to events dating back successively to the time of the patriarchs, the exodus, and the kings. He combines a great number of quotations taken from the books of Genesis, Exodus, and the Prophets (esp. Hosea, Jeremiah, Isaiah and-Malachi) and sometimes comments upon them at length. His purpose is to show that God is faithful to himself and to Israel (9:6), righteous (9:14), glorious, and merciful (9:16, 18, 23ff.; 11:31f.)--when he constitutes, by his free choice and without being influenced by the "works" of his elect, one single people formed of Jews and Gentiles (9:11-12, 24). In the process of Paul's argument the following steps can be distinguished:

(a) 9:6-13. Since the time of the patriarchs, two kinds of children form Abraham's posterity. "Not all from Israel are Israel." It is God's prerogative to decide to whom his gracious promise applies. There are those who are no more than physical children of Abraham; Paul thinks of Ishmael and his offspring. But there are others: Isaac and his posterity owe their birth to God's promise and are called "children of God" and are "counted" as seed of Abraham.[8] Similarly Esau was hated by God while Jacob was loved. "God's word does not fall down"--which means that even within the chosen Abrahamic community God alone decides on election and rejection. Since among the people represented and begotten by Abraham, some are physical while others are spiritual members, some beloved and others hated, the conclusion is unavoidable: Israel, the people of God here described, is a divided people, a nation in revolt and in contradiction. What, for example, in John 7:43; 9:16; 10:19 is called "a schism among the people...among the Jews" (provoked by the coming of Jesus, the Messiah), is described by Paul as an archaic and intrinsic trait of God's people.[9]

(b) 9:14-18. To the *internal* crisis of God's people there corresponds a conflict stemming from *outside* : Pharaoh threatens it. However, even this enemy becomes an instrument in God's hand; by his unsuccessful rebellion against God, the Pharaoh serves as a witness to God's overwhelming power and gives occasion for the worldwide proclamation of God's glorious might and name. The ruler of Egypt proves in his own way what Ishmael and Esau had already demonstrated: God is merciful here and harsh there according to his own free will. But he uses even the disobedient and rebellious for his purpose. When Paul asserts that it is God who "hardens whom he will," he affirms--together with, for example, Isa 6:9-10 (cf. Rom 11:8-9)--that in his freedom God assumes responsiblity even for the one who has been hardened and proves stiff-necked, i.e. for the disobedience of his enemies. It is God who "consigns men to disobedience" (Rom 11:32). By bearing with the hardened, and by overcoming and using them for his own purpose, God reveals the superiority of his mercy over all rebellion. According to Isa 6:9-10 and Rom 11:25, a part of Israel, too, is subjected to this hardening.[10] To those chosen by God there belong people whom we would call reprobate. God's elect people is not unanimously and uniformly a believing and obeying nation; rather it is threatened by external and endangered by internal rebellions. It is precisely this menaced people that is carried in God's arms.

(c) 9:19-24. Is God so arbitrary in his decision to harden some persons and to bear others in mercy that those who are rebellious are exculpated? Paul answers by reference to the authority or freedom of the divine potter to mould different sorts of vessels. There are masterpieces which are gladly exposed to admiring eyes, and there are throw-away pots for base and menial use. Of the first products he is proud, but the others have no future except destruction in anger lest they ruin the potter's name. Have the latter a reason to complain? Certainly not, because God himself "has been bearing them in great patience" for the sake of those which express his ultimate intention. This potter demonstrates the results of both activities: that which in his anger he *can* perform, and that which as a good potter he *will* produce. Ishmael *and* Isaac, Esau *and* Jacob, Pharaoh *and* Israel have been examples of such products. The assembly of people called from Jews and from Gentiles in the Church (9:24) reveals that God's mercy over both, Jews and Gentiles, has been triumphant over his wrath against the rebellion found here and there. The distinction and separation of those elect and those reprobate, of the beloved and the hated, proves now to have been a means to an end, not the final purpose of God (cf. 11:28-32).

(d) 9:25-29. With a daring last step Paul concludes the first section of Romans 9-11. Instead of further distinguishing between two groups, those loved and those hated, the vessels prepared for glory and the pots made for destruction, the apostle speaks of the transformation by God's mercy of the reprobate group into the elect one. He does this by the combination of two verses from the book of Hosea. By God's call "Not-my-people" will be made "My-people," and this will be their name: "Not-beloved" will be called "Loved-one." Hosea had preached to the inhabitants of Israel (the Northern Kingdom); to them he announced their re-union with Judah (the Southern Kingdom). For the apostle the Northern Kingdom represents the Gentiles who will be united with the Jewish people, like Hosea's Israel with Judah. An analogous exegesis and application is found in Eph 2:17. A saying of (the second or third) Isaiah (57:19), originally addressed to *both* Jews living in the land *and* Jews living in exile, is used as pertaining to *Jews and Gentiles.*[11]

The quotations from (the first) Isaiah which in Romans 9 will follow upon the Hosea texts form the transition to the next two sections. Israel's reduction is again called to mind--as if to warn Jewish readers of the boastful assertion: that to our own worth is due the incorporation of Gentiles into God's people. The door opened to the Gentiles indicates a judgment upon Israel rather than the strength or victory of Israel. Only a "remnant" and "seed" of Israel is saved, and it is only because of this remainder that Israel as whole has not been destroyed like Sodom and Gomorrah.

The statements made in Rom 9:6-29 concerning the constitution, essence, and unity of the people of God may be summed up as follows. From its beginning God's people is in a continual crisis and schism. But this does not defeat God; on the contrary, God's election of a rebellious people, his love shown even for those not beloved, turns out to be beneficial for the whole world. The part of Israel that was hardened and rejected is the prototype, substitute, or representative of the gentile nations. At the risk or price of being thrown out of God's house themselves, Ishmael and Esau, the rebels of the Northern Kingdom (according to Rom 9:30-11:32 also those Jews who take offence at Jesus' crucifixion and at the gospel), keep open the door for the entry of the Pharaoh and the Gentiles into the people that praises God's name. Their very existence is like an urgent call going out into the world: "A hearty welcome to you who are the hated and the hardened among humankind. Certainly you have failed to give glory to God. But look here, we are like you, and you are like us. Don't you see that it is only by God's mercy that anyone may belong in God's people? God who tolerates us, the reprobate and guilty, will also receive you into his people. Without you and without us, the riches of God's mercy would not be demonstrated and the seats at his festival table would not be occupied."

This summary of Romans 9--a variation of the Parable of the Great Supper

(Luke 14:15-24)--only seems to go beyond the wording and intention of Paul. It is, in fact, Paul's own conclusion in the text of Rom 11:25-26. Thus, the hardening of a part of Israel is *instrumental* in bringing about the accession of Gentiles. The hardened Pharaoh (Rom 9:17-18) has a partner inside Israel.

In Isaiah 40-55, during the time of the exile, similar things are preached. Precisely when and while Israel suffers God's judgment, this servant of God is destined to be God's missionary to the nations. It is not only the obedient remnant that serves God's honor but in its own way also the disobedient majority of Israel. The totality of God's people will be made up of that remnant, of the majority of Israel, and of the nations which will be joined to them. "God has called us not only from the Jews but also from the Gentiles" (Rom 9:24).

Some Christians have called the Church a sacrament (*mustērion*), either because she is the body of Christ at the same time visible and invisible, or because she administers the sacraments and seems to be constituted by the complementarity of clerics and laymen. Not so the Apostle, least of all in Romans 9! This is the mystery of the people chosen by God: it consists of a variety of members all of whom are children of Abraham, the father of all nations. In his mighty love God embraces all of them, the obedient and the disobedient, the wise and the unwise, using each one of them as his witness. Even Not-my-people, or Not-Israel, is to become Israel, the Beloved. Therefore, the Old Testament people of God, as described in Romans 9, exemplify not merely a disturbing schism within the one people but also foreshadow final unity. Here, persons who are worthy of being condemned are confronted with a holy remnant and kept together by God, in order that all members of this people may become aware that they are chosen and unted by sheer grace.

God's "election by grace" may be described as "double predestination," since doubleness or duality is constitutive for it. Not only Isaac but also Ishmael, not only Israel but also Pharaoh, not only some beloved ones but also all those "not-beloved" are embraced by God's love. How could Paul depict God's people this way? His experience as a missionary of Christ among the Jews cannot have created the conviction that even all those "not beloved" in Israel would in the end be "beloved." Moreover, purely wishful thinking would form a poor basis for his theological reasoning and teaching.

In fact the Apostle builds on other ground: Rom 8:29, where he first introduces the concept of predestination, he asserts that God "predestined us to be conformed to the likeness of his Son." What the Apostle means by "conformity to the likeness" of Jesus Christ is explained in more detail in Rom 6:3-11; 2 Cor 4:7-12; Phil 2:5-11; 3:10, 21. In all these passages, conformity with Jesus Christ consists of participation and unity in Christ by sharing in his death and resurrection. Indeed, shortly after Rom 8:29 (i.e. in Rom 8:32, 34), explicit references are made to Christ's death and resurrection. In the crucifixion and resurrection of Jesus Christ, God's angry rejection *and* God's merciful acceptance are fully revealed: the horror of the former, and the amazing grace of the latter. This archetype of God's covenant with humanity contains in itself God's relation to his whole elect people. For Christ's death corresponds to the rejection of Ishmael, Esau, and Pharaoh; Christ himself was made an object of God's curse.[12] On the other hand, the "acceptance" of the "rejected" people is in Rom 11:15. called "life from the dead"; Jesus Christ's resurrection from the dead would be meaningless without the co-resurrection of a great people (cf. 1 Cor 15:12-18).[13] According to 1 Cor 2:7 (cf. 2:1 *var. lect.)* and especially to Colossians and Ephesians (Col 1:27; Eph 1:9-10; etc. cf. Rom 16:25), the mystery of God which is now revealed is Jesus Christ himself. In summary, the "mystery" of the "hardening of a part" of Israel and the salvation of "the whole of

Israel" of which Rom 11:25-26 speaks is analogous, or rather, essentially equivalent, to the mystery of the crucified and resurrected Jesus Christ.

The following sections will show whether this Christological interpretation of "double predestination" really corresponds to Paul's train of thought.

2. The true Jew: Jesus Christ

The main topic of the second section (Rom 9:30-10:21) is not, as has often been assumed, an exposition of the failure and fall of Israel, although this topic appears at the beginning and the end of this passage (9:30-10:3 and 10:16-21). The center of the text (10:4-18), however, is devoted to Jesus Christ himself and his significance for Israel and the whole world.[14]

The most important verse is 10:4: "Christ is the fulfillment of the law, bringing righteousness for *everyone* who has faith." Here it is affirmed that Christ *fulfilled* the law.[15] The translations, "Christ is the purpose, the aim, or the sum of the law" are equally appropriate; but the version, "Christ is the end of the law" (RSV, NEB, etc.), if understood in the sense of "termination of the law," is misleading. What Rom 10;4 affirms has its closest parallel and clearest interpretation in Rom 3:21-22. "Now, independently of (works of) the law, God's righteousness has been revealed to which both law and the prophets bear witness: God's righteousness [effective] through the faith of (Jesus) Christ for all who have faith." Probably Rom 10:5 denotes *Jesus Christ* as the person who (according to Lev 18:5) shall live, because he does what is written in the law.[16]

At least four supporting statements surround the fundamental assertion made in Rom 10:4-5: (a) Christ became a stumbling-stone to Israel; at this point Paul does not specify whether contempt for Jesus led to the crucifixion of Jesus, or whether the crucified man of Nazareth was the reason for the rejection of the gospel. At all events, Christ's cross and Israel's stumbling (and fall, cf. Rom 11:12) are inseparably connected (Rom 9:32-33).[17] (b) Jesus Christ is the "word...near you" of which Deut 30:14 speaks (Rom 10:6-8). This word is the voice of the living God; nothing else grants and sustains life."[18] (c) Jesus, the resurrected Lord, is the substance and object of that confession, faith, and prayer which assure salvation to all believers without distinction, i.e. to Jews and Greeks (Rom 10:9-13). (d) Finally, it is the "word of Christ" which is preached all over the earth by the apostles as the good news and as the invitation to have faith in him (Rom 10:14-18).

Now, Israel took offence at this Christ, and Gentiles came to believe in him before many Jews did. But Israel's refusal does not negate the fact that the coming and the work of Jesus Christ accomplished for the whole world and manifested to it just what originally had been promised to Israel and required of this people: (a) the fulfillment of the law, (b) the bearing of the curse by the trespasser (Gal 3:13; 2 Cor 5:21), and (c) the destiny to be a light to the Gentiles.[19] In short, Jesus Christ has fulfilled the worship and the mission to which Israel had been called. In him Israel's calling and destiny culminate and are brought to perfection. He is the Jew to whom God gives honor, and who leads Gentiles to praise God's name. (cf. Rom 2:17-29).

God did not, by the disobedience of a part of Israel, let himself be diverted from his faithfulness to Israel. Certainly, Christ himself and the preaching of the gospel, as well as the whole history of ancient Israel, is what is called (in Rom 10:21) a "stretching out of the hands of God to a disobedient and rebellious people." According to the Apostle and the prophets whom he quotes in 9:27 and 11:7, 25, the vast number of Israel constitutes a people lacking faith. Yet God does not let her be "shattered".[20] Rather he makes a native of Israel, Jesus Christ, the people's obedient representative, the one who before God and humanity meets the mark and fulfils the purpose of Israel's election. The stone on which they stumble is made even for them a foundation stone on which they can rely. Their stumbling over the law is the whole story of neither the law nor of themselves. Only Jesus Christ who fulfills the law for them is the culmination of that story.

In Rom 9:1-29, the people of God was described as a *corpus mixtum* whose history included both election and rejection until finally the rejection of the "not-beloved" was overcome by the overwhelming love of God. In Rom 9:30-10:21, Israel is characterized--in spite of all its vicissitudes--as a people which in its entirety exists no longer without the promised Messiah, but rather is perfectly represented by Jesus Christ.[21] His coming, history, and work prevent Paul (and his readers) from gazing exclusively at the status and behaviour of Jews as if Jews could not speak for themselves and decide about their fate without respect to this representative appointed for them by God. "People of God" is a functional and relational concept, rather than a static or self-supporting one. This people is manifest wherever men and women from all over the world are assembled to bear witness to God.

It cannot be denied that the second section of Romans 9-11 includes a "shock-treatment" of Israel. But God himself rather than Paul (as an apostate Jew) is here at work as a healer. Paul might well have quoted (as does Heb 12:5-6) the words of Prov 3:11-12: "The Lord chastises him whom he loves." The negative argument of 9:30-10:3, asserting that Israel had not achieved by its own endeavour the righteousness in store for her, is followed in 10:4-18 by its positive counterpart: Jesus Christ alone has achieved what Israel was lacking. The section reaches a striking conclusion: while those first chosen still continue in their disbelief and rebellion (10:21), a "not-people" or "un-people," even the Gentiles, have seen the light (10:19-20, quoting from Deut 32:21 and Isa 65:1)

3. The Future Gathering of the Whole People

The last part of Romans 9-11 consists of 11:1-32. Here it becomes obvious that the history of the people of God does not end with the schism in Israel, nor with the representation of the people by the Messiah Jesus, nor with the substitution of the former "not-people" for the chosen Jewish people.

The section begins with a warning against a misapprehension. What was said in the polemical sentences at the beginning and end of the last section is protected against cheap realization by the Apostle's return to the discussion of a "remnant." But whereas in 9:27-29 reference to a remnant was made in the context of the threat to reduce drastically Israel's numbers, now in 11:1-10 the positive function of the remnant becomes apparent. As at the time of Elijah so today, the remnant proves that only "some," "a part," "those others" were hardened by God (11:7, 14, 17, 25). Considering the remnant which is "left over" for God and to which the Apostle among others reckons himself as belonging, it is preposterous to assume that God' people Israel is rejected as a whole (11:1-2). Far from indicating a renunciation on God's part, this remnant is in itself an appeal on God's part that is addressed to the totality of the people; it vouches for God's faithfulness to all of them for the sake of the patriarchs (cf. 11:28). The acceptance and salvation of the "whole of Israel" is and remains God's will and promise (11:25-29; cf. 11:12, 15, 23-24). God assumes responsibility, as was stated earlier, for the present drowsiness, blindness, and deafness of the majority of Israel and their consequences (11:8-10). How can they be overcome?

The answer is reached by a peculiar method. The central part of chapter 11 (vv. 11-24) confirms what has already, though more indirectly, been asserted in Romans 9: unwittingly the rebellious part of Israel contributes to the accession and salvation of the Gentiles. "By their downfall," it is now said, "salvation has come to the Gentiles" so that "the world" becomes rich and reconciled to God (11:11, 12, 15). Instead of comparing God with a potter and Israel and the Gentiles with vessels, Paul now likens God to a gardener and the people of God, first, to a lump of dough (11:16a), and then, at length, to an olive tree and its branches (11:16b-25). The divine gardener acts in a way that a human horticulturalist would never imitate: he lops off noble branches in order to graft wild ones in their place so that these may profit from the sap of the noble root. The disobedient part of Israel has to give way to Gentiles in order to let them participate in the holiness of the chosen people. Up to this point it seems that the relation between Israel and the Church is that between a predecessor and a successor, a former people and a new, final people of God, if not of a first covenant-partner and wife of God to another, new wife. However, the beginning of this section (11:1-7) compels us to modify this so-called "succession" or "substitutionary theory" by certain elements of another the so-called "remnant theory." Some of the original branches have not been finally and forever cut away from the olive tree; it is only together with them that Gentiles may receive that holiness which makes of them members of God's people.

Nevertheless, the way which Paul describes is not yet completed. Two consequences of God's procedure are mentioned and discussed in a pastoral manner. The first is a development intended by God and a hoped-for result of the apostle's work among the Gentiles. The hardened, stumbling, cut-off part of Israel is to be made "jealous" of the salvation which is now bypassing them and being given to the Gentiles. If only Israel could become "jealous" of what she has lost and aim at regaining what she has forfeited (10:19; 11:11, 14)! The second consequence is absurd yet real, though it runs contrary to both God's people and the Apostle's intention. The Gentiles who were admitted to God's people are in danger of a cheap triumphalism at the expense of those Jews who at present do not (yet) believe in the Messiah Jesus. The boasting, pride, and (self-) complacency of the gentile Christians is mentioned three times and reprimanded in sharp terms (11:18, 20, 25). Since everywhere in Romans (except in 2:17-29) and particularly in 11:13-24 the Apostle is addressing himself to gentile Christians, his pastoral warning against pride is stronger than his reference to a present or future Jewish jealousy.[22]

With regard to Jews Paul points to a future action of the divine gardener. God has the power and the intention to re-graft the cut-off noble branches into their original stem, even, if need be, at the expense of the foreign shoots (11:23-24). Thus the hoped-for turning to the Messiah by Jews, who up to now are lacking faith, will not remain a mere wish. After the crowds of Gentiles have come in, "all Israel will be saved" (11:26a). Because a remnant, the cut-off noble branches of Israel, and their re-grafting have been mentioned in the same context, the formula "all Israel" cannot imply only "the whole Church" composed of Jews and Gentiles, but must include "all Jews." Whereas for some Old Testament prophets the (gentile) nations' procession to Zion is the pinnacle of hope,[23] for Paul this procession is the penultimate event (for which he takes great pains to prepare, e.g. by organising the collection for Jerusalem).[24] His ultimate expectation is the advent of the "Deliverer from Zion" who comes to forgive the sins of the children of "Jacob," i.e. of the alienated (Northern) part of Israel, viz. of the Jews who stumbled over their Messiah Jesus. Only the (re-)construction of the united, and therefore, whole Israel is for Paul (as in Ezekiel 37) identical with that eschatological resurrection of the dead for which Israel hopes (11:15). As if asked from where he draws his insight, the apostle answers in 11:25-27: it has come from a secret revelation (*mustērion*) which he has read in an apocalyptic book or heard from a Christian prophet or which has been imparted to him directly and/or by his study of the Scriptures.

The doctrinal and pastoral statements of Romans 11 are concluded in vv. 28-32 by the description of the dependence of the Gentiles' salvation upon the history of Israel, and of the solidaity between Jews and Gentiles. It is impossible that one should be played off against the other, for here as well as there disobedience has reigned, and for both sides there is no other salvation than by God's mercy. Solidarity, however, is not the same as uniformity. Solidarity has a long and eventful history through which God shows that, on the one hand, the gentile nations are not saved at the expense of God's mercy upon Israel, and that, on the other hand, Israel is not saved without the extension of God's mercy among the nations. In spite of the disobedience and hardening of both Jews and Gentiles, God proves faithful to Jews and merciful to Gentiles. He carries out the intention of the original election of the patriarchs, that they should be examples and witnesses of the rich blessings to be enjoyed by all families of the earth (Gen 12:1-3, etc.).

The solidarity which Paul has in mind can be illustrated in terms of the relationship between the two sons in the parable of the Prodigal Son after the return of the younger (Luke 15:25-32). This younger brother, first lost from home because of his malice and later admitted to his father's house by sheer grace, has nothing to boast about but much of which to be ashamed. Of course, the elder, by bragging of his works and endured hardships, reveals his own sin. But it is not up to the younger to tell him that, or to consider himself the only true son. Thus, Christians have no right to accuse Jews of self-righteousness and to regard themselves as heirs of the Jews. In both cases, only the goodness of the father overcomes all guilt, a father who loves both sons. On the otherhand, neither the triumph of the father's grace nor its celebration can be fully enjoyed as long as the older brother remains outside in the dark and is missing from the festival table. It is God's will and promise that "all Israel will be saved"!

The information gathered from Romans 9-11 concerning the people of God can now be summed up:

(a) It is God's prerogative to decide who is God's people. This people is constituted by God's choice and promise alone; it is sustained by his faithfulness and power, judged by his righteousness, pardoned by his mercy, and made complete for his honor. Its characteristics and identity, therefore, are not determined by the inclusive or exclusive self-righteousness of either Jews or Christians, except perhaps by the recognition common to both--that each of them is utterly unworthy to belong in this people.

(b) The existence of God's people in ever-changing Old Testament, intertestamental, and post-Christian forms is indisputable. The election, judgment, preservation, and mission of Israel in the midst of the nations shape the history of the Jewish people from the beginning, in the present, and into the future. Therefore, the concept and the reality of God's one people form neither a timeless idea nor a utopia or dream. Its peculiar, mysterious, incomparable, and purposeful existence defies any manipulation by itself or its enemies. Further, it calls for repentance within and outside its border. A particularity of the Jewish people consists in the fact that this nation has among its members represetatives of God's enemies and that it will be saved and completed only together with the nations.

(c) Furthermore, the history of the Church, that is of God's people called from Jews and Gentiles, is unfinished. Just as in the past the identity of the chosen people was determined by the acts of God, so it will be in the future: the coming of the Lord, the resurrection of the dead, and the reunion of the dispersed members will determine its character, number, and life. By their eager waiting for the coming Lord and by their living hope for his gifts, and not by any boasting of a presumed possession, are servants of God recognized.[25]

(d) The unity of Jews and Christians in the Church is a provisional and fragmentary representation of the one people of God, and in itself an urgent appeal to all nations and to the whole of Israel to gather in one house for the service of God.

This completes our discussion of Romans 9-11.

III. GALATIANS 4 AND EPHESIANS 2

At this point an exegesis of Gal 4:21-31, 2 Corinthians 3, and Eph 2:11-12 would be in order. These passages call for an intensive interpretation equal to that of Romans 9-11 since they, too--though each with quite different accents--speak of the relation between Israel and the Church. The description of Paul's special ministry in 2 Corinthians 3 is not so immediately pertinent to the question "Who is God's people? as to require the inclusion of an exegesis of this most complicated chapter in the present context. However, some summary remarks on the other two texts may at least demonstrate their relevance.

1. The Removal of Hagar and Ishmael

In Galatians 4 (cf. 2 Corinthians 3 and Hebrews 8) Old Testament texts are quoted in the framework of a discourse on two covenants which differ widely from each oth er. According to Gal 4:24-25, 29-31, one of these covenants (characterized by the law) is personified by Hagar, the slave-woman of Abraham and mother of Ishmael, the other by Sarah, the free-born wife of Abraham and mother of Isaac. Typologically, Sarah and Isaac represent Christians (the free children of God's promise), Hagar and Ishmael Jews (kept slaves under the law).[26] Paul reminds the Galatians that Hagar, her son, and what they represent, were "thrown out" and disinherited, and the firstborn son of Abraham persecuted the spiritual son, just as in Paul's days, the Church is persecuted by Jews (Gal 4:29-30). In this context Paul does not mention that according to the Genesis story God also looked and had mercy on the suffering Hagar, saved the life of the disinherited Ishmael, and promised to make a nation out of the son of the slave-woman (Gen 16:10-15; 21:13-21). Romans 9-11, however, proves that after the writing of Galatians Paul progressed in his thinking even on this matter.[27]

2. The Naturalization of the Gentiles by Jesus Christ

In Ephesians 2, the same theme is treated in a different way.[28] Regarding assertions about the people of God, some differences from the substance of Romans 9-11 are obvious. In Romans, a split is assumed within Israel between the majority and the remnant, and between the hardened part of Israel and the Church. Ephesians, however, speaks of one single people of God, of the citizenship of Israel, into which Gentiles have been accepted. According to Romans, the crucifixion of Christ apparently is the result and cause of the present schism among God's people; only in his parousia and the resurrection of all the dead will Christ overcome the present division between Jews and Gentiles; no hardening of the Jews, no throw-away "vessels of wrath," no cut-ff branches or thrown-out slaves are mentioned; there is no reference to Israel's foolishness, blindness, callousness, for all these forms of hardening are attributed only to the Gentiles (Eph 2:11-13, 17, 19; 4:17-19). Instead of describing the Jews as a people who reject the Messiah and the gospel, this Letter refers to them as persons who, unlike the Gentiles, have hope (for the promised Messiah and an inheritance, Eph 1:12; 3:6; cf. 2:12), who are circumcised members of a citizenship established by God's promise and covenant, and who are "near," "saints," and children in God's household (Eph 2:12, 17, 19).

In Ephesians 2, three things stand out:

(a) The naturalization and adoption of Gentiles presupposes the destruction of the wall, built up by an intepretation of the law "in statutory ordinances," which separates the people of God from the nations (2:14-15). Just as in Rom 9:12,32 and 11:6, so in Eph 2:9, a brief and sharp outburst occurs against "works (of the law)"; salvation can neither be sought nor secured by obedience to divisive statutes such as sabbath, circumcision, and dietary laws.

(b) The death of the Messiah on the cross is emphatically presented as the means of unification and reconciliation between Jews and Christians (his blood, flesh, body, cross are mentioned in Eph 2:13-16). When, as in Rom 10:9-20 and 11:13, references are made to the resurrection of Christ and the proclamation of the gospel, special emphasis lies always on the unifying power of these events (Eph 1:19-2:16; 2:17;[29] 3:5-12). One of the effects of the (Holy) Spirit (who is not mentioned in Romans 9-11) is to join together diverse members of God's house (Eph 2:18,22).

(c) The result of the peace made by Christ in the "creation of one new person" (Eph 2:16), that is, the "body" and/or the bride of Christ: the Church.[30] She serves the Father in the Spirit, and her growth is described in terms of building a spiritual temple of God (Eph 2:18, 20-22). This body, bride, or temple consists only of these Gentiles and Jews who believe in Christ and are sealed with the Spirit (1:12-14; 4:30). And yet, the sealing of part of the Jews and Gentiles, reveals God's claim upon the whole "circumcision" and "uncircumcision" (2:11). It confirms and manifests the validity of Jesus Christ's rule, and of peace as well, for the whole creation (1:10; 2:17). Ecclesiastical existence is missionary existence.[31] The "body" of Christ reveals God's intimate concern for all bodily beings. The temple is not being built for its own or the building-stones' sake, but is planned and built for a great people. The beauty of the bride will shine abroad (5:27).

It has often been maintained that Ephesians (e.g. in 2:5-6) attests a triumphalist ecclesiology and an enthusiastic anticipation of the end-time. Accordingly, it is frequently repeated that the Letter neglects futuristic eschatalogy and has nothing to say about the parousia of Christ. But clear indications to the contrary are found in the references to the (not yet inserted) keystone (or capstone) of God's temple (2:20-22), in the description of the development of the body which grows not only from its head but also towards its head (4:15-16), and in the allusion to the yearning for the meeting with the "perfect man," that is, the princely bridegroom, Jesus Christ (4:13).[32] The Letter to the Ephesians knows about the imperfection of the embattled Church; otherwise the admonitions given in Eph 4:25-6:20 would be superfluous.

Essential elements of Romans 9-11 are present in Ephesians, partly expressed in even stronger and clearer terms. But only in Ephesians (and Colossians) is the concept "body" and "Messiah" found.[33] Since the expectation of a Messiah promised since David's time is as Jewish as the physical body of a Messiah who has come, the Church of Jews and Gentiles has no right to let herself be called "body of the Messiah (or, of Christ)," nor to call herself "people of God," unless she recognizes and acknowledges that she is participating in the history and community of the Jews. The Jews formed the people of God long before Gentiles joined in. All who would want to have peace on earth apart from the Jewish Messiah, and without community with the people of which Jesus is a native son, would separate themselves from salvation. According to Eph 2:1-10, there is no salvation without resurrection and enthronement together with Christ and with the Jews. An apprehension of salvation as "individual redemption" is, for all practical purposes, excluded. In this Letter (2:1-22; 3:6) Christ's saving action is described as the reconciliation of alienated groups with each other and with God, not as the salvation of individuals. This does not contradict other Pauline Letters which appear to lay the greatest emphasis on the faith of each individual. According to Gal 2:11-21, for example, Paul's doctrine of justification was formulated for the first time in a situation where the unity, the common life, and, quite concretely, the actual eating together of Jews and Gentiles were at stake. And Romans 6-8, with their very personal description of the life of those saved, are framed by Romans 1-5 and 9-11, chapters in which we find described God's righteousness as revealed to Jews and Gentiles at large.

Obviously, our exposition of Romans 9-11 is influenced by Ephesians more than by Gal 4:21-31 and 2 Corinthians 3 not to speak of 1 Thess 2:15-16. If Ephesians were missing in the New Testament, or if Paul had nothing to do with it (with the result that Ehesians would at best have to be deplored as a post-apostolic document), Galatians 4 and 2 Corinthians 3 might well bend the interpretation of Romans away from the testimony of Ephesians and toward the above-mentioned substitution or remnant theories. The eschatalogical orientation, which in Romans 11 is decisive for all affirmations regarding the one people of God, might then be depreciated or ignored altogether.

The situation however is drastically changed when Ephesians is received and respected as authentically Pauline, or when Ephesians 2, even if written by a disciple of Paul, is considered to be a competent explanation and continuation of Romans 9-11, giving special emphasis to eschatalogical hopes which are in the process of realization. In this case, not only do the theories of substitution or a final schism run contrary to Paul's doctrine, but also the restrictive hypotheses of a remnant and of the complementation have to be radically modified. It is necessary and wise to regard the later Letter, Ephesians, as a key to the interpretation of the earlier, Romans. One meets God only on the way on which God himself chooses to meet one, the way on which God leads and accompanies one. To accompany the Apostle and to be led further on the way on which he was led, is certainly the best method by which to understand his witness.

Attempting to summarise the results of our exposition of Romans 9-11 in other terminology we make the following assertion: it is not enough to say that salvation *came* from the Jews; for salvation *comes* from the Jews (cf. John 4:22). Jesus Christ not only was a Jew--in the womb of Mary, on the roads of Galilee, Samaria, and Jerusalem, and on the cross--but he *remains* a Jew as the Resurrected, who intercedes for us at the right hand of God from where he sends the Spirit and the spiritual gifts; he will be the same when he comes again.

These statements are not, as they seem to be, a diversion from the theme "The People of God." Too often the doctrine of the people of God--which should properly be called "laology"--is overshadowed or replaced by ecclesiology. But neither of these doctrines is self-supporting. Christology is the foundation of both, and soteriology (the doctrine of salvation) determines all the traits by which the people of God is recognized. J. Moltmann has attempted to develop a "Messianic ecclesiology,"[34] we would rather call for the unfolding of a "Messianic laology" which embraces all Jews, not merely the "remnant" which believes in the Messiah already come. False decisions and attitudes, taken with reference to the unity of God's people, have the theological weight of Christological heresies; they are tantamount to a rejection of the salvation that has been granted. In the Christians' relation to the Jewish Saviour their relationship with Jews is decided. In the relationship with Jews their relation to Jesus Christ is verified--or falsified.

NOTES

* *Reprinted by permission of the publisher of* ***The People of God.*** *, Sheffield: JSOT Press, 1983, pp. 29--49. With the consent of the author, the title of chapter 2 was changed to "One God, One Christ, One People."*

1. See the documents prepared for the Consultation between officials of the World Council of Churches and of the (now defunct) Near Eastern Bureau of Information and Interpretation, held in Beirut in the autumn of 1972. These documents are available in mimeographed form at the WCC, 150 route de Ferney, CH-1211 Geneva 20.

2 With increasing zeal and passion questions such as the following are asked and answered in divergent ways: Are the chapters Romans 9-11 the substance of an original, independent tractate, or are they a necessary logical link in the structure of the whole of Romans because they include indispensable information on grace, on the history of salvation and of the world, on election, on justification, or on the unity in Christ? Does Paul, in this section of Romans address himself only to gentile Christians, or does he at the same time also intend to be heard and heeded by Jewish Christians and by unbaptized Jews? Are the strong and the weak described in Romans 14-15 gentile and Jewish Christians respectively? Neither these problems nor the issues of election, remnant, mystery, and other individual difficulties will be discussed in detail in the following.

3. Because in Rom 11:26 "all Israel" and in 9:27 and 11:1-7 the "remnant" of Israel is mentioned, it is most likely that the origin of Paul from Benjamin has symbolic significance for the apostle. When after Solomon's death the Northern and the Southern Kingdoms ("Israel" and "Judah") formed separate political entities, only the tribe of Benjamin joined the tribe of Judah in order to remain faithful to the house of David (1 Kgs 12:21; in 1 Kgs 11:31-32, 35-36, and elsewhere, however, only the tribe of Judah is described as loyal to David's offspring). If the note of 1 Kgs 12:21 is reliable, then at the time of the divided realms (according to Jeremiah, also after the destruction of the Northern Kingdom), Benjamin is the quasi-representative of the Northern Kingdom, that is, of the whole of Israel, within the Kingdom of Judah. Thus it is probable that Paul, a Benjamite, considered himself a citizen who, while belonging to Judah, was also representative of "all Israel." In turn (and primarily in those passages in the books of Joshua, Samuel, and Kings that show traces of "deuteronomic redaction"), the term "all Israel" often signifies the united northern and southern tribes; cf. notes 6 and 11. Further, in later Old Testament books "all Israel" signifies all the Jews who returned from Babylon, particularly the members of the former

Southern Kingdom who were reunited in the promised land (Ezra 2:70; 6:16-17; 10:5).

4. So e.g. E. Käsemann, **Commentary on Romans** London: SCM, 1980 253-318; idem, "Paul and Israel," in **New Testament Questions of Today** London: SCM, 1969 194-197. K. Stendahl, however, in his Foreword to J. Munck, **Christ and Israel** Philadelphia: Fortress Press, 1967 viii, insists that the chapters Romans 9-11 are not a tractate--be it on "the interesting theological idea of predestination" or on "justification by faith."

5. An entirely different judgment is passed on the significance of the Old Testament by, for example, P. Vielhauer, "Paulus und das Alte Testament," in L. Abramowski and J.F.G. Goeters (eds.) **Studien zur Geschichte und Theologie der Reformation. Festschrift E. Bizer**, Neukirchen: Neukirchener Verlag, 1969 33-62; **Geschichte der urchristlichen Literatur**, Berlin/ New York: de Gruyter, 1975 770-780. According to Vielhauer, in the proclamation of the gospel of Jesus Christ the Holy Scriptues of the Old Testament fulfilled no more than a "secondary and subsidiary" function; they served "as apologetic and polemical instrument to interpret what God had done in Christ, yet not as a critical norm." Against this opinion speak the similarity and the differences between Pauline hermeneutics and the use of the Scripture made in Qumran, by the apocalyptic literature, and in the Mishnah. L. Baeck, "The Faith of Paul" *Journal of Jewish Studies*, 3 (1925) 93-110, has a better conception of Paul's intention: "Paul was a theologian...not incidentally...by his nationality. As a Jew, his life was contained in the Bible, and as a Jewish scholar he had to justify before the Bible whatever he would say or do," he had to lay bare the meaning of the biblical words, for without biblical interpretation his proclamation could not be legitimate.

6. In the opening of Rom 11:25 reference is made to a *musterion* (mystery, secret). The use of this term may be a signal, saying that the three affirmations made in Rom 1:25b-26a (a part of Israel was hardened; this happened until the fullness of the nations should come in; this way all Israel will be saved) were found by Paul in a (now lost) prophetic-apocalyptic book, or that they stem from a New Testament prophet. What such a book or prophet had said about the fulfillment of Hosea's, Jeremiah's, and Ezekiel's prophecies regarding the reunion of the twelve tribes in one people would then be quoted by Paul--just as in other cases he quotes not only the Scriptures (see e.g. 1 Cor 2:9; 14:34; 15:45; Rom 2:20; Gal 2:16; Eph 5:14). If the citation is taken from a Jewish rather than from a Christian source, the term "all Israel" might have included no more than all proselytes from the nations, not necessarily all nations. Cf. n. 11.

7. For instance, E. Käsemann, **Commentary on Romans**, 253ff., 241ff.; A. Schlatter, **Gottes Gerechtigkeit** Stuttgart: Calwer Vereinsbuchhandlung 1935 291ff.; A. Nygren, **Commentary on Romans** London: SCM Press, 1952 353ff.; E. Gaugler, **Der Römerbrief, II**, Zurich: Zwingli-Verlag, 1952 3ff.; C. K. Barrett, **A Commentary on the Epistle to the Romans** A. & C. Black, 1957 174ff.; J. Huby, **Saint Paul, Épître aux Romains** Paris: Beauchesne 1957 320ff. Agreement prevails particularly in the titles given to part II: the chapter Romans 9 is understood as a reproach of Israel. In deviating from the consensus regarding part III, A Schlatter gives Romans 11 the title, "The Work of Grace in Judaism." The concord regarding Part II is most drastically broken by K. Barth, **Church Dogmatics II** (1957), 213-233, 240-259, 267-305: in his interpretation of each of the three parts, the inclusion in God's election and grace not only of the remnant of Israel, but even of that (part of) Israel which rejects the gospel of Jesus Christ, is explicitly affirmed. This exposition implies a *character indelebilis* conferred upon Israel. U. Luz, **Das Geschichtsverständnis des Paulus** Munich: Kaiser, 1968, also makes steps towards a christological interpretation of these chapters.

8. In Gal 4:21-31, Isaac and Ishmael, the spiritual and the fleshly sons are juxtaposed in corresponding fashion.

9. Analogous is the inclusion of the "rebel" in the community worshipping God through the celebration of the Seder (the Passover Feast), up to the present time. Among the four children sitting at the table and asking ritual questions, one is rebellious. He receives a sharp reply but he is not thrown out.

10. Cf. Rom 9:13; 11:8-10; Isa 6:9-10; Acts 28:26-28; Matt 13:14-15; Job 12:38-40.

11. These Pauline interpretations are rather surprising. But since they are probably influenced by rabbinical exposition of the Scripture, they should not be called arbitrary. For instance, according to some rabbis, Isa 57:19 (the verse announcing peace to those far and near)

was interpreted as referring to the admission of proselytes to God's people; see the references in Strack-Billerbeck, III, 585-586. This rabbinical exposition takes up a tradition traceable already in (the Deuteronomistic) parts of the Old Testament. When, under the influence of Judaean (southern) prophets, the origin of the Northern Kingdom is described in the two books of Kings, much emphasis is given to the introduction of worshipping the calf, among the tribes that had defected from the house of David; the infidel Israelites are shown to have chosen the way of heathens, that is, of idol-makers and idol-worshippers. In 2 Kgs 17:24-41 it is reported that after the destruction of Samaria in 722-21 B.C., the population of the former Northern Kingdom was mixed with gentile elements. Ezekiel 37 (probably composed of pieces that originally were conceived independently of one another) in its present composition and shape illustrates the meaning of resurrection from the dead.The resuscitation seen in a vision (Ezek 37:1-14; cf. Rom 11:15) signifies two seemingly different events: the reunion of the Northern and Southern Kingdoms under one king and around one sanctuary, and the spread of the knowledge of God among the nations (Ezek 37:15-28). Similarly, in the Gospel of John (4:4-42; 10:16), the Samaritan woman represents the sheep of Jesus chosen not from the Judaean (or Jewish?) sheepfold and yet belonging in the flock tended by the one shepherd. It is the Samaritans, who, to our surprise, confess that Jesus is the "Saviour of the World," and not just of Judaea or of Israel.

12. Rom 4:25; Gal 3:13; 2 Cor 5:21.

13. Indeed, Calvin, **Institutes,** III 22:1, 24:5; and, **De aeterna Dei praedestinatione, Corpus Reformatorum, Calvini Opera**, VIII 306, 318, called Jesus Christ "the mirror of election" (electionis speculum). But only by P. Maury, "Election et foi" (1936), repr. in **Foi et Vie** (1956) 199-219; German tr. "Erwählung und Glaube," *Theol. Stud.* 8 (1940), and (following him) by K. Barth, "Gottes Gnadenwahl," *Theologische Existenz heute* 47 (1936), was a new conception of "double predestination" developed. What in the Reformed orthodoxy of the centuries after the Reformation resembled fatalistic determinism, was now shown to be based on the historic tension and unity of Christ's cross and resurrection.The way from Calvary to Easter was shown to be the heart of the mystery of election and reprobation: even the rejected son was elected, in the end. In K. Barth's doctrine on double predestination contained in his Church Dogmatics II/2, 3-506, the theological co-inherence of three pairs is constitutive; (i) Christ's cross and resurrection; (ii) the history of Israel and the church; and (iii) reprobation and election.

14. J. Munck, **Christ and Israel,** 79, uses the words "The unbelief of the Jews toward Christ during his life on earth" as a subtitle *only* to Rom 9:30-10:4, i.e., the first subsection of Part II. But in his comments on the central and main subsection of Romans 10, that is, of vv. 5-13, he writes on p. 84, "Paul is not trying in this passage to point out and prove the guilt of the Jews, but. . . throughout chapter 10 his aim is to show that God has done everything to win the Jews for the faith." He makes similar statements on pp. 89-90 about Rom 10:14-21. Under the subtitle, "God has done everything in order that the Jews may believe and call upon Christ," he asserts, "It is surprising that commentators are almost unanimous in agreeing that the aim of chapter 10, including 10:14-21, is to demonstrate Israel's guilt. . . Of course, Israel's guilt is actually mentioned but it is not stressed as a main theme." See the similar affirmation of U. Luz, **Das Geschichtsverständnis des Paulus**, 1968, 30. K. Barth, **A Shorter Commentary on Romans,** London: SCM Press, 1959 112, speaks of the "human recalcitrance even against the grace of God which was manifested in Jesus Christ." C. E. B. Cranfield, **The Epistle to the Romans,** II, ICC, 1979, 503, affirms that "a hopeful note. . .focusses attention not on Israel's sin but on God's goodness toward Israel."

15. Compare the reference to the obedience of Jesus Christ and the fulfilment of the law in him, in Rom 5:19; Phil 2:8; Gal 2:20; 3:13.

16. See R. Bring, **Commentary on Galatians** Philadelphia: Muhlenberg, 1961 128-142, and C. E. B. Cranfield, "St Paul and the Law," *SJT* 17 (1964) 43-68, esp. 49ff.

17. Cf. 1 Cor 1:18-24; 2:8; Gal 5:11; 1 Thess 2:15-16.

18. Cf. Deut 5:26; 8:3; 30:6, 15, 19-20; 32:47; etc. Is it necessary to conclude that because Paul presents a christological interpretation of the law (called "word") in Deut 30:14, he therefore intended to teach his readers that among Christians Christ has taken that place which the law occupies among Jews? Hardly, for just as Jesus says that he came to fulfil not to destroy the law

(according to Matt 5:17-20), so for Paul Christ is the fulfillment of the law by faith and love. Thus, following Paul, Christ establishes the law and does not invalidate it. "Do we then overthrow the law by this faith? By no means! On the contrary, we uphold the law" (Rom 3:31).

19. Isa 42:6; Gen 12:1-3; Exod 19:6; Jonah *passim.*

20. In Rom 9:31-32 Paul describes Jews as "not succeeding" in fulfilling the law, as "falling over the stumbling stones," and in Rom 11:11-12 he speaks of their fall, trespass, and failure. R. Bultmann's reference to their *Scheitern* ("shattering"; the German term means originally "being shipwrecked"; in his essay "Prophecy and Fulfillment," 206-207, the terms "come to grief" and "miscarriage" are employed by the translator) may have some support in Luke 20:18, "every one who falls on that stone will be broken to pieces; but when it falls on any one it will crush him." But Paul does not have in mind a catastrophe that kills but rather a failure to attain a given goal. According to Phil 3:4-8, he himself had indeed written off as a "loss" all of what he was proud of in earlier years; he called it "manure." At that time, he considered himself "in legal rectitude, faultless," not shattered or crushed.

21. It appears necessary to draw the conclusion that only Jesus Christ in person is the remnant of Israel. Indeed, in Rom 9:27--28, "seed" and "remnant" are used as synonyms, and in a clever exegetical step Paul does not interpret "seed of Abraham" in a collective sense in Gal 3:16, but as a designation of the Messiah to come. However, in Rom 11:1-7, he does not explicitly call Christ "the remnant" or "the seed."

22. It is not only unknown, but highly questionable, too, whether Paul ever urged Jews (e.g., when addressing the Sanhedrin or people assembled in synagogues) to become jealous of the baptised Gentiles. Even more dubious is the presumed right of the Church, especially its gentile-Christian majority members, to encourage Jews to do so. To my knowledge, there is only one single instance of a Pauline speech in which such a motivation on the part of a Jew for conversion to faith in Jesus Christ is touched upon: in Gal 2:15-16 Paul reminds Peter that "we sinners of Jewish extraction" (such as Paul and Peter) "even we, too, began to believe in the Messiah Jesus" because we "had come to know that a person is not justified by works of law, but through the faith of the Messiah Jesus." The "person" (*anthropos*) here mentioned may not be a dogmatical construct, that is, an abstraction or generalisation, but rather Adam (Rom 5:12-21), or Abraham before his circumcision (Rom 4:3-22, esp. 10-12), or persons such as Cornelius, the centurion of Caesarea (Acts 10-11). The use of the phrase "we too" in Gal 2:16 may indeed imply something like jealousy regarding the justification of Gentiles by grace which had contributed to the conversion of Paul and Peter.

23. See esp. Isa 2:2-4; Mic 4:1-4; Isa 60:5-16; 66:19-20; Hag 2:7-9; Zech 14:16-19.

24. This interpretation of the collection for Jerusalem is found in Chapter 10 of J. Munck, **Paul and the Salvation of Mankind,** 1959.

25. In Acts 23:6; 24:15; 26:6-7; 28:20; cf Eph 1:12; 4:4, reference is made to the oneness and sameness of the hope of Jews and Christian. At the meeting of the World Council of Churches at Evanston 1954 a declaration pointing out this particular identity was not adopted. See the "Statement of Hope of Israel," **The Evanston Report, 1954** (London: SCM, 1955) 327-328.

26. The statement made in Gal 4:24, that "these things are said allegorically" (literal translation), does not prove that in the following words Paul proposes what today is called an allegorical interpretation. Because in 4:29 Paul argues, "just as then. . .so also now," Gal 4:21-31 ought rather to be called a typological exercise, as indeed is offered in, for example, 1 Cor 10:6, 11: Rom 5:14. In an allegory the literal sense and the historical events evaporate in favor of their spiritual meanings. In typology, however, a correspondence is stated between earlier and later events on the level of history (cf. R. P. C. Hanson, **Allegory and Event** (London: SCM, 1959) 7.

27. Though literary and historical criteria fail to prove beyond any doubt that Galatians was written before Romans, biographical arguments and the probable development of Paul's doctrine favor the dating of Galatians before Romans. Cf. C. H. Buck, "The Date of Galatians," JBL 70 (1951) 113-127; C. E. Faw, "The Anomaly of Galatians," *Biblical Research* 4 (Chicago, 1960) 25-38; R. Jewett, **Paul's Anthropological Terms** (Leiden: Brill, 1971) 11-48; P. Feine, J. Behm, W. G. Kümmel, **Introduction to the New Testament** (London: SCM, 1965) 197-198.

28. Esp. in Eph 1:12-13; 2:1-3, 11-22; 3:6. In what follows we agree with A. Harnack, E.

Haupt, T. K. Abbott, B. F. Westcott, T. Zahn, J. A. T. Robinson, E. Percy, J. Schmid, R. M. Grant, A Robert, A. Feuillet, and H. Schlier, in considering Ephesians authentic. Arguments for this position are collected in M. Barth, **Ephesians, I,** Anchor Bible 34 (New York: Doubleday, 1974) 36-50; for detailed questions see the Index in **Ephesians, II** 848, s.v. "author." M. Rese, "Die Vorzüge Israels nach Rom. 9,4f. und Eph. 2, 12," TZ 31 (1975) 211-222, makes contradictory utterances on Ephesians. He is certainly right in observing thatEphesians says nothing on the hardening and the excision of Israel, nor on a remnant of this people. On the other hand, he argues that this Letter cannot have been written by Paul because, according to its message and unlike the substance of the genuine Pauline writings, the particularity of Israael has moved to the Church (220, 222). Though this proposition fits the above-mentioned theory of substitution (which claims suport not only from passages such as 1 Pet 2:4-10, but also from many uncontested Pauline statements), it is not substantiated by Ephesians; see especially Eph 3:6.

29. It is hard to decide whether this verse speaks of the proclamation of Jesus Christ, made either between his baptism and his death, or immediately after his resurrection. It is also possible that the world-wide, apostolic proclamation of the name of Christ is in mind. For the way in which Paul handles the text of Isa 57:19, see above, n. 11.

30. Eph 5:25-27; 1:22-23; 4:12, 16; 5:23, 30.

31. Eph 2:7; 3:1-13, esp. 10; 6:18-29; cf. Col 1:5-6, 23-29.

32. Regarding Eph 4:13, see M. Barth, "Die Parousie im Epheserbrief," in H. Baltensweiler and Bo Reicke (eds.), **Neues Testament und Geschichte: Festschrift O. Cullmann** (Zürich: Theologischer Verlag, 1972) 238-250.

33. This is the title of an important book by J. Meuzelaar (Assen: van Gorcum, 1961). The substitution of "one body in Christ" (Rom 10:5) by "the body of Christ" appears already in 1 Cor 12:27.

34. J. Moltmann's work on the Church bears this subtitle.

Romans 9-11 As Scriptural Interpretation And Dialogue With Judaism

BRUCE CHILTON

Paul is, arguably, never more himself than in these famous chapters of Romans, and--for just that reason--they have caused exegetes great perplexity. The main lines of Paul's argument seem reasonably clear, but the form of his argumentation, with its many references to Scripture and deductions from Scripture, strikes most readers as both foreign and convoluted. Why is a basically simple idea wrapped up in an esoteric package? As we shall see, that question will itself require refinement as we encounter Paul's thinking, but it will serve us well as we first approach our text.

I. WHAT IS THE IDEA, AND HOW IS IT PACKAGED?

An observant student could sketch out a précis of Paul's thought in Romans 9-11, without reference to the Scripture he cites. The result would be a reasonable, self-contained address, which could be succinctly delivered:

> Although I am distressed that my people have not accepted the gospel (9:1-5), their failure is not God's: it is just that God has, as always, chosen freely whom he wills (9:6-13). That might seem hard, but God is sovereign in the matter of choice (9:14-23), and he has simply decided to call both Jews and Gentiles (9:24-33).[1]
>
> There is now no distinction between Jew and Greek in the matter of salvation: if you confess the Lord Jesus and believe God raised him from the dead, you will be saved (10:1-21, v. 9). Those who are believers must not, however, imagine that God has rejected his people. After all, Jews do believe in Jesus (11:1-10), and even those who do not believe have in their lack of faith, provided an opportunity for Gentiles (11:11-24). Once the fullness of the Gentiles is accomplished, *all* Israel, including both Jews and Gentiles, will be seen to be saved (11:25-36).

There are, of course, crucial facets within each of the statements in the above précis which remain to be explored, but they are subsidiary to the main lines of argument. What becomes unmistakably clear, when we boil Paul's ornate speech down to its essentials, is that he is making a cogent case for a particular view of how God's saving activity in Christ Jesus is consistent with God's election of Israel. Once it is clear that Israel is *elected*, not sovereign, that divine choice is operative, rather than divine right, Paul's observations follow logically.

Paul's design at this point comports well with the purpose of his Letter to the Romans as a whole, and makes sense within the hellenistic environment in which he functions. In a recent book, Stanley Stowers has explained that the writing of letters, whether at the common level of incidental discourse, or with a refined standard of rhetoric, was conventional within the culture of the Mediterranean Basin and is a natural context in which to understand much of the New Testament.[2] The convention also influenced ancient Judaism, which--despite the impression of an isolated phenomenon which some writers give--was itself a lively constituent within the cultural life of its time.[3] But Stowers is well within the scholarly consensus when he concludes that Judaism did not actively appropriate the convention and transmit it directly to Christianity.[4] Specifically, Paul in Romans appears to be writing a "protreptic letter," by which Stowers means a work designed to convert the reader to Paul's teaching. Stowers is able on the basis of a comparison with Greco-Roman convention to argue that the entire Letter is designed to present Paul's gospel of salvation for Gentiles, and defend it against the charge that it means the loss of Israel's salvation.[5] The analysis of Romans according to its function within its most plausible social setting therefore helps us to resolve the main lines of its purpose. Indeed, the clarity of function which emerges from such an approach may appear curiously at odds with the convoluted character of Paul's argument. Whenever an exegete discovers that his or her explanation of a text is dramatically more homogeneous than the text itself, it is time to consider the possibility that over-simplification has crept in. Even if Romans be a "protreptic letter," the involved argument from Scripture in chapters 9-11 is obviously the result of a dynamic not evidenced by the Letter as a whole. Of course, Scripture does play a crucial role in Romans generally (as it does normally in Pauline thought), but the consistency of recourse to textual argument makes our chapters appear distinctive.[6]

Before we consider why Paul's form of argumentation in Romans 9-11 is exegetical in a way most of the Letter is not, we must first appreciate how the simple, discursive case Paul makes is enhanced by means of reference to Scripture. At each major point in the argument, well known passages of Scripture are cited.

A crucial bridge is provided by narratives concerning Isaac. In Rom 9:7, Paul quotes Gen 21:12, "After Isaac shall your seed be named."[7] Now that reference may appear to be an instance of using a "proof text," chosen pretty much at random from a much larger number of those that might have been cited. But the quotation comes at the climax of a story in which God tells Abraham to accede to Sarah's demand, and cast out Hagar and Ishmael, "for the son of this slave woman shall not inherit with my son Isaac" (Gen 21:10). The analogy with the situation Paul believes he addresses is striking. He spells the analogy out in Rom 9:8, "That is, these children of flesh are not children of God, but children of the promise are reckoned as the seed." Of course, that finding requires that Isaac correspond to the promise, and Paul makes out just that correspondence. In Rom 9:9, he quotes Gen 18:14 (or perhaps v. 10), "At this time (next year) I will come, and Sarah will have a son." That verse is resonant, since it caps the story of God's visitation at Mamre: Sarah laughs (v. 12), and is blessed with Isaac, whose name means "he laughs," because it is God's joke in the end.

The pattern established in Rom 9:6-9 is followed consistently in the chapters we are concerned with. At first, Paul does not cite a specific Scripture in what follows, but he does invoke the general case of Rebecca and Isaac (vv. 10, 11). She conceived twins, and before they did anything, or were even born, Rebecca was told, "The greater will serve the lesser" (Rom 9:12 and Gen 25:23). At issue, of course, is the rivalry between Esau and Jacob, which is a major motif of Genesis. Paul sums it all up with a quotation from Malachi, "I loved Jacob and hated Esau" (Rom 9:13 and Mal 1:2, 3). That Paul can draw upon Malachi's appropriation of the motif in Genesis is especially compelling: he implicitly claims that his analogy has prophetic warrant. The fundamentals of his scriptural reasoning are drawn from the Torah, but the nature of his reasoning, he claims, is in line with that of the Prophets.[8]

It is indicative of the consistency of Pauline rhetoric that he now moves from Genesis to Exodus. That shift in scriptural foundation, at 9:14f., corresponds precisely to the development of Paul's argument (see the précis): having rejoiced in God's sovereign choice as the fulfillment of promise, Paul now defends God's sovereignty against the charge that it is unjust or arbitrary (v. 14). God said to Moses, "I will have mercy on whom I have mercy, and I will show compassion to whom I will show compassion" (Exod 33:19; Rom 9:15). Notably, that statement occurs when God is revealing his glory and his name to Moses (cf. Gen 33:12-23): what is at issue is the very nature of God. A particular case in Exodus of God deciding *not* to have mercy, as Paul says (9:18), is that of Pharaoh, of whom Scripture says, "For this purpose I have raised you up, that I might display my power over you, and that my name might be announced in all the earth" (Rom 9:17; Exod 9:16).[9] God's "name" is at issue in both passages, and their association betrays Paul's almost midrashic logic (see below, part II), in which Scripture is held to address issues coherently. The assumption of that coherence is carried over to the Prophets: Isaiah (29:16; 45:9 in Rom 9:20) and Jeremiah (18:6 in Rom 9:21) are used to demonstrate that it is misguided for a vessel of punishment to answer back to its maker. Consideration of Isa 29:16; 45:9; Jer 18:6 within their literary contexts shows that Paul is still attending carefully to the sense of the passages he cites. In all, the paramount issue is the fate of Israel, as determined by a sovereign God.

The next development of Paul's argument, at 9:24f. (again, cf. the précis) also corresponds to a shift in canonical focus. It is demonstrated by citing Hosea and Isaiah that we who are called by God are from both Jews and Gentiles (9:24). First, Hosea shows--at least, to Paul's satisfaction--that Gentiles are to be included among God's people (9:25, 26). Paul garbles the quotation from Hosea, drawing first from 2:23, and then from 1:10, and here is stretching to make a point. Hosea is contextually concerned with the restoration of Israel, not the inclusion of Gentiles; Paul reads what he takes to be a general truth of Scripture into a passage in which that meaning has not literary place. He returns to his usual, more acute interpretation in 9:27-29 when he cites passages from Isaiah by way of arguing that Jews as such are not chosen, but that a remnant from their ranks is to be saved (Isa 10:22; 28:22 and Isa 1:9). Moreover, he cites a curious and creative mixture of Isa 28:16 and 8:14 in Rom 9:33, in order to show that the principle of selecting from the elect places a stone of stumbling and a rock of offense in the midst of Israel (Rom 9:30-32).

Paul's exegetical method is never more complex than in Romans 9, and we need to pause for breath before proceeding further. Although the details of the Pauline execution may dazzle us (as they were no doubt intended to), the fact is that certain characteristic traits are plain. Paul argues from the Torah that (1) God operates by fulfilling promises (vv. 1-13), and that (2) those promises are kept for those chosen by God (vv. 14-23). He then purports to demonstrate from the Prophets that God has chosen his people from among Jews and Gentiles (vv. 24-33). On the whole, but for two exceptions, Paul cites his passages with care and contextual sensitivity, which means that any reader will better appreciate the argument if he or she is familiar with the Scriptures of Israel. The two exceptions to Paul's care and sensitivity are instructive. He reads Gentiles into Hosea (vv. 25, 26), and splices together two verses of Isaiah (v. 33). As we will see shortly, these are not mere lapses on Paul's part. To his mind, the entry of Gentiles among the ranks of God's chosen, and the coming of Christ as a rock of offense to many in Israel, are facts of experience which co-exist with and interpret facts of Scripture. Paul's "text" is not merely Scripture, but his awareness, and others' awareness, that Jesus is God's son.[10]

Once these interpretative characteristics of Paul's argument are appreciated, Roman 10 and 11 may more briefly be summarized from the point of view of their reference to Scripture. In chapter 10, Paul makes his famous, daring assertion that, in Deut 30:11-14, when Moses refers to the nearness of the commandment, he means not any precise instruction, but the presence of Christ, who can neither be brought down from heaven, nor brought up from the abyss, except by God's power (Rom 10:6-8). How does Paul know the Scriptures, properly understood, adduce Christ? He has just told us in v. 4, "Christ is the point of the law, for the righteousness of every believer."[11] By again citing Isa 28:16, in v.11 Paul may betray his own awareness that he is invoking Christ, rather than deducing Christ, at this point. The other usages in chapter 10--of Lev 18:5[12] in 10:5, of Joel 3:5 in 10:13, of Isa 52:7 in 10:15, of Isa 53:1 in 10:16, of 19:4[13] in 10:18, and of Isa 65:1, 2 in 10:20, 21--fall within the more usual Pauline range, of texts which illustrate a coherent principle.

Chapter 11 may be surveyed even more summarily, because the usages of Scripture are all illustrative. There are no special invocations of Christ or of the motif of the inclusion of the Gentiles. Until this point, the bulk of Paul's references have come from the Torah and the Latter Prophets. Now he brings balance to his case scripturally, by citing the instance of Elijah from the Former Prophets. Again, attention to the contexts of the Scriptures Paul cites richly rewards itself. The assertion that God has not rejected his people in 11:2, drawn from 1 Sam 12:22, comes in a context in which the prophet Samuel assures Israel that, despite their wickedness, God's choice is constant (1 Sam 12:19-25). The close of the passage, however, does threaten, "But if you act wickedly, you shall be swept away, both you and your king" (1 Sam 12:25). In other words, the thought of the remnant, which has been explicit part of the argument since 9:27,28 (by means of the citation of Isa 10:22,23), has remained with Paul throughout. For that reason, the reference to Elijah in vv. 2b-5 (cf. 1 Kgs 19:1-18, and vv. 10, 14 and 18 in particular) is apposite: there is a prophetic analogy of the circumstances Paul finds himself in, where only a radical minority has kept faith. Once it is established that the residue of the remnant can be deliberately hardened in their rebellion (cf. Deut 29:3[14] in 11:8 and Psa 69:22, 23[15] in 11:9), there is no further need of scriptural warrant for what Paul argues. He does, however, make a final citation of Isaiah (59:20, 21 and 27:9) in 11:26, 27, by way of making his comprehensive assertion that "all Israel"--but a chastened, forgiven Israel, not a claimant as of right--is to be saved.[16] At this crucial moment, he must again splice Scriptures, not merely cite them, to achieve the dual stress on deliverance and forgiveness which is the apogee of his argument.

Conclusion of Part I

We may set out mentally, as it were side by side, two analyses of Romans 9-11. Followed along one track, the chapters instance protreptic discourse, in which Paul appeals to his readers to follow his way of thinking. He wishes to convince them that

God's inclusion of believing Gentiles with Jews who accept Jesus as Christ represents a fulfillment of the promise to Israel. Followed along the second track, the same chapters represent a carefully orchestrated argument from all the main sections of the Hebrew canon, cited in translation, which is designed to sweep readers up in the promise that all Israel--forgiven Jews and Gentiles--is to be saved (11:26, 27). It is obvious that the two tracks of analysis are complementary, and neither alone would adequately account for the chapters as a whole. But it is equally obvious that the chapters are crafted as a whole: the references to Scripture are only keyed to major devolpments of the argument, they contribute those developments. It is not a matter of discursive thought merely being illustrated scripturally (although illustration is one function of Scripture in Romans). Rather, logic and interpretation here interpenetrate to a remarkable degree, and give Romans 9-11 a unique character within the Pauline corpus.[17] The questions therefore emerge, What is Paul doing here, which makes the chapters distinctive, and Why does he do it?

II. WHAT IS PAUL DOING, AND WHY?

Our second, major question might be answered quickly, were we able to accept the suggestion--developed in much recent scholarship -- that Paul is here providing his readers with a Midrash.[18] It has become conventional to observe that the noun "Midrash" is derived from the verbal form *darash*, and therefore to infer that "Midrash" refers to any "searching out" of meaning on the basis of Scripture within Judaism. It is fairly obvious that, if one is willing to work with such a free-wheeling definition, Romans 9-11 is indeed "Midrash." But such a description obscures more than it discloses.

When the rabbis produced the documents known collectively as Midrashim, the formal aim was--on the whole[19]--to produce commentaries on Scripture. But the "commentary" was not, as in modern usage, an attempt strictly and historically to explain the meaning of a given document. Rather, the sense which the rabbis explored in their Midrashim was the meaning of Scripture within their practice and liturgy and teaching, which were understood as of a piece with the Torah revealed to Moses on Sinai. That is, Midrash represents a synthesis of written text and rabbinic sensibility, in which both are accorded the status of revelation. Jacob Neusner has written the most compelling, systematic account of the development and character of the Midrashim.20 Amongst other things, Neusner shows that a given Midrash may be composed of four distinct orders of interpretation:[21]

(1) close exegesis, or discussion by each word or phrase of Scripture;
(2) amplification of the meaning of a passage;
(3) illustration of a particular theme by various passages;
(4) anthological collection around a general topic.

The result of the compilations of varying readings, involving different categories of interpretaion, was the eleven distinct Midrashim (on various books of the Bible) which emerged by the end of the sixth century.[22]

When one sets out the Midrashim systemayically, and provides precise examples (as Neusner does), the distance from Paul's activity in Romans is striking. His focus is no single biblical book, so that the general form of Midrash is not at issue. The categories of exegesis and amplification, which Neusner shows were most prominent in the earliest Midrashim (of the second century A.D.) simply do not obtain in the case of Paul. It *might* be said--at a stretch--that the third and fourth categories do characterize Pauline interpretation. But the stretch is considerable, because Paul does not merely illustrate by means of Scripture (although illustration is among his techniques); he argues through it and with it towards a conclusion which Scripture itself does not draw, but--at best--is generally consistent with. And, of course, his over-arching theme, of Jesus Christ's completion of the Torah, the Prophets, and the Writings, could never be described as rabbinic. For all those reasons, to style Paul's interpretation as "Midrash" is misleading.

Having called attention to the inadequacy of any direct identification of Paul's method with the rabbis', a certain analogy remains. Both proceed synthetically, and the synthesis moves in two directions at once. First, both take Scripture as a whole, as making a harmonious, common claim upon the mind.[23] Indeed, it should be pointed out that Paul specifies Torah first, and then the Prophets (by name) and the Writings, more punctiliously than the rabbis do. It appears that Paul wishes to make the point of Scripture's unity, and also that he is making an inherently convoluted argument easier to follow than it would be if he were addressing genuine experts. Second, both Paul and the rabbis also synthesize Scripture with their own sensibilities. The last point is perhaps best illustrated by how differently the rabbis of *Leviticus Rabbah* took Gen 21:12, where Abraham's seed is defined, without justification, as those who believe in the world to come.[24] What was for Paul obviously Christological was for the rabbis (of a later period) self-evidently a halakhah of eschatological belief. Just when the rabbis and Paul seem analogous, their conclusions are antipodal.

Paul has also been compared to the sectarians of Qumran and to Philo, in repect of his interpretation of Scripture. But the famous *Pesherim* of Qumran are designed to relate Scripture exactly to the history of the community, and Philo is concerned to comment systematically on Scripture, so as to elucidate its allegedly philosophical truth.[25] Both the *Pesherim* and the Philonic corpus represent different activities and settings from Paul's: his scriptural interpretation strictly serves the protreptic function of Romans. He shows no sustained interest in historicizing Scripture (as in the *Pesherim*) or in philosophizing with it (as in Philo). Paul is driven by other motives, which is why Romans 9-11 is neither Midrash, pesher, nor philosophical commentary.

Paul is arguing with all the Chistians of Rome, both Jews and Gentiles, in an attempt to promote unity. It is true that Paul had no direct, personal acquaintance with the community at Rome, and to that extent, there is an abstract quality about the Letter to the Romans which sets it apart from other Pauline Letters. Writing at a distance from a church known only at second hand, Paul approximates, more nearly than he ever does, to the presentation of his theology in a systematic fashion.[26] Nonetheless, the central, social issue in the church at Rome was known to Paul: there had been disturbances involving Jews in the city, and probably Christians as well, that resulted in their being expelled in A.D. 49 under the Emperor Claudius.[27] Their gradual reintegration into a single Church with Gentiles, which is Paul's goal, could only be accomplished by means of conveying a coherent vision in which both Jews and Gentiles had a place.

The Letter to the Romans offers just such a vision, which is summed up under the slogan which appears here, and only here, within the Pauline corpus: salvation is for the Jews first, and then for the Greek (1:16; 2:9, 10 cf. 3:9, 29; 9:24; 10:12). Salvation is the possession of neither, but is offered and granted to both, provided it is accepted by means of a willingness to be forgiven.

His Letter to the Galatians presents Paul in such heated controversy with Jews who were also Christians, and with those who demanded that the conditions of Judaism be fulfilled by all followers of Christ (whether Jew or Gentile), that one might have expected Paul to have used the occasion of his Letter to the Romans finally to argue that the gospel of Christ could rightly be severed from its Judaic roots.[28] Having written to the Galatians c.A.D. 53, Paul went on in his Corinthian correspondence (c. A.D. 55-56) himself to appropriate scriptural stories of Israel's salvation directly for the Church (cf., for example, 1 Cor 10:1-4 and even to put believing Christians in the role of teachers comparable to--and greater than!--Moses (cf. 2 Cor 3:7-18). Here, in Rome (c. A.D. 57),[29] was a case in which Judaism had been weakened, to the point that Gentiles in the church were tempted to imagine that the divine right of Israel had been usurped definitively by the non-Jewish Church (cf. Rom 11:13-24). Paul's response is unequivocal: the rejection of many in Israel does not give latecomers any special privilege. Indeed, the implication of the remnant is that the essential promise to Israel is confirmed, although the rebellion of some in Israel demonstrates that no one, Jewish or not, can presume upon God's gracious election. When Paul insists throughout Romans that salvation is to Jews first, and then to Greeks, the implication is that the same dynamics of redemption, initially worked out in the case of Israel, are now available to all humanity by means of Jesus Christ. Romans 9-11 embody that leitmotif in the Letter generally. The salvation effected in Christ is uniquely comprehended by means of Scripture, where "Scripture" refers to the canon of Israel. When Paul turns to his gentile readers alone in 11:13-24, he momentarily drops any reference to Scripture, and argues from an agricultural image.[30] His message is clear: however weak the Jewish component may appear, they are root and you are branch. And it is all Israel, root and branch, which God is determined to save.

III. THE IMPLICATIONS OF PAUL'S ARGUMENTATIVE INTERPRETATION

The salvation which God has effected in Christ Jesus is offerred to all humanity, to whomever understands how rightly to appropriate it. To accept forgiveness for the wrath which rightly hangs over us all (Rom 1:18-2:16) demonstrates a humility greater than naturally comes to most of us, and implies a radical redefinition of how the promises of creation and of Abraham's election may be regarded as fulfilled (Romans 4-6). Paul is wrestling with sweeping issues in Romans. Romans 9-11 provide a precise and dynamic instrument for the understanding of God's offer of reconciliation in Christ: Scripture and Christ together, the past experience of Israel and the present experience of the apostle, are held to be the two, complementary sources of a single revelation. Taken together, in a manner akin to longitude and latitude, a careful reading of Scripture and a critical reflection on the implications of faith in Christ are held to open a vision of a single, restored humanity.

The tragedy of Paul's deep and profoundly theological longing for a single Church, grounded in the promises to Israel and expressed by means of the Hebrew Bible, is that his Letters--particularly Romans--have been plundered for rhetoric in order to fabricate an argument Paul never dreamed of making. In popular Paulinism, from the Fathers until our own day, there is a definite predilection for a supersessionist view of Israel: the Jews have been rejected, in order to make room for the newly chosen people of God. As we have seen, that is a conclusion Paul himself specifically rejected, and it has also been the occasion of a spurious argument in favor of anti-Judaism. Jews can be regarded, on this view, not merely as not saved, but as having rejected salvation.

The notion that Christians have superseded Jews is in many ways fomented by our traditional language. We commonly call "the Old Testament" what Paul simply knew as "Scripture" (*graphe*), and our own interpretation of that corpus of books is often limited to historical observations, as if it merely provided "background" for the actual statement of faith, the New Testament.[31] To meet the challenge of Romans 9-11, however, involves reading the whole of the canon in the light of faith; *particularly, it means becoming familiar with the traditions of Israel as that which best articulates God's action in Christ.*

As Paul demands that we articulate our faith in the terms of reference of Israel, so he presses us on to a dialogue with Judaism. Because we share a heritage with Judaism, we are bound to agree and we are bound to disagree with our Jewish contemporaries regarding the significance of that heritage. Agreement and disagreement of that sort, which is analogous to Paul's ambivalent relationship to the Midrashim,[32] is irreducibly an aspect of our respective, religious identities.

The "Israel" whose salvation Paul sees accomplished in Christ consists of people whom Paul understands as identified by their union with Christ in baptism (Rom 6:1-11). Israel is not a people, in the sense of an ethnic entity, still less a land, and yet the simple fact Paul must acknowledge is that Christ is only manifest by means of the Scriptures of a specific people, his people, who dwell by divine promise in a land which should be their own. For that reason, Abraham is a crucial figure in Paul's argument (Romans 4), in that the patriarch must be seen--to function as a witness of Christ--as opening the promise of faith to all, that the whole world might be possessed by means of the promise to Abraham (Rom 4:13). Circumcision must be seen as a seal of faith, not as its condition (vv. 9-12), and the land of Israel must be understood as the first installment of what is to come to all those who are to be included in Christ (vv. 16-25 and 11:25-27). Abraham is for Paul the paradigm of a univocal promise, of which earlier fulfillments were temporary affairs in the interim before Christ. Paul's account of faith, in other words, requires consistent recourse to, dialogue with, and re-interpretation of Judaism and its Scriptures.[33]

The significance of such dialogue may be seen in historical, intellectual, and/or social terms; for considerations of that sort, Jews might welcome it. For Christians, however, dialogue is no mere option, which particular circumstances or dispositions might favor or disfavor. For those of us who attempt to follow in the steps of Paul, Judaism is not simply a potential field of mission, and still less some sort of embarrassment. Judaism represents an authentic (and relatively straightforward) reading of the Hebrew Scriptures, and the gospel is to be grasped as the intersection between that reading and our experience of Christ. Of course, as compared to a bland rejection of Judaism (or condemnation of Christianity as overly complicated), that position will appear complex. But Paul was the apostle who never feared complexity in his battle to grasp, and to be grasped by, the truth of the gospel.

NOTES

1. A break at v. 24 is more plausible in Greek than in English; cf. the twenty-sixth edition of **Novum Testamentum Graece** (eds. E. Nestle, K. Aland (Stuttgart: Deutsche Bibelstiftung, 1979).

2. **Letter Writing in Greco-Roman Antiquity**: Library of Early Christianity (Philadelphia: Westminster, 1986) 25.

3. Stowers, 41-2. Within the Hebrew Bible, Stowers cites 2 Sam 11:14, 15; 1 Kgs 21:8-10; 2 Kgs 10:1-6; 19:9-14; Ezra 4-5. The last two passages, of course, relate Assyrian and Persian letters (and the second should be extended to 6:12). Moreover, all of the passages cited concern royal, official, or military communication, rather than the sort of cultural activity which is reflected in the New Testament. Stowers's references to Philo, Josephus, and 1, 2 Maccabees are more on target.

4. Stowers does not, however, make reference to the letters of Bar Kokhba and to the evidence of correspondence between Antioch and Palestine; both sorts of letter are of direct pertinence to his theme. Cf. J. A. Fitzmyer, "Aramaic Epistolography," **A Wandering Aramean. Collected Aramaic Essays:** SBLMS 25 (Chico: Scholars Press, 1979) 183-204; W. A. Meeks and R. L. Wilken, **Jews and Christians in Antioch in the First Four Centuries of the Common Era:** SBL Sources for Biblical Study 13 (Ann Arbor: Scholars Press,1978).

5. Stowers, 113, 114. Cf. also M. L. Stirewalt, "Appendix: The Form and Function of the Greek Letter-Essay," **The Romans Debate** (ed. K. P. Donfried; Minneapolis: Augsburg, 1977) 175-206 and Donfried, "False Presuppositions in the Study of Romans," **The Romans Debate**, 120-148.

6. Cf. R. Badenas, *Christ the End of the Law. Romans 10:4 in Pauline Perspective,* JSNT 10 (Sheffield: JSOT, 1985) 90-92.

7. Throughout the present paper, the translations are the author's.

8. Paul appears to have operated with the conventional categorization of the Hebrew Bible in Judaism. That categorization recognized divisions of the canon into the Torah (the Pentateuch), the Prophets (including the Former Prophets, from Joshua through 2 Kings, and the Latter Prophets, more familiarly considered prophetic in English), and the Writings (an essentially miscellaneous category).

9. Generally, Paul's text is practially identical with the emerging text of the Septuagint, but he may have been influenced occasionally (as here) by Targumic interpretations, and by the original Hebrew (cf. Chilton, *God in Strength. Jesus' Announcement of the Kingdom*: The Biblical Seminar (Sheffield: JSOT, 1987) 267, 273, 274.

10. Comparison may be invited with the approach of Jesus to Scripture, in which the kingdom is held to be the hermeneutical center of the Scriptures (cf. Chilton, *A Galilean Rabbi and His Bible. Jesus' Use of the Interpreted Scripture of His Time:* Good News Studies 8 [Wilmington: Delaware, 1984]). For Paul, Christ is that center (cf. Rom 10:4).

11. Cf. Badenas, 144-155. Badenas himself does not render *teos* as "point," but such a rendering would be consistent with his case.

12. Notably, this command, in its context, requires separation from the Gentiles, which supports the understanding that, as in Gal 3:12, Paul cites the passage in order to overturn it with a principle of inclusion.

13. 18:5 in the Septuagint and 19:5 in the Masoretic Text.

14. With reverberations with Isa 6:9, 10; 29:10.

15. 68:23, 24 in the Septuagint, and 69:23, 24 in the Masoretic Text.

16. For the present purpose the Scriptural allusion in the closing hymn in chapter 11, vv. 33-36, are excluded from consideration. The principles of interpretation at work there are nonetheless consistent with those elucidated by the present treatment.

17. Cf. Badenas, 90-92.

18. Cf. W. R. Stegner, "Romans 9:6-29--A Midrash," *JSNT* 22 (1984) 37-52. Stegner's work is essentially based upon that of E. Earle Ellis, **Paul's Use of the Old Testament** (Edinburgh: Oliver and Boyd, 1957) and **Prophecy and Hermeneutic in Early Christianity** (Tübingen: Mohr, 1978). If recent discussion must qualify the description of Romans 9-11 as Midrash, there is nonetheless no doubt but that Ellis contributes signally to our understanding of Paul's manner of thinking Scripturally. Indirectly, the Midrashim shed light on the sort of activity Paul was engaged in; it is only the direct equation of Pauline interpretation with the genre of Midrash which needs to be set aside.

19. In what follows, generalization has been necessary to a higher degree than would be acceptable if the exegesis of the Midrashim were primarily at issue, and it must be remembered that no generalization can replace familiarity with the literature involved.

20. **Midrash in Context. Exegesis in Formative Judaism:** The Foundations of Judaism 1 (Philadelphia: Fortress, 1983).

21. Neusner, pp. 82, 83. It should be noted that these are the modalities of interpretation which Neusner identifies in Talmud, and which he shows were then applied to the Bible in the Midrashim.

22. Ibid., 103.

23. For this reason, the procedures for associating disparate passages are important for both Paul and the rabbis. The famous rabbinic rules of interpretation might be regarded as an attempt to specify how the harmony of scripture may be defined; cf. A. Finkel, **The Pharisee and the Teacher of Nazareth:** Arbeiten zur Geschichte des Spajudentums und seiner Umwelt (Leiden: Brill, 1964) 123-128.

24. The following rendering is that of H. Freedman (*Genesis*: Midrash Rabbah (eds. H. Freedman and M. Simon; New York: Soncino, 1983) at *Genesis Rabbah* 53.12:

> AND GOD SAID UNTO ABRAHAM: LET IT NOT BE GRIEVOUS IN THY SIGHT. . .FOR IN ISAAC SHALL SEED BE CALLED TO THEE (21:12). R. Judan b. Shilum said: Not "Isaac," but IN ISAAC is written here. R. 'Azariah said in the name of Bar Hutah: the beth (IN) denotes two, i.e., [they seed shall be called] in him who recognizes the existence of two worlds. R. Judah b. R. Shalum said: It is written, REMEMBER HIS MARVELOUS WORKS THAT HE HATH DONE, HIS SIGNS, AND THE JUDGMENTS OF HIS MOUTH (Psa 105:5): [God says:] I have given a sign [whereby the true descendants of Abraham can be known], viz. he who expressly recognizes [God's judgments]: thus whoever believes in the two worlds shall be called "they seed ," while he who rejects belief in two worlds shall not be called "they seed."

In order to appreciate the interpretation, which also appears in Talmud (Nedarim 31a), it is necessary to realize that *beth* in Hebrew may mean both "in" and "two."

25. Cf. Chiton, "Commenting on the Old Testament (with particular reference to the pesharim, Philo, and the Mekilta," **It is Written: Scripture Citing Scripture. Essays in Honour of Barnabas Lindars,** S.S.F. (eds D.A. Carson and H.G. M. Williamson; Cambridge: Cambridge University Press, 1988) 122-140.

26. E. P. Sanders, **Paul, the Law, and the Jewish People** (Philadelphia: Fortress, 1985) 31, 46, 59 n. 75, 97.

27. Cf. Wolfgang Wiefel, "The Jewish Community in Ancient Rome and the Origins of Roman Christianity," **The Romans Debate,** 100-119. Wiefel attempts to harmonize the accounts of the New Testament, Suetonius, and Dio Cassius, and in so doing may be reasoning beyond the limits of certainty imposed by the evidence. He argues that Claudius first expelled Jews from Rome (so Suetonius and Orosius) and--after many returned-- attempted to prohibit their meeting in public (so Dio Cassius). F.F. Bruce imagines the precisely opposite scenario: meetings were first banned, and expulsion followed **New Testament History** (London: Pickering and Inglis, 1982) 279-283. But the fact of a disturbance involving Jews is well established; that it had an immediate impact upon Christianity is a second inference (cf. Acts 18:2; Cassius Dio, **Roman History** 60. 66; Suetonius, Claudius 25:4; Orosius, **Seven Books of History against the Pagans** 7.6). In any case, Wiefel is clearly correct in viewing Romans as an appeal for unity to a mixed church, in which Gentiles were in the majority. For further discussion, cf. E. Mary Smallwood, **The Jews under Roman Rule. From Pompey to Diocletian**: Studies in Judaism in Late Antquity 20 (Leiden: Brill, 1976) 210-216 and Francis Watson, **Paul, Judaism and the Gentiles. A Sociological Approach**: SNTSMS 56 (Cambridge: Cambridge University Press, 1986) 91-94 (for positions in support of Bruce's).

28. Yet even in his earlier Letters, Paul's position in Romans may be regarded as adumbrated; cf. 1 Cor 1:21-25; 9:20-23; 10:32, 33; 12:13; Gal 3:28.

29. The dates here offered, which are well within the range of the scholarly consensus which has emerged, are those of Chilton, **Beginning New Testament Study** (Grand Rapids: Eerdmans, 1987).

30. A.G. Baxter and J.A. Ziesler, "Paul and Arboriculture: Romans 11:17-24," JSNT 24 (1985) 25-32,. Their argument is especially telling, in that the purpose of the grafting -- which was not considered outlandish in antiquity--was to re-invigorate the tree in which the scion was implanted. The authors cite a contemporary of Paul's Columella (*De re rusticus* 5.11.1-15 and *De arboribus* 26-27); cf. 27-29.

31. The designation "New Testament" by no means implies necessarily that the Hebrew Bible is the "Old Testament." On the principle that those who originate works have the first call on naming them, "Hebrew Bible" and "New Testament" can stand side by side without contradiction or embarrassment.

32. Cf. H. J. Schoeps (tr. H. Knight), **Paul, The Theology of the Apostle in the Light of Jewish Religious History** (Philadelphia: Westminster, 1961) 244.

33. In just this sense, Watson's argument, that Paul is attempting here to show "*the consistency of the Pauline view of God's activity with the OT Scriptures*" (Paul, 162) is apposite. For Watson, however, that observation contributes to the finding that Romans was written in order to convince "the Jewish Christian congregation in Rome to separate themselves from the Jewish community, to accept the legitimacy of the Pauline Gentile congregation in which the law is not observed, and to unite with it for worship" (173). A detailed consideration of Watson's views is merited, and cannot be provided here. Obviously, I would concur with the emphasis on Paul's desire for unity. But I do not believe Watson has adequately accounted for the relative flexibility of Roman Judaism (cf. Harry J. Leon, **The Jews of Ancient Rome**: The Morris Loeb Series [Philadelphia: The Jewish Publication Society of America, 1960]), where baptism in Jesus' name need not have implied automatic exclusion from the synagogue at the time Paul wrote, nor can I see Paul demanding the sort of separation from Judaism which is presupposed in Hebrews. Notably, Watson himself observes that Romans 11 is far more positive in respect of Judaism than his thesis would allow (170-173).

THE SALVATION OF ISRAEL IN ROMANS 11:25-32 A RESPONSE TO KRISTER STENDAHL

SCOTT HAFEMANN

One of the most pressing issues for the Church in the last decades of the twentieth century is once again the question of her attitude toward the Jewish people. After centuries of relative neglect, modern Zionism, the Jewish holocaust, and the reestablishment of the state of Israel have raised anew in a poignant and especially painful way the age-old question of the relationship, both religiously and politically, between Jews and Christians. The daily newspaper and nightly television have brought those Christians who have never heard of Section 4 of the Second Vatican Council's "Declaration on the Relation of the Church to Non-Christian Religions," *Nostra Aetate*,[1] nor ever even met a Jew, face to face with the question of the Church's responsibility and role toward the people from whom she has received her history, Scripture, and Lord. And since 1948 literally millions of Christians have been introduced to a dispensationalist view of the central place of Israel in the future timetable of the eschatological drama.[2]

Indeed, the roots of this question go back to the writings of the New Testament itself.[3] And nowhere is this more apparent than in the writings of the apostle Paul, where the themes of the relationship between the law and the gospel, old covenant/new covenant, and Israel/Church are explicitly and repeatedly treated. It is no wonder then that in the last twenty-five years much of the renewed focus on the question of the relationship of the Church to Israel has centered on the theology of Paul, particularly his extended treatment of this theme in Romans 9-11. The renewal of interest in this question in Romans 9-11 has also been tied to the recent renewal of interest in the classical questions of Pauline interpretation as a whole, especially those surrounding Paul's theology, and the nature of Paul's opposition in his various churches.[4] In both of these areas Pauline studies is going through a radical reinvestigation of its most cherished convictions, so much so that some have concluded that a fundamental "paradigm shift" has already occurred.[5] How one understands these more fundamental issues in approaching Paul will therefore have a great effect on one's understanding of the salvation of Israel in Romans 9-11. In any hermeneutical circle, one's grasp of the whole will inevitably effect the interpretation of the part. The issues are thus complex and interrelated, and together all have a direct bearing on the overarching question of the relationship between the Church and Israel in Paul's thought, in the New Testament as a whole, and in the life of the Church today.

The focus of this essay is the very specific question of the nature of the salvation of Israel in Rom 11:25-32 in order to ask, in turn, what bearing this text might have for understanding the more fundamental issues of Paul's theology that undergird it. In other words, the question is not, "Given Paul's understanding of the law, the heart of his gospel, and his response to his opponents, what must he think about the salvation of Israel in Rom 11:25-32?" Rather, in this paper we ask the more specifically exegetical question, "Given his understanding of the salvation of Israel in Rom 11:25-32, what implications does this have for understanding Paul's theology?" For when faced with the hermeneutical circle of the whole and the parts, it is always sounder, methodologically, to begin with the part..

"Iron sharpens iron" (Prov 27:17), so that any interpretation benefits greatly from dialogue with a partner. And since one of the most influential interpretations of Paul's understanding of the salvation of Israel in Romans 11 within the framework of the current debate and perspectives on Paul has been the work of Krister Stendahl, the purpose of this paper is to reexamine Rom 11:25-36 against the backdrop of Stendahl's thesis in order once again to pose the question of the means and nature of Israel's salvation within the theology of Paul.

I. KRISTER STENDAHL'S PARADIGM FOR UNDERSTANDING PAUL

Since Stendahl's interpretation of Rom 11:25-36 cannot be understood apart from his interpretation of Paul as an apostle and his view of the driving force of Paul's thought, an analysis of his view of Rom 11:25-36 must begin here. For when Stendahl first pointed out the need for a radical reinvestigation of Paul's thought almost thirty years ago, his goal in reevaluating the question of the salvation of Israel in Rom 11:25-36 was the same as his purpose in rethinking the questions of Paul's self-understanding as an apostle and the center of his theology.[6] In all three cases Stendahl wanted to place Paul back into the historical context in which he belonged and from which he must be interpreted, namely, "the lost centrality of Jews and Gentiles" in Paul's self-conception and theology (pp. 3, 7, 12, 15, 127, 130-31).

In regard to Paul's theology, Stendahl's concern grew out of his conviction that Paul's teaching concerning justification by faith, under the influence of Reformation dogmatics, had been "removed from its setting within the relationship between Jew and Gentile" and had become inappropriately transposed into the very center of his "teaching about salvation" (p. 5). To posit that "justification by faith alone" is the center of Paul's theology thus "blocks our access both to the original thought and the original intention of Paul" (p. 3). Specifically, it obscures the "specificity of Paul's arguments" within his various letters and makes it possible "to homogenize Pauline theology since the common denominator could easily be found in generalized theological issues" (p. 5). For in Stendahl's view,

> Paul's doctrine of justification by faith has its theological context in his reflection on the relation between Jews and Gentiles, and not within the problem of how man is to be saved, or how man's deeds are to be accounted, or how the free will of individuals is to be asserted or checked (p. 26; cf. pp. 27, 37, 40, 68).

The ultimate result of this misappropriation of the context of Paul's theology is that the Pauline problem of the relationship between Jews and Gentiles becomes captive to and is finally replaced by the Western problem of the introspective conscience (cf. pp. 87, 93). Rather than speaking to the status of Gentiles within God's plan for the world, justification by faith becomes the abstract doctrinal response either to the despair provoked by humankind's failed attempts to live up to the moral demands of the law of God, or to the pride caused by humanity's self-deceived attempt to justify themselves (pp. 87-88, 91-92).

As a corollary to this misguided analysis of Paul's theology, Stendahl argues that interpreters have also wrongly universalized Paul's Damascus Road experience into an abstract conception of "that inner experience of conversion which Western theology has taken for granted" (p. 12). Consequently the "I" of Paul's writings has been equated with the experience of "the Christian," interpreted through the lenses of persons like Luther or Calvin, rather than with Paul himself in his specific role as "the Apostle to the Gentiles" (p. 12; cf. p. 5). Paul's Damascus Road experience thus becomes the archetype of the modern conception of a conversion from one religious system to another in order to escape the sinfulness and guilt of the human predicament.

To counter these false conclusions, Stendahl contends that "Paul's argument about justification by faith neither grows out of his 'dissatisfaction' with Judaism, nor is intended as a frontal attack on 'legalism'. . . ," but instead "was hammered out by Paul for the very specific and limited purpose of defending the rights of gentile converts to be full and genuine heirs to the promises of God to Israel. Their rights were based solely on faith in Jesus Christ" (pp. 130, 2). For Stendahl, therefore, Paul's view of justification by faith served merely as that apologetic doctrine which " 'justified' the status of gentile Christians as honorary Jews. . . ." (p. 5, cf. p. 130). Thus, Paul's "call" to be the apostle to the *Gentiles*, not some deep-seated moral or theological problem with the law, was the impetus for the development of this doctrine. Hence, rather than "the pervasive, organizing doctrinal principle or insight of Paul . . . the doctrine of justification originates in Paul's theological mind from his grappling with the problem of how to defend the place of Gentiles in the Kingdom--the task with which he was charged in his call" (p. 27).

Specifically, Paul's task and ministry are to bring the Good News to the Gentiles that, justified by faith, they "will become part of the people of God without having to pass thought the law. This is Paul's secret revelation and knowledge" (p. 9). Viewed from this perspective, Paul's Damascus Road experience is not a conversion to a new religious persuasion, but a "new and special calling in God's service. God's Messiah asks him a Jew to bring God's message to the Gentiles. . . . Rather than being 'converted,' Paul was called to the specific task--made clear to him by his experience of the risen Lord--of apostleship to the Gentiles. . . ." (p. 7).

Stendahl supports his view by showing that Paul's "call rather than conversion" in Gal 1: 13-16 (cf. Acts 9:15; 22: 14-15, 21; 26:16-18) is patterned after the prophetic calls of Isaiah and Jeremiah in which Paul too is commissioned for service, this time to go to the Gentiles with the message of salvation (cf. Jer 1:5; Isa 35:5; 42:7, 16; 49:1, 6; 61:1) (pp. 8-10). Paul has been called as a Jew, not to preach the new message of a new religion, but to a new mission as a Jew on "a new understanding of the law which is otherwise an obstacle to the Gentiles" (p. 9). From beginning to end, therefore, Paul's self-conception, as well as his theology, derive from his concern as a *Jewish* apostle called to the *Gentiles*. For Paul to be a Christian *is* for him to be an apostle and vice versa (p. 12). "There is not--as we usually think--first a conversion, and then a call to apostleship; there is only the call to work among the Gentiles" (pp. 84-85).

Conversely, our job as Paul's interpreters is not to make Paul a prisoner of our convictions and concerns by replacing the Pauline problem of the relationship between Jews and Gentiles with the Western problem of the introspective conscience. Justification by faith must not be transformed into the center of Paul's thinking. A conversion from helplessness and guilt must be kept from becoming the focal point of his self-understanding. Instead, we are to let Paul once again be the first century Jewish Apostle to the Gentiles who found himself between Jews and Gentiles both personally and theologically. Once this takes place, the real issues of Paul's theology and life will come back into focus: (1) What happens to the law (the Torah, the actual law of Moses, not the principle of legalism) when the Messiah has come? (2) What are the ramifications of the Messiah's arrival for the relation between Jews and Gentiles? (p. 84).

For Stendahl, these then are the perspectives and questions that ought to guide any interpretation of Paul's letters today, especially Paul's Letter to the Romans with its explicit treatment of these themes in chapters 9-11. For of all of Paul's writings, "the lost centrality of 'Jews and Gentiles' is most clearly to be felt in a study of Romans" (p. 3).

II. THE IMPLICATIONS FOR READING ROM 11:25-36

For Stendahl, Paul's Letter to the Romans is not an abstract theological treatise on the doctrine of justification by faith alone. Nor is it Paul's polemical defense against the criticisms of a group of gentile or Jewish-Christian "Judaizers" in an attempt to win them over to his law-free gospel. Indeed, Stendahl sees no attempt in any of Paul's writings to draw out the implications of his doctrine of justification by faith alone for Jewish Christians. (p. 2). Rather, Paul's Letter to the Romans is his attempt to introduce his apostleship to the church in Rome in the hope of making clear how his mission to the Gentiles fits into God's total plan and scheme for the world (pp. 3, 27).

In Romans Paul thus addresses himself to his gentile audience, but the focus of his attention is on the Jews. For in Stendahl's view, Paul outlines his doctrine of justification in Romans not only to defend the right of the Gentiles to be members of the people of God without keeping the law, but also to counter the Gentiles' propensity to pride in view of the Jews' rejection of Jesus (pp. 4-5, 132). In Stendahl's words, "Paul's reference to God's mysterious plan is an affirmation of a God-willed coexistence between Judaism and Christianity in which the missionary urge to convert Israel is held in check" (p. 4). For according to Stendahl, Paul has come to see that in spite of the Jews' rejection of Jesus as the Messiah, "God has mysterious and special plans for the salvation of Israel" (p. 4). Paul's burden in Romans is thus to argue for the inclusion of both Gentiles and Jews within God's people, the former because of and in Christ, the latter outside of him.

Stendahl therefore argues for a different evaluation of the center and gravity of Romans itself. From the perspective of Paul "among Jews and Gentiles," Romans 9-11, with its crescendo in 11:25-36, is no longer to be read as an appendix to Romans 1-8, nor even as some sort of secondary digression in the development and application of Paul's central thesis on justification by faith in chapters 1-8 and 12-15, but as the very climax of the letter (pp. 4, 28, 85, 132). For in Romans 9-11 Paul addresses the question of the relationship between Jews and Gentiles directly in order to bring his argument for the inclusion of the Gentiles to bear on the question of the future of Israel. It is here that the "mystery" of God in regard to the Jews finds its explicit expression (cf. 11:25) so that the pride of the Gentiles can be decisively denounced (cf. 11:25 with 11:18-24).

Stendahl's specific arguments for his conclusion that in Romans 9-11 Paul teaches the separate coexistence of Jews and Gentiles within the salvific plan of God are based on five exegetical observations. First, Paul is silent concerning the means of Israel's salvation in 11:26.

> It should be noted that Paul does not say that when the time of God's Kingdom, the consummation, comes Israel will accept Jesus as Messiah. He says only that the time will come when "all Israel will be saved" (11:26) (p. 4).

Second, once Paul turns his attention to the future of Israel in 10:17-11:36 there is no more mention of Jesus Christ (p. 4). Third, the striking nature of this absence of any mention of Jesus Christ after 10:17 is accentuated by the fact that Romans 9-11 end with the only doxology in Paul without a Christological element (p. 4). Fourthly, as this *theological* doxology indicates, the issue at stake in Romans 9-11, especially 11:11-36, is not the future of Israel *per se*, but the pride of the Gentiles as expressed in 11:18, 20, 25 (p. 132). For as Stendahl puts it elsewhere, the purpose of this "striking absence of overt Christology" and a doxology which is "totally in 'God language,' i.e. without any reference to Jesus or Christ" was "to upbraid gentile Christians for their haughty attitude toward the Jews."[7] Why?

> Presumably for the reason that he had found something unnerving in the missionary zeal of his bragging gentile converts over against the Jewish people. . . he reminds them that the consummation is a mystery--not we winning over them--'lest you be wise in your own conceits' (11:25). . . Paul, the missionary, actually puts brakes on the missionary urge and instinct. He unmasks it as a secularised style of thinking, soiled by hubris on the part of Gentiles.[8]

Finally, as this passage makes clear, Stendahl suggests that Paul's reference to the "mystery" (*mustērion*) in 11:25 is meant to convey that its future fulfillment is unknown or "mysterious" so that no one can predict its details (cf. pp. 4, 132).[9] But one thing is clear, "The expression 'And so the whole of Israel will be saved, *sōthēsetai*, does not indicate any acceptance of Jesus as the Messiah."[10]

Two reasons account for this rather lengthy restatement of Stendahl's position. First, the influence of his views requires that they be taken seriously. But even more important, the interrelationship between his paradigm for understanding Paul in general and his specific interpretation of Rom 11:25-36 is crucial for understanding his train of thought. For in tracing his postion, it becomes readily apparent that Stendahl reads Rom 11:25-36 the way he does because of his views concerning Paul's conversion and his understanding of the role of justification in Paul's thought. Paul's message of justification by faith in Jesus cannot be intended for Israel if Paul was never "converted" from his Jewish faith when he met Christ on the road to Damascus. On the other hand, Paul cannot condone a Christian mission to the Jews by the Gentiles if the role of justification is merely to support the inclusion of the Gentiles as "honorary Jews." Instead, "the central issue claiming Paul's attention was that of the inclusion both of Gentiles and Jews" in God's plan of salvation, each in their own, independent way (p. 28). Unfortunately, Paul's original intent was lost when his gospel was taken captive by Western theology and psychology. Once this happened, Paul's message for the Gentiles could be *misapplied* to the Jews, since the "introspective conscience of the West" universalized the Pauline gospel by misinterpreting it to refer to the common modern dilemma of guilt-ridden failure, a dilemma which did not exist in Paul's day.

III. ROM 11:25-36 WITHIN THE CONTEXT OF ROMANS 9-11

Doubtless many of Stendahl's observations concerning the destructive influence of the Reformation paradigm for understanding Paul's self-conception and view of the law are very helpful and have rightly been a programmatic stimulus for a rereading of Paul's letters. And certainly Rom 11:25-36 must be so read if Stendahl's overall thesis concerning Jew/Gentile relations in Paul's thought is to stand without modification. But since Rom 11:25-36 is the only explicit treatment of the question of the future of Israel,[11] any alternative interpretation of this key text would create an anomaly for Stendahl's own paradigm too great to be ignored. Does this passage then, in fact, support Stendahl's thesis? And if not, what necessary adjustment(s) must be made? In order to answer these questions, we must examine the argument of Romans 9-11 itself.

1. The Centrality of Rom 9:6 in Romans 9-11

Students of Paul are generally agreed that the impetus for Paul's argument in these chapters is the extreme anguish Paul himself feels over the fact that his own people are rejecting Jesus as the Messiah (cf. 9:2-3 in view of 9:31-33). As Stendahl himself has emphasized, for Paul the "genetic center" of all that is said about Jesus is that he is the Messiah and that the messianic age has dawned.[12] Thus, Paul's pain is increased by his realization that, of all peoples, it is the "Israelites" who seemingly should have responded to Jesus, since they are the ones to whom the covenant blessings and promises have been given and from whom the Messiah has now come (9:4-5). Only *some* of the Jews of Paul's day, however, are following Jesus as Christ (cf. Rom 9:3; 10:16; 11:14).

But, as the switch in focus in 9:6 from Paul's feelings and wish and the Israelites' privileges to the question of God's word indicates, even more important for Paul is the theological question that Israel's rejection of the Messiah raises for God *himself*! For as Hans Hübner has recently pointed out once again, the ultimate issue for Paul in Romans 9-11, as introduced in 9:6, is not the rejection of Jesus by Paul's contemporaries, but the problem this rejection creates for the character of God.[13] Israel's rejection of the Messiah seems to call into question God's faithfulness to the very covenant promises and privileges outlined in 9:4-5, promises and privileges which entail and imply the eschatological redemption of Israel.[14] For Paul it is thus *God's* word and consequently *his* trustworthiness which is ultimately at stake. John Piper states the issue well: "Rom 9:1-5 states the problem: it appears that what God has guaranteed is in fact not happening--the end-time salvation of Israel. Has then the word--the reliability--of God fallen, and with it the Christian hope as well?"[15]

The main theme of Romans 9-11, therefore, is not the relationship between Jews and Gentiles, the nature of Paul's mission in the plan of God, the future of Israel, the scheme of salvation history, the identity of true Israel, nor even the nature of God's election and predestination, *per se*.[16] These are all penultimate concerns. The central issue in Romans 9-11 is whether God's faithfulness to himself and to his promised redemptive, saving activity can be maintained in spite of Israel's rejection of Jesus.[17]

Paul's answer to this question is clear. In spite of the fact that most of Israel are rejecting the Messiah, God's word has *nevertheless* not failed (9:6a). This, not Paul's assertion in 9:6b that "not all those who are from Israel are Israel," nor any other assertion or sub-section, is the main point and controlling motif of the argument of Romans 9-11.[18] Everything from 9:6b onward (note the chain of argumentation introduced with the *gar* in 9:6b) is designed to support this declaration, with the possible exception of the doxology in 11:33-36, where Paul's argument in support of 9:6a has ceased and his concluding personal response begins. For Paul, theology naturally evolves into doxology.[19] Thus the main point of the argument of Romans 9-11 remains Paul's bold assertion in 9:6a that in spite of most of Israel's rejection of Jesus, God is still faithful to his covenant promises to physical, national, ethnic Israel (9:4-5). His word has not failed.[20]

The implication of this structural observation for understanding 11:25-32 becomes evident. Rather than the climax of Romans 9-11 (or for that matter of Romans as a whole),[21] or the summary of these chapters,[22] Paul's argument in 11:25-32 functions to support Paul's *a-fortiori* statement in 11:24 that the "natural branches" of ethnic Israel who believe (cf. 11:23) will be grafted back into the "olive tree" (cf. the *gar* of v. 25). In so doing, vv. 25-32 provide the last and perhaps most important support for the point of 9:6a. Why has God's word not failed? Because, just as God has promised, "all Israel shall be saved" (11:26).[23] But before Paul can draw this conclusion, he must first answer why the *current* rejection of the Messiah by the vast majority of Israel has not *already* overthrown God's word. It is one thing to posit a future salvation of Israel that will fulfill God's word, but it is quite another to show how God is being faithful *now* to his promises to Israel in spite of the fact that most of those who belong to Paul's "kinsmen according to the flesh" (9:3) have rejected the Messiah. In regard to the trustworthiness of God's character, faithfulness in the future is worthless without faithfulness in the present. Thus, unless we decide that Paul is hopelessly inconsistent at this point,[24] any interpretation of the future of Israel in 11:25-36 must therefore be related to his view of Israel in the present.

2. The Identity of True Israel in Rom 9:6b-13

Paul's answer to the problem posed by Israel's present rejection of Jesus is first given in 9:6b-7 and then interpreted and supported in 9: 8-13. Paul's answer is short and to the point: God's word to ethnic Israel in 9:4-5 has not failed because God's promise to Abraham never included a promise of salvation to his descendants based on their ethnic identity. This is the point of Paul's play on the word "Israel" in 9:6b: "All those from [ethnic] Israel are not [spiritual, true] Israel." In 9:7 Paul puts the same point in different words: God's promises to Israel have not failed "because (*hoti*) the seed of Abraham (= ethnic Israel) are not all children (of the Abrahamic Covenant=children of God, cf. v. 8) [spiritual Israel]. But 'through Isaac shall a seed be called to you'." Rom 9:8 offers an interpretation of this promise to Abraham quoted from Gen 21:12. The children of the flesh are not the children of God, only "the children of promise" are Abraham's true seed (9:8), that is, only those *within* ethnic Israel who have also been given the promise of redemption. God has no commitment, therefore, to save *all* of ethnic Israel, but only those whom, in his sovereign call (9:7), he has unconditionally elected to be part of his spiritual people (9:11). The examples from the patriarchs in 9:9-13 are then given to support this interpretation of the distinction between ethnic and spiritual Israel as paradigms of how God preserves his purpose of election (9:11b).[25]

Paul's point is clear. Since God never promised to save all ethnic Israelites, the rejection of Jesus by the majority in Paul's day caused no problem for the integrity of God's word. Moreover, it is instructive to note that the introduction of the themes of

God's call, promise, and election in 9:7-13 in order to distinguish between ethnic Israel and the true Israel of God's covenantal obligation is offered as the *solution* to the problem of the rejection of the Messiah in 9:3. This indicates that, for Paul, ethnic Israel's rejection of Jesus as the Messiah must be a sign of being outside of the Abrahamic covenant and the people of God (9: 7-8).

In contrast, those ethnic Jews who are part of "true Israel" will continue within the covenant people of God by accepting the Messiah in fulfillment of God's call and promise in their lives. Hence, if Paul parallels the elect within ethnic Israel with those who accept Jesus as the Messiah, then the contrast between true Israel and ethnic Israel in 9:6b-13 must be equivalent to that between the Jewish-Christian and the non-Christian Jew of Paul's day.[26] And in each case, one's status before God is determined by God's unconditional, sovereign election (9: 11).

God's word thus also stands because God is the one who has determined who from within ethnic Israel will respond to his call in Christ, just as he chose which one of the twins would be the child of promise (9:11). God therefore remains faithful because God's promise to ethnic Israel is a *self*-commitment rather than a response to their ethnic distinction. On the one hand, God need not elect any from within ethnic Israel simply because they are ethnic Israelites. On the other hand, God has committed himself to Abraham to elect those from within ethnic Israel whom he chooses. As long as he does both of these, so that those who are part of true Israel are always children of God by *promise* (9:8), God's word to Abraham and to ethnic Israel stands.

3. The Questions of Romans 9-11

Paul knows that this answer to the problem of ethnic Israel's rejection of the Messiah will spawn a host of objections. Thus, in typical diatribe style, he now proceeds to take up these questions by anticipating where his argument will lead his reader and then posing the next logical question *himself* in order to answer it. As a result, each of these rhetorical questions marks a turning point in Paul's argument so that Rom 9:13-11:32 can be structured around these pivotal questions. Moreover, the major breaks in Paul's thought can be distinguished from the minor moves in his argument by the different style of rhetorical questions used.

The first two major breaks are thus signaled by the use of the same question "What therefore shall we say?" in 9:14 and 9:30, in distinction to the various other types of questions used by Paul to move the argument along within these sections (cf. 9:19, 20-21, 22-23, 32; 10:14-15, 18-19). Similarly, the second two sections of Paul's argument are marked off in 11:1 and 11:11 by a rhetorical question introduced with the same phrase, "I say, therefore. . . " in contrast to the rhetorical question in 11:7 and possibly 11:24. Moreover, three of the four of these major thesis-like questions are denied with the characteristic phrase *mē genoito*, 9:14; 11:1; 11:11) while none of the interior questions are negated. The argument of Rom 9:14-11:32 is therefore built around these four significant turning points, with the main point of each section leading to the next. The structure of 9:14-11:32 can thus be summarized as follows:

(1) Paul's support for the integrity of God's word, which leads to the question of 9:14a: "Is God unjust?"
(2) The justice of God in 9:14-29, which leads to the question of 9:30-31: "Why did the Gentiles attain righteousness while Israel did not?"
(3) The failure of the Jews in 9:30-10:21, which leads to the question of 11:1:

"Has God therefore rejected his people?"

(4) The role of the remnant as a sign of the faithfulness of God in 11:1-10, which leads to the question of 11:11: "Has Israel stumbled so that they have fallen?"

Paul, therefore, bridges the gap between his final answer concerning the future of Israel in 11:25-32 and his first answer concerning Israel in the present by means of a step-by-step argument regarding the nature of God's relationship to ethnic Israel during the interim period in redemptive history between the promise to Abraham (9:7) and the consummation of this age (11:26-27). The scope of this paper does not permit a detailed analysis of each of these sections. It will suffice for our purpose, however, to trace briefly the basic flow of Paul's argument as it crystallizes around these four rhetorical questions in anticipation of his argument in 11:12-32. For having given his answer to the question of God's commitment to ethnic Israel in the present, the question that Paul must eventually answer is why he can assert that "all Israel shall be saved" in the *future* (11:26) if God has no necessary commitment to save ethnic Israel as a whole in the *present*. Attempts to solve this problem by interpreting "Israel" in 11:26 to refer to the "true" or "spiritual Israel" throughout time, or to the Church as a new spiritual Israel comprised of both Jews and Gentiles, rather than to ethnic Israel, prove unconvincing (see below.)[27] The answer lies in bridging the gap between the integrity of God's word to ethnic Israel in the present (9:6b-13) and its integrity in the future (11:11-32) when the content of these words appears distinct.

IV. THE ARGUMENT FOR THE INTEGRITY OF GOD'S WORD IN ROM 9:14-11:10

1. Is God Unjust?

Paul's support for his distinction between ethnic and true Israel on the basis of God's sovereign election naturally raises the question of God's justice in 9:14a. How can God be just if he elects without regard for human distinctives by choosing the children of promise before they are even born? Paul's answer is a complex one that hinges on the definition of God's glory found in Exod 33:19 and quoted in 9:15.[28] According to this text, God's glory consists in his ability to bestow his kindness freely as an act of unconstrained mercy. And "the most fundamental characteristic of God's righteousness is his allegiance to his own name, that is, to his honor and glory."[29] Hence, for God to be just he must preserve his glory and the honor of his name. God is, therefore, just in electing his people apart from their human distinctives (good or bad) since, by so doing, he is acting to maintain his glory as revealed in his acts of mercy. But as the example of Pharaoh demonstrates, this also means that God is just when he "hardens whom he wills" (9:17-18). In addition, it is equally unjust for humankind to protest God's sovereignty since God has the right (*exousia*) to use his vessels as instruments and/or objects of wrath as he pleases (9:20-21). Moreover, God's justice is shown to be predominantly characterized by mercy since the vessels of wrath serve the penultimate purpose of providing the means to display God's glory on the vessels of mercy (9:17b, 22-23). Thus, in 9:14-23 Paul's reader is encouraged not only to accept God's sovereign election as an expression of his justice, but also to acknowledge the good and merciful end of God's "purpose according to election" (9:11), even in the vessels of wrath.

Paul's point in 9:22-23 prepares us for his conclusions in 11:12, 15, 30-32. This becomes especially apparent when we realize that in defining who the vessels of wrath are, Paul has introduced a chiasm in 9:24-29 in order to stress the salvation of the Jews (cf. Jews [24a]/Gentiles [24b]/Gentiles [25-26]/Jews [27-29]). Indeed, Dahl sees the emphasis in 9:24-29 to be on the inclusion of the Jews to such a degree that his impression is that "Paul adds almost as an aside that there are Gentiles among these vessels of mercy. . . ."[30] This latter reality is supported, by way of analogy, from a quotation taken from Hosea 2:25 and 2:1 (LXX) in 9:25-26. In their original context these texts refer to the salvation of disobedient Israel at the time of her restoration. For this reason commentators have often suggested that Paul used these texts without regard for their original sense.[31] But it is more probable that Paul was drawing a *comparison* between the calling of the Gentiles from unbelief and the restoration of Israel from exile and judgment. Just as God can bring Israel back from the dead, he can also call Gentiles to new life. Such a reading of the function of the quotes in 9:25-26 is supported by the use of the introductory formula "as" in v. 25a and the absence of any referent in the introductory formula such as the explicit referent "concerning Israel" found in 9:27. If such a reading can be sustained, then here too Paul is preparing us for chapter 11 in which he will compare the future salvation of Israel with the present salvation of the Gentiles, just as he now compares the present salvation of the Gentiles with the past description of the salvation of Israel (cf. 11:17 with 11:23).

In addition to the chiastic structure of the passage, the point of 9:30-32 concerning *Israel's* failure to attain what she was seeking (not the Gentiles' success) also indicates that Paul's focus of attention in 9:24-29 is on the mixed quotes from Isa 10:22-23; Hosea 2:1; and Isa 1:9 in 9:27-29. Paul's discussion of the justice of God in electing some to mercy and some to destruction therefore closes with the realization that the salvation of the Gentiles in great numbers is to be balanced by the salvation of only a meager number of ethnic Israel. Rom 9:27 is thus the key to *both* the nature of God's righteousness in 9:14-29 and the integrity of God's word in 9:6a. God is just toward ethnic Israel in the present because "he hardens whom he wills" for the sake of showing mercy to others, even if this means hardening the majority of ethnic Israel in order to save the Gentiles (9:18, 23, 25). At the same time, God's word has not failed because Isaiah foretold that at the time of the exile, God's judgment would be so severe on ethnic Israel that only a *remnant* would be saved (9:28-29). In the same way, ethnic Israel's rejection of the Messiah is the same kind of divine judgment on "vessels of wrath prepared for destruction" (9:22). Here too Paul prepares us for his argument in chapter 11, this time by introducing the concept of the remnant which will play such an important role in 11:1-5.

But before Paul returns to the significance of the remnant for the future of Israel, he must first deal with one last question about the present. For Paul's proclaiming an unexpected reversal in the plan of redemptive history, in which the inclusion of many Gentiles is taking the place of the restoration of ethnic Israel,[32] as part of God's faithfulness to his word was certainly shocking.[33] And it was all the more so, given the seemingly hopeless prospect in this text for the salvation of much of ethnic Israel at all. There is no hint of the future in 9:27-29. This stress on ethnic Israel's judgment in vv. 27-29 is so shocking, in fact, that it leads to the anticipated question of 9:30-31.

2. Why did the Gentiles Attain Righteousness while Israel did not?

It is not the purpose of this essay to confront the difficult questions surrounding Paul's view of the law in 9:30-10:13. It is enough for our purposes to observe that what ethnic Israel did not obtain *after the Messiah came* was the law (9:31) (however this reference to the law is to be understood in the context of v. 31) and that the reason she did not attain it was because she pursued it "as from works" (9:32) (however this notoriously difficult phrase is to be interpreted). What is crucial for our study is simply the *result* of this failure on Israel's part to reach her goal: "They stumbled over the (stone of) stumbling" just as Isaiah once again said they would (9:32-33). This "stumbling" can only be a reference to their failure to follow Jesus as the Messiah.[34]

However we understand the nature and role of the law in this passage, the main point to be made is that the Gentiles attained righteousness despite their past neglect of it, while ethnic Israel failed despite her pursuit of it, because the Gentiles "believed in the stone of stumbling" and ethnic Israel did not. Moreover, it is also clear in this context that Paul again emphasizes that for ethnic Israel to reject the stone of stumbling is for her to be excluded from the salvation he wishes so desperately that she would enjoy (10:1; cf. 9:2). This is indicated not only explicitly in the content of Paul's prayer in 10:1, but also implicitly in the way Paul distances himself from ethnic Israel. He addresses his fellow Christians as "brothers," but refers to ethnic Israel in the third person without any personal attachment. Rom 10:1 thus hearkens back to Paul's careful distinction in 9:3 that ethnic Israelites are his "kinsmen" only by race, that is only "according to the flesh."

The rest of this section details why the vasy majority of ethnic Israel was led astray from the Messiah through her pursuit of the "law of righteousness" (cf. 10:2-13) and why she should have known better (cf. 10:14-21). Israel is thus fully responsible for her rejection of the Messiah (10:18-20) within the context of God's hardening activity (11:7-8). Yet once again, Paul's eye is on the future as he describes the present, this time through his allusion to the jealousy-provoking role of the conversion of the Gentiles in the future salvation of Israel (cf. 10:19 with 11:13-14). But it is just an allusion waiting to be developed. This section too ends with the judgment and rebellion of ethnic Israel (cf. 10:21). Yet God's word has not failed. God himself proclaimed through Moses and Isaiah that he would not save all of ethnic Israel, but indeed judge her for her rejection of the message of the gospel which was brought to her in the past and is now being brought to her once again in the present.

3. Has God therefore Rejected his People?

Against the backdrop of the severe judgment of 9:27-29 and 10:18-21 it is no wonder then that Paul begins his transitional section from present to future in 11:1 by now making explicit the question which was implicit behind 9:6: "Because of her sinful disobedience to the coming of the Messiah, has God therefore rejected his ethnic people?" That Paul has ethnic Israel and not true Israel or the remnant in view in the question of 11:1 is clear by the answer Paul gives: God has emphatically not rejected his ethnic people because Paul himself believes in the Messiah and he too is "an Israelite, a descendant of Abraham, of the tribe of Benjamin" (11:1b). God's word to Abraham has not failed. The Lord is still calling people in the present from within ethnic Israel to be true children of Abraham just as he promised in Gen 21:12 (9:8).

At this point in his argument, however, Paul begins to develop the significance of the themes which he has introduced in chapters 9-10 in a new direction, i.e. *toward the future*. Thus, Paul now ties his own present experience of God's call to be one of the few vessels of mercy elected from ethnic Israel (11:1; 9:24) to the fact that he is also a member of true Israel, the elect "children of promise" within ethnic Israel (9:8), which in turn means that he is now a present part of the chosen "remnant" he referred to in 9:27

(cf. 11:5). Paul's rehearsal of his ethnic pedigree in 11:1b is thus intended to make the point that God has not rejected his ethnic people in spite of their disobedience and rebellion (10:21) because Paul himself is a part of the remnant which has been chosen from within ethnic Israel. Therefore, since Paul himself is living proof that a remnant now exists, he can be confident that "God has not rejected his people whom he foreknew" (11:2, taking v. 2a to be an implied inference from 11:1b)

But it is not readily apparent how Paul's thought at this point should be construed. Many have argued that Paul can be confident that God has not rejected his ethnic people because Paul is a Jew and therefore Jews are presently being saved. In this view, the remnant to which Paul belongs is understood in 11:1 to *replace* disobedient ethnic Israel as God's people, so that the same contrast found in 9:6b is also at work here. Paul's point in 11:1-7 is thus still the same as it has been in 9:6b-10:21 and Paul's focus is still on the present salvation of those few Jews who make up the remnant.[35]

But such a view fails to take into consideration both the significance of the remnant motif itself, as introduced in the reference to the experience of Elijah in 1 Kgs 19:10ff., and Paul's own interpretation of its significance in 11:2b and 11:5-11. Once these are taken into account, it becomes apparent that Paul has switched his focus from the present to the future salvation of Israel in 11:1-10. In 11:2 Paul grounds his conclusion that God has not rejected his ethnic people by calling our attention to Elijah's response when confronted with Israel's apostasy. Faced with the same disobedience among Israel (cf. 10:21), Paul's first point is that Elijah pleaded with the Lord "against Israel," i.e. for Israel's judgment! At first glance, therefore, Paul's reaction as one of the elect in 11:1 might be to follow Elijah in viewing himself as the substitute for faithless Israel in the expectation of the latter's judgment. Indeed, one cannot help wondering if Paul does not see his own suffering and rejection on behalf of the gospel in Elijah's complaint in 11:3 (cf. 1 Cor 4:9ff.; 2 Cor 4:7ff.; 11:23ff.; and especially in this context Gal 5:11; 1 Thess 2:14-16).

Paul's emphasis, however, lies on the *adversative* response of God from 1 Kgs 19:18 quoted in 11:4: Elijah is not alone! God has called out for himself a larger remnant of the faithful. And as the narrative in 1 Kgs 19:17-18 makes clear, this remnant of 7,000 will be kept from the coming judgment on the rebellious. The point of the parallel to Elijah is not that Elijah or Paul or the small remnant of the Jews that are currently being saved (cf. 9:27-29) are all alone. The point is the promise to Elijah and to the remnant of Paul's day that their experience points forward to the salvation of a greater number. Rather than judgment on all the rest, the significance of the small, persecuted remnant is that their experience is a symbol of hope for the future of the people.

This reading of 11:1-5 finds support in the fact that, as Dan Johnson has recently pointed out, the motif of the remnant in the OT can either be a word of judgment (Isa 10:22, as in 9:27) or a word of hope (Gen 7:23; 2 Kgs 19:30-31; Isa 11:11-12, 16; 37:31-32; Mic 2:12; 4:7; 5:7-8; Zech 8:12).[36] In Romans 9 Paul has used the remnant within the context of the judgment of God to stress Israel's current rejection and hardening. But in 11:1-5 he uses it as a sign of hope for the future of God's ethnic people and a testimony to the faithfulness of God, not a substitution for the rest of Israel.[37] Johnson concludes, therefore, that in 11:1 Paul is introducung the "overriding theme" of Romans 11, namely, that "all Israel will be saved" (11:25).[38] The future salvation of ethnic Israel is thus implicit in the remnant motif of 11:1-6 and in the temporary hardening referred to in 11:7-16. But it becomes explicit in reference to the full inclusion of ethnic Israel in 11:12, 15, and 24.[39] Otfried Hofius has made this same point by comparing Paul's argument in Romans 11 to the Qumran community's conception of themselves as the remnant of God, whose salvation as the "true Israel" *takes the place* of God's promises to the larger ethnic community both now and in the future. Hofius' point is that it is precisely this hope for the future of ethnic Israel in Rom 11:11-32 as an extension of the remnant concept from 11:1-10 that marks Paul's thought as distinct.[40]

This reading of Romas 11:1-5 is also undergirded by Gerhard Hasel's extensive study of the motif of the remnant in the ancient Near East and OT traditions.[41] Hasel's study led him to conclude that "in the Abraham-Lot story the remnant motif is used in connection with revolutionary reflections about God's righteousness: for the sake of divine righteousness the minority of a righteous remnant has a preserving function for the wicked majority."[42] In the same way, "the theophanic reply of Yahweh to Elijah's complaint that he 'alone is left' climaxes in the assurance that Yahweh will leave a remnant of 7,000 in a future judgment. Israel's apostasy will be punished by the sword (war) from within and without, but this judgment will not lead to complete annihilation."[43] It is precisely these two "remnant" traditions that Paul uses to frame his argument in Romans 9-11, moving from the remnant within Abraham's descendants and its implications for understanding God's relationship to Israel in the present to the experience of Elijah as a type of this remnant and its implications for God's relationship to Israel in the future.

Finally, such a switch in perspective in Rom 11:1-32 is also corroborated structurally by the change in the rhetorical style of question with which Paul introduces the last two sections of his argument. The sections dealing with the present salvation of true spiritual Israel were both introduced with the first person *plural* "What therefore shall we say?" (9:14, 30), whereas the last two sections dealing with the future salvation of ethnic Israel are introduced with the first person *singular* "I say therefore . . . ." (11:1, 11). Thus, both in terms of content and structure, there is good reason to take 11:1-5, as the introduction to the question of the future salvation of ethnic Israel. Hence, it is the role of the remnant as a sign of the faithfulness of God to his ethnic people in 11:1-5 that bridges the gap between the integrity of God's word of judgment to the majority of ethnic Israel in the present (9:6b-13) and its integrity in the future (11:11-32) when the content of these words is distinct.

V. THE FUTURE OF ISRAEL IN ROM 11:11-36

If my reading of Rom 11:25-36 is correct (*supra* 16-21), then the present hardening of the "rest" of ethnic Israel who have not been chosen as part of the remnant in 11:7-10 is God's penultimate word to Israel. Although faithful to this word in the present, the very existence of a remnant in the present is evidence that God has not rejected his people *as a people*. This is the point of 11:1-2. But if this is true, then the final question of Romans 9-11 can now be asked and answered: "Has ethnic Israel stumbled in their unbelief in Christ in such a way that they are no longer linked to the implied promise of the remnant from their own people?" (cf. 11:11a with 9:32-33)?

1. The Purpose and Potential Problem of the Gentile Ministry.

Stendahl is right in emphasizing that Paul raises and answers this question in 11:11-24 for the sake of the Gentiles whom he is addressing and that he is writing from the perspective of his own ministry, not to the Jews, but to the Gentiles (cf. 11:13, 17-21).

Paul's answer regarding the relationship between present day ethnic Israel and the salvation of the Gentiles, when placed against the backdrop of 9:22-24 and 11:7-10, is clear. According to 11:11b, 12a, 15a, 17a, 19-20a the majority of ethnic Israel has now been hardened and has therefore "stumbled" for the penultimate purpose of bringing mercy to the Gentiles (and to the small remnant minority from within ethnic Israel who have also been elected to believe, cf. 9:27 and 11:5). Stendahl is also right, therefore, in emphasizing that the problem Paul has in mind in addressing the Gentiles is their potential arrogance over the Jews (cf. 11:18, 20).

Though written to Gentiles to address a gentile problem, this emphasis on the salvation and pride of the Gentiles in 11:11-12, as the question of 11:1 itself indicates, is not Paul's main point, however. The salvation of the Gentiles, their response to it, and even Paul's own ministry, are all of penultimate importance in Paul's argument. His main point in 11:11-24 is that although ethnic Israel is now hardened for the sake of the Gentiles, *nevertheless* there is still a future for ethnic Israel, as testified to by the Jewish Christian remnant which now exists, while no such divine commitment exists for any gentile ethnic group. For only this realization, and not the nature of the salvation of the Gentiles or the role of Paul's ministry *per se*, can keep the Gentiles humble.

Paul makes this point in 11:16 by using two analogies, the first fruits of the dough and the root of the olive tree. In both cases, the reference can either be to the patriarchs (as in 11:28) or to the remnant (as in 11:14-15). But on the basis of the parallel usage in Rom 16:5 and 1 Cor 16:15 and the fact that the latter fits better into the immediate context, a reference to the remnant is to be preferred,[44] although of course the remnant itself is an expression of God's prior commitment to the patriarchs so that the theological principle remains the same in either case. As in Num 15:20-21 regarding the offering of the first fruits of the dough for the whole, or in the realm of nature in regard to the relationship between the root and the branches, the quality of the former determines and even guarantees the nature of the latter.[45] Since the remnant (or the patriarchs) are already "holy," so too the rest of their people. The present salvation of the remnant guarantees the future blessing of their people. What is implicit in the role of the remnant in 11:1-5 is now made explicit in the analogies of 11:16.

It is this link between the remnant and ethnic Israel that explains the purpose of Paul's ministry in 11:11-24. It is often suggested that Paul conceived of his ministry as the beginning of the fulfillment of the prophetic hope for the pilgrimage of the Gentiles to Zion, which in a strange twist of events now *precedes* the restoration of Israel rather than follows it.[46] As the Apostle to the Gentiles, Paul "magnifies (his) ministry" in order to make ethnic Israel jealous and as a result "save *some* of them" (11:14). But since 11:14 explicitly says that Paul's aim is not to bring in the fullness of ethnic Israel (cf. 12), but only "some" of them, i.e. more of the remnant,[47] it seems more appropriate to see the ultimate purpose of Paul's ministry to be the securing of the elect in the present. Paul's ministry aims at saving Gentiles in order that he might cause ethnic Israel to be jealous, and in so doing, save the elect from within her (11:11, 14). The hardened rest will simply be further alienated by their jealousy, as Paul has already indicated in 10:20-21. Yet in realizing that his ministry will thus have an effect on only a small number of Jews, Paul is not forgetting the future of his people or the final redemption of the creation. Just the opposite! For Paul knows that the remnant is God's "down payment" on the future salvation of his people and the final fulfillment of God's promises to his creation. Thus, just as the present "transgression" of ethnic Israel means salvation in the present for Gentiles, i.e. "riches" and "reconciliation for the world" (11:12a, 15a), so too the remnant's present "acceptance" means "life from the dead" for

Israel in the future (11:15) and in turn, their eventual "fullness" will mean eschatological riches for the creation (11:12).[48] Paul's ministry is an essential link in this chain of events.

The essential connection between the remnant ("root") and the future salvation of Israel (the "branches") also destroys gentile hubris caused by their own present salvation (cf. 11:17-24). First, Gentiles must realize that they owe their own salvation completely to God's prior commitment to Abraham and the same promises and covenants referred to in 9:4-5. It is therefore the "root" which supports the Gentiles and not the other way around, since the gospel came to them through the death of the Jewish Messiah, in response to the covenantal promises given to the Jews, as proclaimed to them by the remnant (11:17-18). The gospel, after all, is to the "Jew first" (Rom 1:16) both temporally and theologically. Moreover, the purpose of the salvation of the Gentiles is to make ethnic Israel jealous (11:11b). To be a gentile Christian is thus to derive one's existence *from* Israel and to find the earthly purpose of one's existence in relationship *to* Israel. Second, Gentiles must realize that their salvation itself, like the present hardening of ethnic Israel, is a matter of faith or unbelief in the unmerited and unconditionally electing grace of God as now expressed in Christ (11:20; cf. 9:18; 9:30-32; 10:9; 11:5-6). The danger of pride to faith is manifest, and the danger of unbelief is equally real for the Gentile (11:20b-22). Fear, not arrogance, is the watchword of the faithful, since the basis of salvation is not our human distinctives, but God's election. This means, therefore, that at any time God may graft back into the olive tree of God's covenant people the unbelieving ethnic Jew. In fact, one day God will save such a great number of ethnic Jews that the hope of the remnant will be fulfilled. This is the implicit point of the *a-fortiori* argument of 11:24: If Gentiles, who "according to nature" are not ethnic Jews and thus have had no hope anchored in a remnant, have been grafted into the people of God, *how much more* will those who are of ethnic Israel be grafted in, i.e. the ones who are part of the root "according to nature"?[49] This point, now made rhetorically in v. 24, is the explicit point of the last section of Paul's argument.

2. The Future of Israel in Rom 11:25-36

The purpose of 11:25-36 is to offer support for the assertion of 11:24 that Israel "according to nature" will one day be grafted into the "cultivated olive tree" of true, spiritual Israel and in so doing to warn the Gentiles once again against pride over their having been grafted in already. Paul's point concerning Israel in 11:25 is thus essentially the same as the one he has just made in 11:11-24. The mystery which has now been made known is that ethnic Israel has been partially hardened in the present to allow for the grafting in of the Gentiles. What is new about 11:25 is Paul's assertion that this hardening is not only tied to the coming in of the Gentiles in the present, but that its removal is also tied to the time when God will cease grafting in Gentiles as well. This is the sobering reality that the Gentiles must come to grips with that will keep them from being "wise in their own estimation." The Gentiles are not now being saved *because* they are Gentiles any more than the remnant are saved because they are Jews. God's mercy to the Gentiles will also be limited. The mystery is that the time of Israel's hardening *and* the Gentile's salvation are *both* limited. The time of the inclusion of the Gentiles will come to an end, just as the time of Israel's hardening.

But it is at this point that the parallel ends. For unlike the Gentiles, God has a "remnant promise" to keep to ethnic Israel. Thus, when the "fullness of the Gentiles " has come in, God's work among the nations is finished. But the salvation of the remnant within this same period, brought about through the jealousy of the mission to the Gentiles, does not bring an end to God's commitment to ethnic Israel. Instead, it necessitates that the corresponding "fullness" of Israel be brought in. This is the second half of the mystery as proclaimed in 11:26-27 and then summarized in 11:28-32.

Once we give full due to the temporal designation within 11:25 ("until") the debate over the meaning of the introductory phrase *kai houtōs* in 11:26 takes on a different light. In view of our interpretation of 11:1-24, the "until" of 11:25 is itself enough to posit the future salvation of ethnic Israel![50] Hence, the weight of interpreting 11:26 as a future reality does not rest on whether *kai houtōs* or *kai* by itself (with *houtōs* referring forward to v. 26b) can be rendered consecutively,[51] or on whether the "deliverer" in view is God himself or Christ. Even if 11:26 is intended merely to describe the manner ("and in this way") of Israel's salvation and the deliverer cannot be identified with Christ, the Israel in view is still ethnic Israel and the salvation in view is still future.

Rom 11:28 is especially important in this regard since it makes clear that the Israel of 11:26 must be ethnic Israel, since it is clearly ethnic Israelites that are now "enemies for the sake of the Gentiles" in 11:28a and ethnic Israelites who are "beloved because of the fathers" and "according to the election," which in view of 9:11 and 11:5 is to be taken as a reference to the remnant. God elected ethnic Israel in Abraham as the people from whom he would draw the remnant of his children of promise. In turn, his preservation of the remnant thoughout Israel's history, and now even after Israel's rejection of the Messiah, are evidence that God has not forsaken them (11:1, 11; and now 11:28). Why has God not abandoned his people? "Because the gifts and calling are irrevocable," gifts and calling which were initiated in Abraham and confirmed in the remnant (11:29; cf. with 9:6a). The future salvation of ethnic Israel in 11:25-32 is thus the last step in God's demonstration of his own righteousness and glory. For with the end of the period of the ingathering of the Gentiles and the consequent salvation of a great number of ethnic Jews ("all Israel") it will become clear that salvation has always been by the sovereign, electing grace of God (11:32) and that God's word has not failed (9:6a). Paul's closing doxology is therefore a theological doxology rather than a Christological one since the issue which has been guiding Paul's discussion throughout Romans 9-11 has been the question of God's character and faithfulness. The final salvation of ethnic Israel causes Paul to pause and extol the One who has worked throughout redemptive history to reveal his mercy and power and the riches of his glory (cf. 9:16-17, 22-23). Moreover, since Paul has been thinking of the future ever since 11:1, and specifically of the consummation of history since 11:11-32 (cf. 11:12, 24, 26-27), it also seems appropriate that he would close this section with a doxology that reflects the same ultimate theocentric goal of history which he sets forth in 1 Cor 15:24-28. If the last act of redemptive history is for Christ himself to be subjected to the Father so that "God may be all in all" (1 Cor 15:28), then it is only fitting that Paul would close his thoughts on the future salvation of ethnic Israel, which for him is the last chapter of salvation history on earth (11:26), with praise to God the Father.

VI. IMPLICATIONS FOR UNDERSTANDING PAUL: A RESPONSE TO KRISTER STENDAHL

In a sense, my reconstruction of Paul's argument in Romans 9-11 is a response to the position of Krister Stendahl. But if my understanding of Paul's thought in Romans 9-11 is correct, then certain things may be said by way of summary. First, Paul is not silent about the means of Israel's salvation in 11:26. For the future salvation of ethnic Israel must correspond to the nature of the remnant's salvation in the present, since the future nature of ethnic Israel is inextricably tied to the present nature of the remnant (11:16). It is also clear that by definition, the "remnant" are those who have not stumbled over the gospel of Jesus Christ (cf. 11:11 in view of 9:30-10:4 and Paul's own protest to be one of the remnant in 11:1). This is confirmed by Paul's impossible wish in 9:3 and the basic conviction that Jesus is the Messiah which Stendahl himself recognizes undergirds all of Paul's thinking (cf. 9:5). The fact that Paul does not mention the name of Jesus after 10:17 is thus more than made up for by his references to the remnant in 11:1-5, 14, 15 as an extension of this motif in 9:27, where it is clearly in a Christologically focused section. Moreover, as E. P. Sanders has pointed out in response to Stendahl, "a place in the kingdom" always implies for Paul a way of salvation based *only* on faith in Jesus Christ so that in the present, as well as after his discussion of the future in 11:26-27 (cf. 11:30-32 with its emphasis on mercy!), Paul applies the requirement of faith to both Jew and Gentile.[52] Further, it is "beyond objection" that faith for Paul is never a general attitude, but "always means 'faith in Jesus Christ'. . . . If this is granted, Rom 10:17-11:36 is not so non-christological as Stendahl's observation about the appearance of the name 'Jesus Christ' would at first lead one to think."[53] Indeed , faith (in Jesus Christ) is explicitly referred to as the way to salvation for both Jews and Gentiles in 11:20 and 23. Hence, by the time Paul gets to 11:25-26,". . . the condition of faith in Christ has been so often repeated that he does not need to repeat it again."[54]

Second, Stendahl's main point concerning 11:25-32 is that, as the culmination of Paul's argument against the pride of the Gentiles, this passage could not be referring to the same way of salvation as followed by the Gentiles without undercutting his own purpose. Paul is a "pastoral theologian," not a systematic theologian, so that we must read his argument from that perspective.[55] But Paul's argument against the pride of the Gentiles is that they are not to place their experience in a separate category (which could lead to a new pride of the "better way"), but to see their dependence on Israel for the *same* way of salvation. Both the future salvation of Israel *and* the present salvation of Gentiles grow out of the same root and lead to being grafted into the same tree (11:24). Both need the same faith (11:20-23). In this light, it is the promise of the future salvation of Israel *in Christ* that deflates the Gentile's pride since it makes clear that Gentiles too stand in faith in the present only as a result of God's mercy and grace (9:16; 11:5-6). This mercy is not their private possession, but a gift from God that ought to stir them up to fear rather than conceit (11:20). Paul's God-centered doxology, therefore, is not an attempt to downplay the Gentile allegiance to Jesus, but is intended to show the Gentiles that all, both Jews and Gentiles, will one day be worshipping the same Father together for the same reason, namely, his electing mercy in Christ (cf. the parallel between 11:35 and 9:16).

As elsewhere in Paul, "mystery" in 11:25 does not refer to some undisclosed and "mysterious" idea or series of events, but to that which was once hidden, but has *now* become clear in Christ and is given to the Church to proclaim.[56] Rather than not predicting its details or nature, the point of 11:25-32 is to do precisely that, i.e. to state clearly the answer to the question originally asked in Rom 3:1. The mystery is indeed that at the consummation of redemptive history a great number of ethnic Israel will accept Jesus as the Messiah and thus the Kingdom of God will be ushered in.[57] Stendahl's earlier view was, therefore, correct and should not have been corrected![58]

What then can be said about Stendahl's paradigm for reading Paul in general in the light of our discussion of Romans 9-11? There is no basis from Romans 9-11 for calling into question Stendahl's critique of the "introspective conscience of the West" and its implications for rethinking Paul's view of the law. This project is well underway by Pauline scholars and ought to be continued. But there is reason to doubt Stendahl's thesis that Paul's doctrine of justification by faith applied only to Gentiles and that Paul never attempted to draw out the implications of this doctrine for unbelieving Jews or Jewish Christians. However we may understand the contrasts between "faith" and the "law" and "grace" and "works" in these texts, it cannot be denied that the parallel between 9:30-33 and 11:5-7 indicates that Paul's doctrine of justification by faith alone through grace is to be applied equally to both Gentiles and Jews. Moreover, justification by faith also occupies a role in the context of the eschatological future for both Jews and Gentiles (cf. 11:30-31). Hence, arguments may differ concerning how close to the center of Paul's theology his doctrine of justification by faith actually is, but Stendahl has moved it too far away.

If the results of my exegesis hold up under further scrutiny, Stendahl's stark contrast between Paul's "call" and "conversion" will have to be rejected. Certainly Paul was called as a Christian to be the Apostle to the Gentiles so that there is no separation between Paul's call to Christ and his call to take the gospel to the Gentiles. But the reason for this is not because Paul did not experience a radical change in religious conviction in his Damascus Road experience. Rather, Paul was called to the Gentiles precisely because he did undergo a decisive conversion--the conversion from unbelief to belief in Jesus as the Messiah. Paul did not just change "job descriptions," he changed allegiances, from God's will as revealed in the covenants of the Torah, to God's will as revealed in the new covenant of the Messiah. The degree of continuity and discontinuity between these allegiances must be determined. But that Paul's call was also a conversion and his conversion also a call must not be denied.

In conclusion, what is the role of the Church today in relationship to Israel on the basis of Romans 9-11? Stendahl is right in insisting that nowhere in Romans 9-11 is it said that the Church should have an organized mission to Israel. And Stendahl is also right that Paul's ministry was to the Gentiles. But if even the basic outline of my reconstruction can stand, then there is every reason to believe that Paul was also in full agreement with Peter's mission to the Jews (Gal 2:7-8) and that any mission to Gentiles could expect to reach Jews as well (Rom 11:13f.). For as we have seen, it is in the creation of a remnant by faith in Jesus as the Messiah that God ratifies and keeps his covenant promise to ethnic Israel alive. For God's word not to fail, there should at all times be those members of ethnic Israel who are also part of the remnant. God is saving both Jews and Gentiles to demonstrate his mercy and display his power (9:24), and the Church, made up of Gentiles and true Israelites, with its proclamation of the message of the gospel of Christ is his means of doing so (11:14).

Stendahl does not think that Paul supported a mission to the Jews and would thus cast his vote against it. E. P. Sanders, who rejects Stendahl's limitation of faith to the Gentiles in Paul's theology and argues strongly for Paul's "exclusivist Christian soteriology," would nevertheless for other reasons also cast his vote against any proposal that said "the only way to be saved was through Christ Jesus."[59] One cannot treat a theme like the salvation of Israel in Romans 9-11 without dealing with this question. Nor can one refuse to give his or her opinion. I would cast my vote for such a conviction and support such a mission, and then pray for humility and the fear of God (Rom 11:20).

NOTES

1. See **Vatican Council II**, ed. Austin Flannery (Collegeville, MN: Liturgical Press, 1975) 740-742.

2. For example, the influence of popular books such as Hal Lindsey's **The Late Great Planet Earth** (Grand Rapids: Zondervan, 1977) and the preaching of the televangelists on the role of Israel and the Jewish people has been immense both religiously and politically in American culture. See Merrill Simon, **Jerry Falwell and the Jews** (Middle Village, NY: Jonathan David Publishers, 1984).

3. For perhaps the most well-known, and certainly controversial treatment of the NT's attitude toward Judaism see Rosemary R. Ruether, **Faith and Fratricide, The Theological Roots of Anti-Semitism** (New York: Seabury Press, 1974) 64-116. For a critique of Ruether's contention that the theological roots of "anti-Judaism" are to be found in the "christological midrash" of the early Church and NT itself (cf. 94-95); see Franz Mussner, **Tractate on the Jews, The Significance of Judaism for Christian Faith**, tr. Leonard Swidler (Philadelphia: Fortress Press, 1984) 228-232, 239-40.

4. See Douglas Moo, "Paul and the Law in the Last Ten Years," *SJT* 40 (1987), 287-307 and Stephen Westerholm, **Israel's Law and the Church's Faith, Paul and His Recent Interpreters** (Grand Rapids: Eerdmans, 1988).

5. So, e.g. Robert Jewett as quoted by D. Moo, "Paul and the Law," 287-88.

6. Stendahl's programmatic essays, "Paul Among Jews and Gentiles" and "The Apostle Paul and the Introspective Conscience of the West," were originally presented in 1963 and 1960 (in Swedish) respectively. The latter was first published in English in *HTR* 56 (1963) 199-215. References from these two articles are taken from K. Stendahl, **Paul Among Jews and Gentiles and other Essays** (Philadelphia: Fortress Press, 1976) 1-77 and 78-96 and will be indicated in the body of the text along with other quotes from this work.

7. K. Stendahl, "In No Other Name," **Christian Witness and the Jewish People**, ed. A. Sovik (Geneva: Lutheran World Federation, 1976) 48-53, 52-53.

8. Ibid., 53.

9. For a concise summary of Stendahl's basic thesis, including a reprint of his earlier essay "In No Other Name," cf. his essay "Christ's Lordship and Religious Pluralism," now in K. Stendahl, **Meanings. The Bible as Document and As Guide** (Philadelphia: Fortress Press, 1984) 233-244, esp. 243-44.

10. Stendahl, "Judaism and Christianity I: Then and Now," in **Meanings**, 205-215, 215 n. 1. This view is a reversal of his earlier position as originally published in this 1963 essay (cf. p. 213). But even there Stendahl argued that this return of the Jews to the Messiah would not come about as the result of a mission by the Gentiles but would result from God's own mysterious way of reaching them (cf. p. 213). For this same point see "Judaism and Christianity II: A Plea for a New Relationship," in Meanings, 217-232, 223.

11. Nils A. Dahl, "The Future of Israel," in **Studies in Paul** (Minneapolis: Augsburg, 1977) 137-158, 137 argues convincingly against taking the only other two possibilities, 1 Thess 2:14-16 and 2 Cor 3:16, as referring to the future of Israel as a people.

12. **Meanings**, 210, 211-213.

13. Hans Hübner, **Gottes Ich und Israel. Zum Schriftgebrauch des Paulus in Römer 9-11, FRLANT 136** (Göttingen: Vandenhoeck & Ruprecht, 1984) 14-17, 20.

14. For an interpretation of 9:4-5, which demonstrates the salvific implications of these benefits, see J. Piper, **The Justification of God: An Exegetical Study of Romans 9:1-23** (Grand Rapids: Baker, 1983) 5-30.

15. Ibid., 30.

16. Cf. James W. Aageson, "Scripture and Structure in the Development of the Argu-

ment in Romans 9-11," CBQ 48 (1986) 265-289, 265-266 for a review of the attempts to find the center of Romans 9-11 in these various theological concepts and the relevant literature.

17. See also J. C. Beker, "The Faithfulness of God and the Priority of Israel in Paul's Letter to the Romans," *HTR* 79 (1986) 10-16, 15.

18. This point has been argued most recently by Mary Ann Getty, "Paul and the Salvation of Israel: A Perspective on Romans 9-11," *CBQ* 50 (1988) 456-469, 464-65, though I am not convinced by her apparent interpretation of the meaning of 9:6b itself as a reference to the inclusion of the Gentiles into the people of God.

19. Cf. the same response in Rom 9:5 and in Rom 6:17; 7:25; 16:27; 1 Cor 15:57; 2 Cor 1:3; 2:14; 8:16; 9:15; Gal 1:5; Phil 4:20.

20. See G. Bornkamm, Paul (New York: Harper & Row, 1971) 150; Dahl, "The Future of Israel," 143; and Hübner, **Gottes Ich**, 60, for this same conclusion.

21. So e.g., Beker, "The Faithfulness of God."

22. So e.g. Getty, "Paul and the Salvation of Israel," 457ff.

23. See U. Wilckens, **Der Brief an die Römer (Röm 6-11), EKK VI/2** (Zürich: Benziger Verlag; Neukirchen-Vluyn: Neukirchener Verlag, 1980) 263-267 for an insightful analysis of 11:25-36 as the final answer to the "problem of Israel from the standpoint of salvation-history" first raised in 9:1 and already anticipated in Rom 3:1-6.

24. For the relevant literature, see Piper, **Justification** 9ff.

25. For an interpretation of God's purpose in his election "by which God aims to preserve his complete freedom in determining who will be the beneficiaries of his *saving* promises, who will be the 'Israel' within Israel (9:6), see Piper, **Justification** 34-54.

26. So too Hübner, **Gottes Ich**, 17-19 and the literature cited there. Hübner points to 1QS 5:5f; 6:13-14; 8:5, 9; 9:5 and 1QM 10:9 as examples from Qumran of the ability to make the distinction between "true" and ethnic Israel so that Paul's way of thinking was already present in the Jewish thinking of his day (cf. 19-20, n. 23a). Otfried Hofius, "Das Evangelium und Israel. Erwägungen zu Römer 9-11" *ZThK* 83 (1986) 297-324, 305 makes the same point and adds 1QH 2:12f.; 7:10, 12; 14:15; 4QpPs 37 II 5; III 5; IV11f.; 1QpHab 5:4; 10:13; 1Qs 8:6; but for Hofius' view on the distinction between Paul and Qumran on the issue of the remnant, see below.

27. For an outline of these three views of "all Israel" in 11:26 see Charles M. Horne, "The Meaning of the Phrase 'And thus all Israel will be Saved' (Romans 11:26)," *JETS* 21 (1978) 329-334.

28. For this view I am indebted to J. Piper, **Justification** 55-101.

29. Ibid., 90. Piper argues for this view on the basis of passages such as Pss 23:3; 31:1-3; 79:9; 143:1-2, 11; Dan 9:7, 13-19; Isa 43:6-7, 21, 25; 44:23; 46:13; Jer 13:11; 14:7, 9, 20-21; Ezek 16:59-63; 20:9, 14, 22, 44, etc. (cf. 90ff.).

30. "The Future of Israel," 146.

31. So, e.g., Käsemann, **Commentary on Romans** (Grand Rapids: Eerdmans, 1980) 274.

32. Cf. Peter Stuhlmacher, "Zur Interpretation von Römer 11:25-32," **Probleme biblischer Theologie, FS Gerhard von Rad zum 70. Geburstag**, ed. H.W. Wolff (Munich: Chr. Kaiser Verlag, 1971) 555-570, 561 n. 29, who points to Isa 2:2f.; Mic 4:2; Isa 56:7; 60:3; Psa Sol 17:30ff. as examples of the expectation that the Gentiles would come to Zion after Israel had been restored.

33. Rom 9:27-29 thus encapsulates what Martin Rese called the thesis of Romans 9-11 as a whole, namely, that God's word remains valid and true in spite of the unbelief of Israel; "Israel und Kirche in Römer 9," *NTS* 34 (1988) 208-217, 212.

34. So too Hofius, "Das Evangelium und Israel," 298-99. Cf. Gal 5:11; 1 Cor 1:23; Luke 2:34; 1 Peter 2:5-8.

35. E.g. Horne, "'And thus all Israel will be saved '," 330 and O. Palmer Robertson, "Is there a Distinctive Future for Ethnic Israel in Romans 11?" **Perspectives on Evangelical Theology. Papers from the Thirtieth Annual Meeting of the Evangelical Theological Society**, ed. K. Kantzer and S. Gundry (Grand Rapids: Baker, 1979), 209-227, 210.

36. Dan G. Johnson, "The Structure and Meaning of Romans 11," *CBQ* 46 (1984), 91-

103, 93.

37. Ibid., 96

38. Ibid., 92.

39. Ibid., 101

40. Cf. Hofius, "Das Evangelium und Israel," 305-306 and 1QH 6:8; CD 1:4-5; 2:1ff. ; 1QM 13:7ff. ; 14:8-9; 1QS 1:8,10.

41. Gerhard F. Hasel, **The Remnant. The History and Theology of the Remnant Idea from Genesis to Isaiah** (Berrien Springs: Andrews University Press, 1972).

42. Ibid., 389.

43. Ibid., 391 (emphasis his).

44. So too Dahl, "The Future of Israel," 151 and Johnson, "Structure," 98-99.

45. For this point and a treatment of these two analogies in Romans 11 against their development within Jewish tradition, see K. H. Rengstorf, "Das Ölbaum-Gleichnis in Röm 11:16ff. Versuch einer weiterführenden Deutung," in **Donum Gentilicium. New Testament Studies in Honor of David Daube**, ed. E. Bammel, C. K. Barrett, and W. D. Davies (Oxford: Clarendon Press, 1978) 127-164, esp. 129, 135-36.

46. For biblical references, see n. 32 above.

47. So too Johnson, "Structure" 97-98.

48. Contrary those who, like U. Wilckens, H. Hübner, and Robertson, argue that "fullness" in 11:12 refers to the gradual ingathering of the present day remnant over time to a full number. For the former, see Hübner, **Gottes Ich**, 107 and the literature cited there; for the latter, see Robertson, "Ethnic Israel," 214-15. But the remnant, by definition, is small and partial (cf. 9:27 and 11:3, 5), and the superior nature of the "riches" to come as a result of this fullness implied in the *a-fortiori* argument of v. 12 speaks against this view. In addition, the "fullness of the Gentiles" in 11:25 clearly does not represent a small, minority status within the new covenant people of God.

49. Cf. Rom 5:9-10 for this same use of an *a-fortiori* argument with a future passive verb in which the focus is clearly on a temporal future in relation to the supporting clause.

50. So too, Stuhlmacher, "Zur Interpretation," 560, 562.

51. Ibid., for this latter view, 560.

52. E. P. Sanders, "Paul's attitude toward the Jewish People," *Union Seminary Quarterly Review* 33 (1978) 175-187, 182-83.

53. Ibid., 182.

54. Ibid., 183.

55. This is Stendahl's main response to Sanders' critique of his position as found in an epilogue to Sanders, "Paul's Attitude," 190.

56. See Rom 16:25; 1 Cor 2:1, 7; 4:1; 13:2; 15:51; Eph 1:9; 3:3-4, 9; 5:32; 6:19; Col 1:26-27; 2:2; 4:3.

57. See, in addition to the texts referred to above in n. 32, Hosea 3:5; Mic 4:1 and *Test Dan* 5:3-7.

58. See above, n. 10.

59. "Paul's Attitude," 185.

Calvin's Understanding of the Relation of the Church and Israel Based Largely on His Interpretation of Romans 9-11

I. JOHN HESSELINK

I. INTRODUCTION

Heiko A. Oberman, in his recent study, **The Roots of Anti-Semitism: In the Age of Renaissance and Reformation,**[1] focuses on "three strange bedfellows," viz., Reuchlin, Erasmus, and Luther. What united them was their confidence that "a renewed, impartial, and scrupulous study of the biblical sources would provide the key to wisdom, which would in turn unveil truth in its pure condition and revive both Church and society."[2]

Unfortunately, according to Oberman, despite their lofty goal, these three did not progress much beyond the traditional medieval anti-Judaism which was characteristic of the Middle Ages. "Even the sixteenth century, so self-consciously at odds with the Middle Ages, did not to any measurable degree surpass its counterpart where the Jews were concerned."[3]

In this regard, Oberman only deals with Calvin in passing. The question of the Jews and Judaism was not a primary concern of his. Accordingly, with Calvin the task is both simpler and more difficult; simpler, because Calvin has far less to say on the subject, more difficult, because he wrote no treatises on the subject. In his **Institutes of the Christian Religion** there is no formal discussion of the subject, so one must look for scattered references in the commentaries and sermons.

As a result, the secondary literature on Calvin in regard to this question is very limited[4] and is concerned only with Calvin and the Jews, not Calvin's understanding of the relation of the Church to Israel, the proper subject of this paper. Oberman touches on the subject very briefly in **The Roots of Anti-Semitism**. He points out that one reason Calvinists may have been more tolerant of the Jews than their Protestant counterparts (including, surprisingly, the Anabaptists) was the fact that they too were largely refugees and, like the Jews of old, were forced to live a diaspora existence. Moreover, there can be found in the late sermons of Calvin on Jeremiah and Lamentations "a growing sense of the fate shared by Christians and Jews in their homeless state of persecution and diaspora."[5]

This is an important consideration, but one must also take into account a fundamental difference between Luther and Calvin, viz., their differing approaches to the relation of law and gospel. This difference is not as great as imagined by many Lutherans, for as I have shown elsewhere,[6] in their exegesis of key passages in Galatians, their exegesis is surprisingly similar. Nevertheless, the general perception that Calvin stressed the unity of the covenants and accordingly the *substantial* unity of law and gospel,[7] broadly conceived, more than Luther is an accurate one. This is sometimes held against Calvin, with the allegation that he taught an Old Testament religion or had a legalistic tendency, but in this case his positive view of the Old Testament and appreciation for the people of Israel works in his favor. For these presuppositions dispose him toward a positive view of Israel, its past, present, and future.

Whereas he may have inherited the antipathy toward the Jews characteristic of the medieval church and the Reformers (this is implied by Oberman), *theologically* he was more inclined to see the relationship between Israel and the Church in a positive light. This will become apparent as we investigate his interpretation of Romans 9-11.

II. THE TREATMENT OF THIS THEME IN THE INSTITUTES

In the meantime, it is not irrelevant to our theme to note the theological substructure for the relationship of the Church and Israel in the **Institutes**. After devoting a chapter to the uses of the law (in the context of salvation history), Calvin exposits the decalogue (II.7 and 8). Then follow three chapters which deal with the relationship of the old and new covenants, sometimes referred to as law and gospel. The titles are significant and set the stage for the following examination of Calvin's exposition of Romans 9-11:

Chapter IX: "Christ, Although He was Known to the Jews under the Law,
Was at Length Clearly Revealed Only in the Gospel"[8]
Chapter X: "The Similarity of the Old and New Testaments"
Chapter XI: "The Difference Between the Two Testaments"

The thesis of these chapters is that "The covenant made with all the patriarchs is so much like ours in substance and reality that the two are actually one and the same yet they differ in the mode of dispensation" (II.10.2). The differences are numerous and are not unimportant, but they are all relative. The New Testament saints see, understand, and experience more clearly the grace of God which was only adumbrated in types under the old covenant. Despite all the differences, however, both covenants have the same substance and foundation, viz., Christ. Calvin will not countenance the notion that God's relation to the Jews under the old covenant was characterized by law, whereas his relationship to his children under the new covenant was basically evangelical. No, the Old Testament, like the new, "was established upon the free mercy of God, and was confirmed by Christ's intercession" (II.10.4).

Citing John 8:56--"Abraham rejoiced that he was to see my day; he saw it and was glad"--Calvin further asserts, "Who, then, dares to separate the Jews from Christ, since with them, we hear, was made the covenant of the gospel, the sole foundation of which is Christ?" (II.10.4).

These chapters are full of such positive references to the Jews, the Old Testament patriarchs, the "saints" of the old dispensation. Granted, Calvin is thinking here not of contemporary Jews, i.e., his peers, but of Jews prior to the coming of Christ. Yet it is noteworthy that in these three key chapters which contain Calvin's fullest and most formal treatment of the relation of Israel and the Church there are no remarks which betray an animus against the Jews, past or present.

When enemies of the gospel are cited and excoriated in this context, they are not Jews but rather "certain madmen of the Anabaptist sect," that "rascal Servetus" (II.10.1), and earlier the Turks (II.6.4).

However, at one point Calvin does see a parallel between the Jewish people of his day and those of the New Testament era whose minds were hardened so that when they read Moses a veil lay over their eyes and they failed to see the glory of God in Christ (2 Cor 3:13-15). Calvin minces no words in the one comment of this type in these chapters. Contrasting the Jews of his time with the Sadducees of the New Testament, Calvin comments: "Nor would the obtuseness of the whole Jewish nation today in awaiting the Messiah's earthly kingdom be less monstrous, had the Scriptures not foretold long before that they would receive this punishment for having rejected the gospel" (II.10.23).

As indicated above, this is the sole remark of this sort. In the next chapter, however, Calvin does seem to denigrate the special significance and continuing role of the Jews as a chosen people. One of the last differences he cites between the two covenants (or law and gospel) is that under the old covenant "the Lord set apart one nation within which to confine the covenant of his grace" (II.11.11). With the advent of Christ, the wall between Jew and Gentile was broken down (Eph 2:14-16), so that there is "now no difference between Jew and Greek (Gal 3:28), between circumcision and uncircumcision (Gal 6:15), but "Christ is all in all" (Col. 3:12) (II.11.11).

So far so good. The argument is biblical and incontrovertible. But when Calvin in the next section suggests that the Gentiles have replaced the Jews as God's chosen instrument, one wonders whether he has forgotten the Apostle Paul's rhetorical question, "Has God rejected his people? (Rom 11:1). For Calvin says that "by this public calling the Gentiles not only were made equal to the Jews, but it also was manifest that they were, so to speak, taking the place of dead Jews" (II.11.12).

This is a curious statement on which Calvin unfortunately does not elaborate. What does he mean by "dead Jews?" Apparently, in the light of other statements, not Israel as a whole, but those Jews who even under the old covenant were faithless and unbelieving.

Even so, it is strange that the reformer who had such a lofty view of the Old Testament and the revelation given to Israel is so unconcerned about the abiding significance of Israel as a nation and the place of the Jews as a chosen people in God's plan of salvation. Calvin does not even raise this question in the **Institutes**, let alone discuss the issue in a substantive way. There is no reference to Rom 11:1 in the **Institutes**. The answer to Paul's question given in 11:2 is cited in a chapter on election (III.22.6), but Calvin's only interest in the verse is in Paul's use of the verb "foreknow" ("God has not rejected his people whom he foreknew").

For Calvin's understanding of the continuing significance of Israel and her place in the economy of salvation we must turn to his exegesis of the key passage, Romans 9-11.

III. CALVIN'S INTERPRETATION OF CHURCH AND ISRAEL IN ROMANS 9-11

Before investigating the salient passages in Calvin's commentary on Romans,[9] it may be useful to place it in the context of his writings and of other commentaries on Romans written during the first half of the sixteenth century.

As T. H. L. Parker points out, in a special study of this subject,[10] in one decade alone--1532-1542--no fewer than thirty-five commentaries on Romans were published! Roman Catholics were as zealous in this regard as their Protestant counterparts, partially, Parker suggests, to show the errors of Protestant exegesis on controverted themes such as grace, works, and justification by faith. Parker focuses on eleven of these commentaries, six by Roman Catholics, five by Protestants, the latter being Bucer, Bullinger, Pellican, Calvin, and Melanchthon. (Luther's **Lectures on Romans** were written in 1515-16 and were not published until 1938.) Hence Calvin had access to a number of recent commentaries on this Letter when he first undertook his own study of Romans shortly after arriving in Strasbourg in 1539. In particular, he had available to him one or more editions of his friend Melanchthon's commentaries on Romans, probably the 1530 edition (although his 1540 edition was published in both Wittenberg and Strasbourg in May, 1540. Calvin's first edition was published in Basel the same year, but the dedicatory epistle was written in October, 1539.).

We know that Calvin utilized Bullinger's commentary on Romans (1533) and the large commentary on Romans by his mentor and colleague in Strasbourg, Martin Bucer. The latter commentary appeared in 1536 and "crushed into insignificance all but two or three . . . other works, and its influence for a few years was immense."[11] Its influence on Calvin was considerable, as Calvin acknowledges. In his dedication to Simon Grynaeus, with whom he had studied Greek in Basel, Calvin mentions the commentaries of Melanchthon, Bullinger, and Bucer. He apologizes for adding yet another commentary on this Letter but justifies it on the basis that it will be comprehensive (in contrast to Melanchthon's) and brief (in contrast to Bucer's). Unfortunately, the commentaries of his illustrious predecessors are not readily available and accordingly cannot be used as a basis for comparison.

Within Calvin's own corpus, however, his commentary on Romans has a special place, perhaps only second to the **Institutes**. As soon as he completed the greatly revised second edition of his classic in the summer of 1539, his next major publishing venture was to complete his exposition of Romans. Since his life in Strasbourg was relatively idyllic, he was able to expend more care on this commentary than almost any other. Moreover, it is the only commentary he was able to revise twice, first in 1551, and again in 1556.

Thus, the final edition of his **Romans** was composed about the same time as the final edition (1559) of the **Institutes** and actually post-dates much of the material found in chapters 9-11 of Book II which was cited earlier. (Only Chapter IX is new to the 1559 edition.)

Consequently, there can be no playing off of reflections about the Jews or Israel in the Institutes against the commentary on Romans. Both have roots in the thought of the young Calvin, but the final editions of both reflect the experience and thought of the reformer at the height of his career.

Before proceeding to an analysis of Romans 9-11, we can gain some insights into Calvin's approach to this question by taking a brief look at the outline (*Argumentum*) of the contents of the Letter. This is a straightforward summary of the argument of Romans without much elaboration. As he follows the apostle's argument that both Jews and Gentiles, each in their own way, are guilty before God, Calvin shows no particular animus toward the Jew. In short, there is here no incipient anti-Judaism! On the other hand, he is reluctant to attribute any superiority to the Jews. In his summary of Romans 4, for example, he notes that "the Jews have no reason to exalt themselves above the Gentiles, since this blessedness is common to both."[12]

When he comes to Romans 9, he makes a point in passing that will prove to be crucial later on, viz., that biological descent means little as far as salvation history is concerned. For Paul in these chapters "divides the children of Abraham into two classes (*duplex genus*) to show that not all those who were his physical descendants are to be regarded as his seed and share in the grace of the covenant. On the contrary, even strangers become his children if they are brought into the covenant of faith."[13] Calvin has good reason to make this claim, for in this chapter the contrast is made between Jacob and Esau, both full-blooded children of the patriarch Isaac. So, in a sense, Calvin's point is an obvious one, but we shall be seeing that there is a tendency to minimize the distinctiveness of being Jewish. Rather, he constantly stresses that it is the faith connection that is important. In the last analysis, it is God's gracious election, not one's blood line, that counts.

Nevertheless, he does not totally ignore the significance of being a Jew. He combines both motifs--God's election and the significance of being a Jew--in the following statement which is found in his summary of Romans 11: "Finally, he [Paul] asserts that the covenant remains even in the physical descendants of Abraham, but only in those whom the Lord has predestined by his free election."[14]

Thus, the matter is not a simple one for Calvin--nor for Paul, for that matter. This will become even more apparent as we turn now to the salient points in the exposition of Romans 9-11. This analysis cannot be exhaustive but must focus on those comments which are relevant to the theme of Israel and the Church.

A constant concern of Calvin's in these chapters--not unrelated to the Apostle's--is the constancy and faithfulness of God. An important assumption is what Calvin terms "the destruction of the Jewish nation."[15] This is why Calvin says little about the future of Israel as a *national entity*.

At the same time, Calvin stresses again and again that the destruction of the nation Israel and the passing over of the Jews as an ethnic group does not in any way render the covenant with Israel invalid. It might be argued that since God had chosen the Israelites and had made his covenant with them, the validity and permanence of the covenant depended on the future of the nation Israel. For "God by his covenant had so highly exalted them [the Jews], that if they fell, the faithfulness and truth of God himself would also fail in the world. The covenant would have been made void. . . ."[16]

However, such a notion is unthinkable, for "the abolition of the covenant would be more strange than the sad and ruinous upheaval of the whole world."[17] God will be faithful even though his people prove faithless. Thus the infidelity of the Jews as a whole cannot undercut or break the covenant whose stability depends on God's faithfulness, his gracious election, and sure promises. For

> although the Jews had blasphemously separated themselves from God by their defection, yet the light of the grace of God had not wholly been extinguished among them, as he has said in Rom 3:3. Although they were unbelievers and had broken his covenant, yet their perfidy had not rendered the faithfulness of God void, not only because he preserved for himself some seed as a remnant form the whole multitude, but also because the name of a church still continued among them by right of inheri-

tance (italics mine).[18]

This is an important passage for it shows that: (1) Calvin considers the covenant with the Jews still valid and operative despite their defection. (2) The basis of this continuity, though ultimately dependent on God's faithfulness, rests in a remnant. (3) By virtue of this special relationship--they have been chosen and adopted by God--the Church continues to exist among them.

However, the people as a whole, having rejected God and his covenant, experience the "greater condemnation" precisely because of their privileged status.[19] Still, the *promise* of salvation "belongs to all who trace their natural descent to Abraham, because it is offered without exception." However, "his *inheritance* does not relate to all of his descendants without distinction."[20] This is the way Calvin understands 9:6: "Not all who are descended from Israel belong to Israel"; and 8: "It is not the children of the flesh who are the children of God but the children of the promise are reckoned as descendants."

Again, the ultimate basis of such distinctions is found in the election of God, although the specific ground for this separation between Israel after the spirit and Israel after the flesh is the ingratitude of those who reject their adoption. In this connection Calvin makes a futher distinction between *general* election and what might be called *particular* election (although he does not use the word "particular" in this context). In his own words:

> The general election of the people of Israel does not prevent God from choosing for himself by his secret counsel those to whom he pleases. God's condescension in making a covenant of life with a single nation is indeed a remarkable illustration of undeserved mercy, but his hidden grace is more evident in the second election, which is restricted to a part of the nation.[21]

In other words, there is an election within the election of the chosen people, or, more particularly, a secret election within the general election, an interior call within the outward or external call.[22] Israel after the flesh corresponds to the former, the true Israel to the latter. The same can be said of the Church and Calvin's (and Augustine's) familiar distinction between the visible and invisible Church.

This, for Calvin, is the explanation for the choice of Isaac over Ishmael and Jacob over Esau. It is also the basis for his controverted doctrine of double predestination, which is beyond the scope of our concern here.[23]

Much of the rest of chapter nine is concerned with the theme of God's election--and mercy, a key word in 9:15-18. In 9:24-26, however, the Apostle takes again the theme of Jew and Gentile, pointing out that "the vessels of mercy" (9:23) include both Jew and Gentile (9:24-26). On the basis of the quotation from Hosea (cited in 9:25-26), Calvin observes that God hereby declares that he "has put the Gentiles on a level with the Jews."[24] Yet he sees in 9:27-29 and allusion to the return of the Jews to Jerusalem after their exile in Babylon and thus a typological pointing to the renewal of the Church in his own time. "That physical restoration of the Jews prefigured the true renovation of the Church of God which is accomplished in Christ, and indeed was only its beginning."[25]

Romans 9 concludes with a contrast between the righteousness of faith and the righteousness of the law. The Gentiles attained the former, although they did not seek it, whereas the Jews "stumbled" because they sought God's righteousness on the basis of works. Calvin draws the lesson that "This example of the Jews should inspire with fear all those who strive to obtain the kingdom of God by works.[26]

In Romans 10 Paul begins by expressing his burden for the salvation of his fellow Jews and then returns to the theme of God's righteousness, the righteousness of faith, as over against human attempts at achieving righteousness. There is no advance here on the theme of the relationship of Israel and the Church except for the observation in 10:12 that "there is no distinction between the Jew and the Greek; the same Lord is Lord of all and bestows his riches upon all who call upon him." Calvin adds that the reason for this is, "If the One who is the creator and maker of the whole world is the God of all mankind, he will display his kindness to all by whom he has been invoked and acknowledged as their God."[27]

This chapter concludes on a negative note as far as the Jews are concerned because they were specially privileged with the revelation of God's law and covenant but spurned God's grace and became "a disobedient and contrary people"(10:21b). Calvin asks, "How is it that strangers and non-Jews should run to the light held up to their view afar off, while the holy race of Abraham reject the light which they have close at hand?"[28] Calvin does not give a direct answer to his question. Paul's quotation from Isa 65:2 in 10:21 indicates that the problem was that the Jews were "disobedient and contrary." Calvin sees the root cause as idolatry, based on the context of the quotation from Deuteronomy 32:21 in 10:19. For the Jews "had forsaken the true God and whored after idols." Their sin was compounded after the coming of Christ, for they "denied that God the Father was revealed to them in Christ, his only-begotten Son. This is the ultimate form of godlessness."[29]

In his discussion of 10:19 Calvin makes two comments in passing that would seem to indicate a low view of any continuing role for Israel as a whole, i. e., "after the flesh." In one place he says," Paul proves from this statement of Moses that there is nothing irrational in God's preferring (*praeferat*) the Gentiles to the Jews. "A few lines later he refers to God's having "repudiated (*repudio*) the Jewish people."[30] This is saying more than the text would seem to allow. Moreover, the main point of Romans 11 is that God has not cast off his people!

This brings us to the key question in regard to Calvin's view of Israel over against the Church. We have seen in various contexts that whereas Calvin does not appear to share the animus toward the Jews of his time characteristic of many of his contemporaries, whether Catholic or Protestant, at the same time he does not assign a significant continuing role to the Jews or the people of Israel as an ethnic entity. In other words, the evidence thus far would seem to deny any eschatological meaning to Israel. Recall that in the **Argumentum** Calvin had stated that "God's covenant has not wholly departed from the seed of Abraham," but that the continuing validity of the covenant only applies to a predestined remnant.

Now, as he considers the critical question raised by the Apostle at the beginning of Romans 11--"Has God rejected his people?"--a more definitive answer can be given. Calvin begins by pointing out that Paul's argument thus far could be taken to suggest that with the advent of Christ--and his subsequent rejection by the Jews--that the promises to Israel were now offered to the Gentiles. However, according to Calvin, Paul now "qualifies what he had previously stated concerning the *repudiation* (italics mine) of the Jews in such a way as to prevent any from supposing that the covenant which had formerly been made with Abraham was now abrogated, or that God had so forgotten it that the Jews were now completely estranged from his kingdom, as the Gentiles were before the coming of Christ."[31]

The difficulty here is in reconciling what seems to be contradictory assertions. On the one hand, because the Jews had rejected God's way of righteousness, they were "repudiated," "cut off" (*excidisse*) from the covenant," and rejected. On the other hand, Calvin maintains that the covenant with the Jews was not "abrogated." The solution to this apparent contradiction is found in two important qualifications Calvin makes on several occasions. The first is that while Israel, *as a whole*, may be cut off and rejected by God because of their idolatry and faithlessness, from God's side the covenant "stands firm and inviolable."[32] "The rejection of the Jews, therefore, is not of such a character as to render void the promise of God."[33] The second qualification or distinction is one noted earlier, viz., that whereas Israel after the flesh was rejected, the true or spiritual Israel, the *ecclesiola in ecclesia*, so to speak, by virtue of God's secret election, continues to enjoy God's favor. As Calvin puts it,

> God has by no means rejected the whole race of Abraham, by acting contrary to the trustworthiness of his covenant. The effect, however, of his adoption is not found in all children of the flesh, because his secret election precedes adoption. Thus the general rejection was not able to prevent some seed from being saved, for the visible body of the people was rejected in such a way that no member of the spiritual body of Christ was lost.[34]

Note how this principle is at work not only among the Jews but also among members of the Church. Whether Jew or Gentile, it is not the external calling but the inward that counts, and where the latter obtains, there true faith will be found. So Calvin concludes his comments on the phrase, "God has not rejected his people whom he foreknew" (11:2), with a general application: "Although God invites all the people to him without distinction, he does not inwardly draw any except those whom he knows to be his own and has given to his Son, and whom he will also keep faithfully to the very end."[35]

This may appear speculative or hyper-Calvinistic to those of non-Reformed background, but it must not be forgotten that Paul himself a few verses later asserts that "at the present time there is a remnant chosen by grace" (11:5). Again in 11:7 we read: "What then? Israel failed to obtain what it sought. The elect obtained it, but the rest were hardened." Concerning the latter verse Calvin suggests that "Israel had labored in vain in seeking for salvation, because it strove for it with misplaced zeal."[36]

We come now to the crux of this whole section, for in 11:11-12 Paul treats first the role the Jews play in making possible the salvation of the Gentiles and then turns the argument around by pointing out that the final result will be the conversion of Israel. The argument is a complicated one and need not be repeated here, nor Calvin's particular exegesis of these fascinating verses.

Two points, however, have a special bearing on our subject. The first is that Calvin does not understand the rejection of Christ by the Jews as having infinite and universal consequences. To do so--and this has been done throughout the ages in certain Christian circles--would be a rationalization for anti-Judaism and the alleged reason for the curse upon the Jews.

Calvin, on the contrary, in commenting on 11:11-12, first warns against confusing the Jewish nation with Jews as individuals. Even though "the majority of Jews were opposed to Christ," this does not mean that there is no hope of repentance" for the Jews. Paul, he says, "rightly denies here [11:11] that the salvation of the Jews was to be despaired of, or that they were so rejected by God that there was no restoration to come, or that the covenant of grace, which God had once made with them, was completely abolished, since there always continued to remain in the nation the seed of blessing" (*semen benedictionis*).[37] It is true that some Jews found Christ to be a stumbling stone (9:32-33), and were hardened and blind to the truth (11:7-10), but "the nation itself has not so fallen that one who is a Jew must necessarily perish or be estranged from God."[38]

Not only that, on the basis of 11:16-21--"if the root is holy, so are the branches"--Calvin does not hesitate to affirm that "because the Lord sanctified Abraham to himself on condition that his seed also should be holy, and therefore bestowed holiness not only upon the person of Abraham, but also upon his whole race, Paul rightly argues from this that *all Jews have been sanctified in their father Abraham*"[39] (italics mine). One could say this is the obvious meaning of the text, but more than one interpreter takes a less inclusive view of the term "branches" and interprets them to mean not Israel as a whole but "the faithful remnant whose latest representation is the church."[40] This may be the majority view among contemporary commentators, but quite apart from the correctness of Calvin's interpretation, it shows a positive view toward the whole Jewish race.

When it comes to the other *crux interpretum*, however, viz. 11:26--"And so all Israel shall be saved"--Calvin takes a view which is both narrower and broader. Most modern interpreters understand "all Israel" not to mean every last Israelite or Jew but in a general corporate sense, i.e., the nation of Israel as a whole.[41]

Calvin, however, interprets "all Israel" to include "all the people of God," by which he means both Jews and Gentiles. "The salvation of the whole Israel of God, which must be drawn from both, will thus be completed, and yet in such a way that the Jews, as the first born of the family of God, may obtain the first place."[42]

This is an unusual, if not unique, interpretation which finds little favor today, but Calvin sees a parallel in Gal 6:16: "In the same way, in Gal 6:16, he [Paul] calls the Church, which was composed equally of Jews and Gentiles, the Israel of God, setting the people, thus collected from their dispersion, in opposition to the carnal children of Abraham who had fallen away from faith."[43] However, as the doughty Calvinist, John Murray, has pointed out, Calvin errs in appealing to Gal 6:16 because there is no contrast between Jew and Gentile there whereas here in 11:26 "there is the sustained contrast between Israel and the Gentiles."[44] Yet, as we saw above, Calvin does include in the "all" the restoration of Israel as a people. Accordingly, Calvin does not narrow the scope of the passage, but rather broadens it so that the new, eschatological Israel includes both Jew and Gentile![45]

It is evident from comments on succeeding verses (11:28-34) that Calvin does not intend to spiritualize away the significance of Israel as an ethnic entity. Concerning 11:29, for example--"The gifts and the call of God are irrevocable"--he comments: "If, therefore, it is completely impossible for the Lord to depart from the covenant which he made with Abraham . . , then he has not wholly turned his kindness away from the Jewish nation." Moreover, in this context he also qualifies an earlier assertion to the effect that Israel had been "cut off from the covenant" (on 11:1), for here he adds that Israel "has not been cut off *by the roots (sed a radice excisa non fuit*"[46] --italics mine).

Thus, despite some exegetical flaws and an occasional remark which would appear to minimize the significance of the Jews as a people, Calvin turns out to be surprisingly positive about the relation of Israel to the Church. It also appears that he has transcended, in large part, the anti-Judaism which the Reformers inherited from their late medieval predecessors. Even though Calvin did not fully appreciate the eschatological significance of Israel in *Heilsgeschichte*, particularly in the **Institutes**, in his exegesis of Romans 9-11 he shows considerable appreciation for the significance of Israel, not only for an elect remnant who have become a part of the Church, but for the people as a whole, for all the seed of Abraham. Thus it appears that Calvin does leave room for the possibility of the eventual salvation of Israel as a whole.

If this appraisal is correct, the brief analysis of Heiko Oberman should be modified to the extent that Calvin is viewed as having a more positive picture of the place of Israel than most of his contemporaries.[47]

NOTES

1. Philadelphia: Fortress, 1984.

2. Ibid., 22.

3. Ibid. This is one of the theses of Oberman's book.

4. See "Calvin und die Juden. Zu einem Streitsgesprach," in *Judaica* 2 (1946) 203-08, reprinted in **Christen und Juden. Ihr Gegenüber vom Apostelkonzil bis Heute**, edited by W. D. Marsch und K. Thieme (Mainz: Matthias-Grünewald Verlag, 1961) 141-46; and the essay in Dutch, "Calvijn en de Joden," **Kerk en Israel** 17 ('s Gravenhage, 1963).

5. Op. cit., 141. Cf. 145, n 7.

6. See my essay, "Luther and Calvin on Law and Gospel in their Galatians Commentaries," *Reformed Review* 37/2 (Winter, 1984).

7. In relation to law and gospel, Calvin makes a threefold distinction: a unity of the substance of the doctrine, a *distinction* in the form or mode of instruction, an *antithesis* of letter and Spirit. I have elaborated on this distinction in an essay, "Law and Gospel or Gospel and Law? Calvin's Understanding of the Relationship," in **Calviniana**, Robert V. Schnucker, Editor, Vol. X Sixteenth Century Essays and Studies (Kirksville, Mo.: Sixteenth Century Journal Publishers, 1988), 17ff.

8. Quotations from the **Institutes of the Christian Religion** are from the Library of Christian Classics edition, edited by John T. McNeill and translated by Ford Lewis Battles (Philadelphia: Westminster, 1960).

9. I shall be using the translation by Ross Mackenzie in the edition edited by David W. Torrance and Thomas F. Torrance, Vol. 8: **The Epistles of Paul to the Romans and Thessalonians** (Grand Rapids: Eerdmans, 1961). I am also checking critical phrases or passages in the original Latin text as found in the **Calvini Opera** of the **Corpus Reformatorum** Vol. 49 (Brunswick, 1892).

10. On this subject see T. H. L. Parker's **Commentaries on Romans 1532-1542** (Edinburgh: T. & T. Clark, 1986).

11. Ibid., 34-35.

12. Torrance edition, 7.

13. Ibid., 9.

14. Ibid., 10.

15. On 9:2, 191.

16. On 9:3, 192.

17. On 9:3, 192. Translation modified.

18. On 9:4, 194. "The favor of God could not fail the Israelites without abolishing the covenant . . . . Paul shows nonetheless how the grace of God would constantly remain among the Jewish people, however great their blindness, so that the truth of the covenant might stand firm." On

9:6, 196.

19. On 9:5, 196. One is reminded here of the judgment pronounced on Israel through the prophet Amos. "You only have I known ["chosen"--NIV] of all the families of the earth; *therefore* I will punish you for all your iniquities" (3:2).

20. On 9:6, 197.

21. On 9:6, 197-98. Cf. the same distinction made in the **Institutes** III.21.6: "We must now add a second, more restricted degree of election, or one in which God's more special grace was evident, that is, when from the same race of Abraham God rejected some, but showed that he kept others among his sons by nourishing them in his Church."

22. See on 10:17, 232, and Comm. on Amos 5:4-6.

23. Just one comment in connection with 9:10. Calvin here states three "propositions," the first of which is: "As the blessing of the covenant separates the people of Israel from all other nations, so also the election of God makes a distinction between men in that nation, which he predestines some to salvation, and others to eternal condemnation" (on 9:11, 199-200).

24. On 9:25, 214.

25. On 9:27, 215.

26. On 9:32, 218.

27. On 10:12, 229.

28. On 10:19, 135.

29. Ibid.

30. Ibid.

31. On 11:1, 238.

32. On 11:1, 239.

33. On 11:2, 239.

34. Ibid.

35. On 11:2, 240. As he proceeds to exposit the latter part of this verse it is apparent that Calvin is no longer thinking of the Jews but of the Church of all time which is "nourished by the secret providence of God."

36. On 11:7, 243.

37. On 11:11, 246.

38. Ibid.

39. On 11:16, 249.

40. So T. W. Manson in Peake's **Commentary on the Bible,** revised edition, edited by Matthew Black and H. H. Rowley (London: Thomas Nelson & Sons, 1962), 949. So also C. K. Barrett: Paul is not yet speaking of the relation of Israel to the patriarchs, but of the remnant . . . he regards the *Jewish Christians* as the pledge of the eventual salvation of all Israel" (italics mine). **The Epistle to the Romans** (New York: Harper & Row, 1957) 216.

41. So C. E. B. Cranfield, C. K. Barrett, F. F. Bruce, and Ernst Käsemann, commentaries, *loc. cit.*

42. On 11:26a, 255.

43. Ibid.

44. The **Epistle to the Romans** (Grand Rapids: Eerdmans, 1965) 96-97, n. 51.

45. However, a few lines later Calvin makes a slight qualification: "Although in this prophecy [verse 26] deliverance is promised to the spiritual people of God, among whom the Gentiles also are included, yet because the Jews are the firstborn, it was necessary that what the prophet declares should be fulfilled particularly in them. The fact that Scripture calls all the people of God Israelites is ascribed to the excellence of that nation, which God preferred to all others" (On 11:26, 256).

46. On 11:29, 257.

47. See **The Roots of Anti-Semitism,** 141. The question is whether Justas Jonas was the only reformer "even to approximate [a] future oriented view" of Israel in relation to the Church.

"RECOVERING THE REAL PAUL": THEOLOGY AND EXEGESIS IN ROMANS 9-11

STEPHEN R. HAYNES

I. INTRODUCTION

The last two decades have witnessed calls for genuine "paradigm shifts" in the disciplines of Christian theology and biblical studies. Before the Nazi Holocaust and the founding of the state of Israel in 1948, only a few radical thinkers were concerned with the "Jewish question" and its significance for Christian faith. Jacques Maritain, James Parkes, Erik Peterson, and George Foot Moore are among the few twentieth-century Christian scholars who were sympathetic to the problem of Christian anti-Judaism in the pre-Holocaust era.[1] Recently, however, revelations of Christian silence and complicity during the destruction of European Jewry in the 1940s, and the growing recognition that traditional Christian attitudes toward Jews are at the root of much religious anti-Judaism and pagan anti-Semitism, have led to calls for wide-scale reformulations of Christian theology, exegesis, liturgy, catechesis and seminary education. In the last fifteen years in particular, this reconsideration of Christian traditions vis-a-vis "Israel" has become an obsession--and it shows no signs of abating.[2]

The first major wave of Christian theology sensitive to the implications of the Holocaust broke onto the scene in the early 1970s.[3] This "Holocaust theology" argued, first, that the events of recent Jewish (and world) history had inescapable implications for the way Christians think and talk about God, and, second, that the roots of Jewish genocide in the twentieth century must ultimately be sought in Christian theology of the first. This approach went well beyond a critique of anti-Jewish biases on the part of Christian scholars,[4] and returned to early Christianity itself, establishing anti-Judaism as the (necessary?) concomitant of christology.[5] Although the approaches and conclusions of "Holocaust theology" have been a source of controversy, its influence has been substantial for both biblical studies and theology.

Our present study is concerned particularly with one result of the changes described above: the return to the documents of the New Testament as an arena for theological and exegetical revision in light of the Holocaust and the establishment of the state of Israel. Both Jewish and Christian biblical scholars have reopened the New

Testament in recent years and discovered fresh resources for ecumenical dialogue and Christian-Jewish coexistence. Markus Barth recently described this new atmosphere of return *ad fontes*!:

> Because unity in matters of faith depends upon truth, and because brotherly conduct in daily life is based on faithfulness, it has been necessary to go back once more to the biblical evidence, to assess critically the major (and some minor) currents in both the Jewish and Christian usage of Scripture, and to issue a plea for honest repentance and courageous action.[6]

The results of this renewed engagement with the documents of the New Testament have been revolutionary: the sources which traditionally have been interpreted as the "last word" on Christian condemnation of "the Jews," are now being looked to as the source for a new "first word" of reconciliation. In fact, in their attempts to wrestle with passages of the New Testament which have been labelled "anti-Semitic," scholars have rediscovered the "Jewishness" of Jesus, Paul, and the New Testament environment. They have also set their focus on recapturing the original intention of passages like Romans 9-11, which promise to provide a fresh foundation for a positive Christian understanding of Israel.

In 1969 Alan T. Davies could describe the importance of Romans 9-11 only with regard to its image of the Jew as a special species of non-believer. Today, these chapters are the focus of a flury of exegesis seeking to discover a different Paul--one who has much to say to the Church on the topic of its understanding of "Israel." This scramble to "recover the real Paul" (to use Paul van Buren's words) has occupied New Testament scholarship every bit as much as did the elaboration of the "Jewishness" of Jesus.[7] Biblical scholars from Baur to Bultmann understood Paul in terms of one or another aspect of his "Greek" environment,[8] and Paul's relationship with the Palestinian Judaism of his time was understood as "basically antithetical."[9] Now, however, the pendulum has swung almost completely in the other direction. Interest in the Jewish "background" to Paul, his Letters, and his theology is now the dominant orientation in Pauline studies.[10]

The great focus on Paul and his Jewish environment has had at least three foci. First, there has been tremendous interest in the extent and character of Paul's "Jewishness," and the nature of his relationship to Palestinian/Rabbinic Judaism. Second, Paul's understanding of the "law" has been a topic of keen interest.[11] Third, a fierce battle has been waged over the location of the "center" of Paul's theology.[12]

Each of these foci are linked to our present topic, but the third is particularly salient for understanding recent theological interpretation of Roman 9-11.[13] This is because one's interpretation of these chapters really revolves around the question, "What is Romans about?" The answer to this question has traditionally been, "justification by faith," but contemporary scholars have suggested another answer: "entering and being the people of God." In taking this view, these scholars have focused on Paul's sociological situation at the time he wrote Romans, forsaking a traditional "introspective" approach based on Paul's apparent concern with personal salvation.[14] New Testament scholarship of the last decade is rife with new studies of Romans 9-11, and together they represent a new consensus which views these chapters as central to the Letter,[15] and as the interpretive key for Paul's view of "Israel," if not his entire theology.

The purpose of the following essay is to examine this recent renewal of interest in Paul and the significance of Romans 9-11 in its relationship to theology. We will pursue this relationship in three ways: by exploring the seminal work of Karl Barth and Krister Stendahl as examples of the importance which Romans 9-11 plays in formulating a positive Christian understanding of "Israel;" by critically considering the methodological significance of what we have called the "recovery of the real Paul;" and by anticipating problems which result from the great theological burden which Romans 9-11 is increasingly asked to bear.

II. PAUL AMONG JEWS AND GENTILES

The work of the Swedish New Testament scholar Krister Stedahl is particularly representative of the recent changes in the way Paul is understood. Although its approach is "far from esoteric" (Stendahl, 7), Stendahl's **Paul Among Jews and Gentiles** has been well-received by the academy. This simple, yet profound and programmatic book owes its success, in part, to its accessibility relative to works like Sanders' **Paul and Palestinian Judaism**, and to the author's compelling style. In the decade or so since its publication, many studies of Paul and Romans have been produced which reflect Stendahl's approach. Although it is usually difficult to pinpoint the sources of a particular scholarly orientation, many writers have confirmed the seminal nature of Stendahl's work.[16] Precisely why, we must ask, is Stendahl such a "provocative starting point for the recent discussion" of Paul, the Church, and Israel?[17]

Part of the answer to this question lies in Stendahl's method. He works along the line suggested by Jesus' statement, "you have heard it said. . . but I tell you. . ," calling time-honored traditions into question in an attempt to establish a new "center" in Pauline interpretation. In fact, Stendahl sees his work as an "attempt to renew our acquaintance with Paul after nineteen hundred years" (Stendahl, 78). Drawing inspiration from the work of Johannes Munck,[18] Stendahl argues that "the main lines of Pauline interpretation. . . have. . . been out of touch with one of the most basic of the questions and concerns that shaped Paul's thinking in the first place: the relation between Jews and Gentiles" (Stendahl, 1).

An important corollary of Stendahl's redicovery of the "Jews and Gentiles" theme in Paul is the displacement of the doctrine of "justification by faith" at the thematic center of Romans, so that justification is now placed in service of this new center, rather than vice versa.[19] Stendahl believes that as Pauline theology became "homogenized" soon after canonization, the message of Romans was "spiritualized," and the Letter came to be viewed as a "theological tractate on the nature of faith." As a result, Paul's own concern in Romans was gradually lost in the history of interpretation (Stendahl, 5).

A second corollary to Stendahl's focus on "Jews and Gentiles" in Romans is his insistance that chapters 9-11 are the "real center of gravity" in the Letter (Stendahl, 28). This amounts to a structural shift--chapters 9-11 replacing the traditional favorites, chapters 3 and 7, as the "climax" of Romans--which complements the thematic shift described above.

This two-pronged strategy, in which Stendahl displaces traditional understandings of Paul and his Letters, has been adopted in outline by many exegetes. In fact, there seems to be something like a scholarly consensus emerging with regard to Romans 9-11--a consensus which treats these chapters as a thematic whole, views them as comprising the centerpiece (or at least a key element) in Paul's argument in Romans, and treats the breakdown between Jewish and Gentile communities as a result of sociological conditions rather than Christology or conflicting views of the "law." Stendahl's approach to Romans 9-11 has nicely complemented its use as a key text by the theologies of "coexistence" and "continuity" which currently abound.[20]

Before considering more fully the implications for theology of Stendahl's work on Romans, we must point out a rather important element in his approach which is easily overlooked. To put it simply, Stendahl's interpretation of Romans relies on an "historical" approach which has fallen out of favor among many biblical critics. In his attempt to overcome perennial misinterpretations of Paul and his Letters, Stendahl distinguishes between the "original" meaning of Romans and that imposed by later interpreters:

> . . . it is precisely *his* (Paul's) language and original meanings which in these chapters we are attempting to recapture and revitalize. The problem I am addressing . . . is what did *Paul* actually mean? What did Paul actually think?[21]

Stendahl's quest to discover what was in the mind of Paul as "author" of Romans may be expressed in terms of his desire to get "behind the hermeneutical to the exegetical level" (Stendahl, 36). That is, Stendahl believes that description of what a text "meant--understood in its own terms--comprises a separate and necessary "descriptive task" which precedes a determination of what the text "means"--that is, the "hermeneutic question."[22] Though this distinction appears simple enough, it is based on dubious premises: first, it assumes the ability of the scholar to ascertain the "original" meaning of a text, and second, declares that this "original" meaning must underly all others. Both these ideas have come under severe attack as the hegemony of the "historical-critical method" is challenged by "literary" and other forms of criticism. Although biblical scholarship has not completely abandoned the "diachronic" methods associated with the "historical" method, these methods have been increasingly forced to share time with various "synchronic" methods which locate meaning somewhere between the text (and its "structures") and the reader.[23]

Despite its apparent methodological naivety, however, Stendahl's admonition to "seek ye first the original meanings" (Stendahl, 36) has been carefully heeded by the majority of recent interpreters of Romans 9-11. "Structural," "semiotic" and "literary" treatments[24] of this passage are few indeed, compared with those which approach it with the conscious intention of ascertaing its "backgrounds," understanding its original theological intent, or elaborating the sociological conditions it reflects. Furthermore, many of these historically-oriented interpretaions follow Stendahl in moving confidently from a determination of "what the text meant" to affirmations about "what it means"--usually with contemporary ecumenical relations in mind.[25] Perhaps then it is not surprising that so many of these arrive at the same general conclusions as Stendahl: the continuing election of the Jewish people and the permanence of the Jewish covenant(s), established on the basis of their clear affrmation by Paul himself, in his struggle "among Jews and Gentiles."[26]

III. THE ELECTION OF THE COMMUNITY OF GOD

Stendahl's insistence that it is two closely interrelated religious "communities"--and not "Judaism" and "Christianity" as we have come to know them--

which are the subject of Romans, provides a transition to our consideration of another exegete/theologian whose work on Romans 9-11 has been very influential: Karl Barth. Barth, too, understood "Church" and "Israel" in terms of "community," viewing them as organically connected as two forms of the same "indissoluble" people of God. Interestingly, it was not in his early commentary on Romans (**Der Römerbrief**, 2nd ed., 1921), but in his later interpretation of the doctrine of election that Barth undertook a serious exegesis of Romans 9-11. Despite the "historical and philological weaknesses"[27] which some have associated with his **Der Römerbrief**, Barth's exegesis of Romans 9-11 in **Church Dogmatics**, II: 2 is a lasting testimony to his exegetical competence.

Though Barth was undoubtedly a "pre-Holocaust" theologian, and though his understanding of "Israel" remained at best "dialectical,"[28] his theological/exegetical approach to the relationship of "the Church and Israel" continues to exercise a provocative influence on theology. After briefly reviewing the main elements in his mature understanding of "Israel," we will explore Barth's contemporary influence on this issue, with particular regard to Romans 9-11.

For those of us sensitized to the problems of religious pluralism and coexistence, and influenced by the ongoing campaign to rid church and acdemy of anti-Jewish biases, Barth's discussion of "the election of the community" (para. 34 in the **Church Dogmatics**) may at first glance seem exceedingly traditional. This 100+ page section which includes Barth's exegesis of Romans 9-11, resounds with God's "No" to Israel," which is made all the more tragic because it falls within Barth's classic exposition of divine election. Barth uses the term "Synagogue"-- which is employed derisively in the confessions of the Reformed tradition[29]--to describe Israel as a whole, and seems particularly influenced by Augustine's doctrine of the Jews as a "witness people," preserved by God but only as a witness to judgment.[30] Furthermore, despite his emphasis on the irrevocable election of "Israel," it is not at all clear whether Barth intends to include in "Israel" Judaism or individual Jews *post Christum natum.*

Given some of Barth's other references to "Israel" in the ***Church Dogmatics***,[31] and his admitted personal aversion for living Jews,[32] it is tempting to understand Barth's discussion of election as cleverly deferring on the significance of contemporary Judaism. Furthermore, Barth's attempt to take "Israel" into his theological system may lead to other problems. In particular, his view of Jews as "mirrors" of human self-sufficiency (based on a Pauline view of Jewish religion that has recently been challenged), allows him to incorporate anti-Judaism into the structure of salvation history.[33]

On the other hand, Barth's treatment of "Israel" is precedent-setting in some important respects. First, Barth rediscovers Romans 9-11 as a "catalyst" (Davies) for modern theology by basing his theology of "Israel" on this particular passage, rather than on Jesus' reproaches to "the Jews," Westminster "covenant theology," or later antagonisms between Christians and Jews. Second, the systematic context for Barth's treatment of "Israel and the Church" is his discussion of divine election. This means, among other things, that the concepts of "grace" and "mercy" (not "law") are the background on which the question of "Israel's" meaning is posed. This in itself is a radical departure from the theological tradition inherited by Barth. Related to this departure is Barth's interpretation of Christ as the "goal" (Greek, *telos)* of the law in Romans 10:4. Barth's "teleological" interpretation of this passage has been increasingly supported by contemporary exegetes.[34]

Third, Barth was radical in his understanding of the "one community of God in its two-fold form." This emphasis on fundamental continuity between Church and

"Israel" (though its implications remain unclear in Barth) is still a popular option in contemporary discussions of Church/Israel relations.[35] Whether a one or two covenant "model" is used to make sense of this relationship, Barth's approach to the "one community of God" allows for the drawing of parallels between Jewish and Christian worship, belief, and mission.[36]

Finally, it is significant that Barth's interpretation of Paul's treatise on "Israel" in Romans 9-11 comes in the context of his systematic theology. Although some would not deem this an advantage, arguing that the "descriptive task" of exegesis, "biblical theology," and "systematic theology" must all remain independent,[37] the need for a systematic context in which to develop a Christian theology of "Israel" is still very acute. It is an open question whether today, almost fifty years after Barth completed this section of the **Church Dogmatics**, a successful "Christian theology of Israel" has yet to appear.[38]

We now turn to some specific examples of Barth's influence on contemporary thinking on the relation between the Church and "Israel." On the Protestant side, Barth's legacy has been particularly important in the work of Paul van Buren. In fact, van Buren's recent attempt to construct a "theology of the Jewish-Christian reality," has been carried out in dialogue with Barth. Although Barth's influence is clear in **Discerning the Way** (volume 1 of van Buren's project) it is in volume 2, **A Christian Theology of the People Israel**, that what van Buren calls the "experience of wrestling with Barth's **Church Dogmatics**" is particularly evident.[39]

Although van Buren is appreciative of the help his former mentor's theology has provided for his own task, he is also aware that Barth saw "far too dimly" the reality of postbiblical Israel.[40] Yet van Buren seems destined to labor in Barth's vineyard, as it were, and currently, having completed three volumes of his "theology of the Jewish-Christian reality," is once more working through Barth's paragraph on "the election of the community" for the benefit of a new generation of theologians and pastors.[41]

Another Protestant scholar whose work is concerned with a renewal of Christian-Jewish theological relations, and who is open about his debt to Barth, is C. E. B. Cranfield, whose commentary on Romans has been widely praised for its detailed exegetical analyses, testifies to a change in his thinking about "Israel:"

> If we would be true to Paul's teaching, we must surely repudiate altogether the notion, which is very widespread among Christians and has often been expressed by theologians (including--God forgive him!--the present writer) that the Jewish people, having rejected Jesus Christ, has been dispossessed of its election and simply replaced by God by a new Israel namely the Christian church.[42]

In this passage we are reminded of Barth's words in the **Church Dogmatics**:

> We cannot, therefore, call the Jews the "rejected," and the Church the "elected community. The object of election is neither Israel for itself nor the Church for itself but both togather in their unity.[43]

Cranfield makes his dependence on Barth explicit in the second half of his Romans commentary, referring to the "decisive amendment of doctrine" brought about by Barth's "magnificent section on God's election of grace." In particular, Cranfield goes on, Barth's "suggestive and penetrating exegesis" of Romans 9-11, and his innovative account of the two forms of the one community "illumines many of the difficulties" inherent in a Christian understanding of Israel.[44] A specific point at which Cranfield follows Barth's exegesis can be found in his "teleological" interpretation of Romans 10:4.[45]

Barth's influence on Catholic thinking on this issue of the relationship between "Church and Israel" is not to be overlooked. In fact, in a recent account of Barth's influence on Catholic theology, Philip J. Rosato identifies Barth's emphasis on the "unique and continuing role of the Jews in the communication of humanity's election by the Word of God" as a major source of inspiration for Catholic theology.[46] We see a concrete example of this inspiration in the recent attempt of Franz Mussner, a Catholic New Testament scholar, to construct his own "Christian theology of Judaism" in **Tractate on the Jews**. Mussner does not write in dialogue with Barth to the same extent as van Buren, but clearly reveals the influence of Barth's approach nonetheless. For example, Mussner's "outline for a Christian theology of Judaism" (chapter 1) is based on "the election of Israel" and its continuing covenant with God. Furthermore, Mussner credits Barth with having "rediscovered Israel for Christian theology,"[47] and quotes approvingly from Barth's Church Dogmatics. In the tradition of Barth, and in keeping with the approach of New Testament scholarship after Stendahl, Mussner treats Romans 9-11 as his interpretive key, not only for Romans and Pauline theology, but for his entire Christian theology of Judaism.[48] Clemens Thoma's **A Christian Theology of Judaism** is another recent study by a Catholic scholar in which the influence of Barth's approach to the interrelatedness of Church and Israel is evident.[49]

Although Barth's understanding of the significance of "Israel" for the Church may appear from our point of view as traditional in some places as it is radical in others, the lasting influence of Barth's "dialectical" assessment of "Israel" cannot be denied. Barth is important for our study in another sense, however. His work places before us the question of the relationship between theology and biblical exegesis. Despite, perhaps because of, the traditional impasse between Barth and "the exegetes,"[50] this question must be taken very seriously in our present context.

IV. WHERE THEOLOGY AND EXEGESIS MEET

Although the cleavage between biblical and theological disciplines[51] may be a stubborn reality in the academy, we have seen that concern for the relationship between "Church" and "Israel" has led scholars to ignore this cleavage and build bridges between theology and exegesis wherever possible. Particularly in the case of Romans 9-11, a recovery of Paul's original situation, intention, and "meaning" is often motivated by a new sensitivity to the Church's estrangement from the Jews, and its ongoing consequences.

Several Christian scholars have identified the insidious theological biases which have prejudiced exegetes *against* taking Jewish religion seriously on its own terms. So it should not be surprising to find a conscious reversal of this trend in contemporary scholarship. One question which this reversal prompts us to ask, however, is, "to what extent have theological concerns governed exegesis on this important issue?" Peter von der Osten-Sacken provides one kind of answer to this question. It is one which reveals the theological burden which interpreters of Romans 9-11 must bear:

> Romans 9-11 has the same constitutive function for the question about the relationship between Christians and Jews as the words of institution

> have for the interpretation of the Lord's Supper. These chapters are therefore the source providing guidelines for a theology in Christian-Jewish dialogue.[52]

This question of the relationship between theology and exegesis is not the primary focus of this study, however. Instead, we shall be content to consider some of the theological issues on which any exegesis of Romans 9-11 inevitably touches, and some of the potential dangers which a "recovery of the real Paul" entails.

If we agree (following Stendahl and Barth) that the central theological thrust of Romans 9-11 is the affirmation that "Israel" is and remains God's chosen people, a whole host of theological issues come to the fore. Perhaps the most obvious of these is the nature of the relationship between the original covenant with "Israel" and the extension of this covenant to the Gentiles in Jesus Christ. Are these covenants (or "ways", to use van Buren's term) essentially the same? If they are not the same, and the ("new") Christian covenant somehow replaced or "fulfilled" God's original covenant with the Jewish people, does the "old" covenant retain salvific efficacy, or not?[53] It would seem that Reformed theology, with its strong covenant tradition, would be a likely resource for tackling such questions. In fact, however, the Reformed tradition, while emphasizing the notion of covenant, contains a good deal of ambiguity with regard to their number and nature.[54]

Many theologians have told us that the traditional model of "promise" and "fulfillment" is no longer useful for describing our understanding of "Israel's" relationship to the Church.[55] This may be true, but it is also true that models of complementarity or continuity, based on the affirmation of God's irrevocable election of "Israel" (Romans 9-11), cannot be integrated theologically as long as the notion of covenant remains confused. This is a case, then, where theology and exegesis desperately need each other.

A second potential difficulty which any theology of "Israel" must anticipate lies in the area of "mission." The essential problem here is the same as described above. If Israel's election is unconditionally affirmed, then questions are raised concerning Jewish evangelism. The problem has come up frequently at the denominational and pan-denominational levels,[56] and is often framed in terms of the choice between "evangelism" and "dialogue" and in view of past persecution and proseletyzing, as well as the perdurance of "Israel's" covenant, "liberals" call for genuine "dialogue" between Christians and Jews. "Conservatives," on the other hand, see such attitudes as violations of the Great Commission, and as threats to the belief in Christ's uniqueness.

This is not a new debate, of course, but has been present at World Council of Churches Assemblies since 1948.[57] One solution to this dilemma has been to stress a mutual "witness" between Jews and Christians which combines faithfulness to one's own calling with respect for the other's integrity. Even conservative scholars have advanced this view,[58] and the relatively non-threatening notion of "mutual witness" may hold the key to ameliorating the "evangelism dilemma" for many Christians. But this issue's inevitable connection with Romans 9-11 is suggested by Stendahl's claim that, in Romans, we see "the God-willed coexistence between Jews and Christians in which the missionary urge to convert Israel is held in check."[59]

Another theological issue which emerges when treating these chapters surrounds the rendering of Romans 10:4, "Christ the end (*telos*) of the law. . . ." Translating (and thus interpreting Paul's intention in using) the polysemous *telos* has occupied exegetes for centuries, and there is still no consensus concerning the word's meaning in Roman 10:4. The three recognized options--the temporal (*telos* as "termination"), perfective (*telos* as "fulfillment"), and teleological (*telos* as "goal") interpretations[60]--imply three different ways of understanding the Church's relationship to "Israel." This relationship, in other words, is intimately connected with the continuity or discontinuity perceived between Christ and the "law."

The traditional, and perhaps still dominant view, is that Romans 10:4 refers to Christ's "termination" of the law as a way of salvation.[61] It is clear that a theology of radical "discontinuity" between Christianity and Judaism is implied by this temporal understanding of *telos.* While interpreting *telos* in a perfective sense (as "fulfillment") may lead to either a continuous or discontinuous understanding of Christ and the law,[62] the teleological interpretation of *telos* tends to establish Romans 10:4 as the example *par excellence* of a Pauline belief in continuity between the law and Christ.[63]

Based on these observations, we might argue that *if* its main intention is to establish the irrevocable election of "Israel" and its "mysterious" salvation, and *if* Paul's concern is not the opposition of "law" and "faith," but the coexistence of Gentile "branches" with their Jewish "roots," then perhaps we are justified in arguing for a teleological understanding of *telos* (as "goal) on the basis of this verse's context. Since, as we have seen, these conditions can be established exegetically, this is an example of theology in the service of exegesis, and not vice versa.

At this point we must take up the most obvious, and most difficult, theological question related to Romans 9-11: "what do we mean by 'Israel'?" The question is difficult enough when confined to the exegetical realm, that is, when we ask "what did *Paul* mean by 'Israel' in Romans 9-11?" Paul is somewhat clear in suggesting what "Israel" is *not* ("for not all who are descended from Israel are Israel," 9:6), but is not as helpful when the question turns to what Israel *is*. The problem is intensified by the fact that statements about "Israel" in this passage (e.g., "All Israel shall be saved," 11:26) are not illuminated in Paul's other writings.

We must now broaden the scope of our inquiry and concern ourselves with the "recovery of the real Paul" and its implications for theology and exegesis. First, we return to the problem we touched on in relation to Stendahl's work: the priviliging "historical" interpretation. Although the number of biblical scholars who exclusively employ "literary" methods in interpreting the Bible is not as great as one might think,[64] we are struck nevertheless by the brashness with which Stendahl and others have sought to leap across the "ugly ditch" of history in search of the "original" Paul and his thoughts. On the other hand, if there is any issue important enough to warrant attempts at historical reconstruction, it is that of renewed Jewish-Christian relations in the wake of the Jewish Holocaust. Furthermore, it is difficult to deny the positive resources this new reliance on original meanings has offered for the Church's theological overtures toward "Israel."

We may look at the matter another way. Even an exponent of exegesis according to the "linguistic paradigm" has argued that the preunderstanding underlying a particular exegesis must coincide with that of the exegete's "culture."[65] If we allow "culture" in this case to include the religious community in which the scholar's work must live, then perhaps the historical "recovery of the real Paul" and his understanding of Israel becomes justified. In other words, exegesis according to the "historical paradigm" may be necessary in the context of a contemporary church which is concerned with its *historical* relationship to "Israel."

Second, it appears that the attempt to (re) establish the coexistence of Jews and Gentiles at the center of Pauline theology seems often to entail a polemical stance against the "Lutheran" doctrine of "justification by faith." As long as this battle remains intra-Lutheran, that is, as long as it is Stendahl and Käsemann who are exchanging blows, this contest over what Romans is "about" is probably healthy. But this question must not dominate the discussion to the extent that Christians are fighting to defend their individual traditions of interpretation (i.e., justification, covenant theology, etc.) rather than working together to put their common house in order vis-a-vis Israel. It is true that in many ways this issue is a "Christian problem," and E. P. Sanders' observation that the legalistic picture of Rabbinic Judaism is a "projection onto Judaism of the view which Protestants find most objectionable in Roman Catholicism"[66] suggests its complexity. But the Church's attempt to reevaluate the significance of "Israel" must avoid becoming bogged down in internal struggles, or the Church will miss the *kairos* which is at hand.[67]

On the other hand, of course, thoughtful resistance to the reformation in the way we read Paul and understand "Israel" may be occasionally be in order. When the integrity of the Church and its theological task are in danger of being sacrificed at the altar of exegetical expediency, dissenting voices must be heard. With considerable courage, and at the risk of appearing traditional and (much worse) "anti-Jewish," a few scholars have expressed caution about the results of "exegesis after Auschwitz."

For example, in response to the important statement on Christians and Jews issued by the State Church of the Rhineland in 1980, Erich Grässer has charged that some of the exegesis behind this statement "prejudices and even changes the original meaning of the text."[68] Another example is Ernst Käsemann, whose critique of Stendahl includes a general objection to the project of "recovering the real Paul." Käsemann observes, quite correctly, that "the ecumenical movement furthers the tendency to stress what binds rather than what divides, and looks for the same disposition in the New Testament."[69] Behind this statement lies Käsemann's suspicion that this "ecumenical" tendency imposes certain theolgical biases ("salvation history," in Stendahl's case) on exegesis, and thereby threatens the integrity of the exegetical enterprise.

We have not mentioned resistance which is primarily theological, but much of it is substantial.[70] There is, however, one final note of caution which needs to be sounded. It concerns the possibility that a reaffirmation of "Israel's" election, which is not accompanied by specific admonitions to love and respect individual Jews, may have the inverse of its intended effect.

V. CONCLUSION

It is appropriate to express explicitly what we have alluded to often up to this point, namely, that the renewal of the relationship between "Church and Israel" cannot be carried out entirely exegetically, or entirely theologically, because exegesis and theology need each other. On this point, the words of Paul van Buren are quite salient:

> I believe that Paul, especially when understood on his own terms as a Jew and a Pharisee, can nourish the Church's efforts to turn toward the Jewish people in a spirit of reconciliation and cooperation. . . because God requires of his Church its own living response to Paul.[71]

This "living response," I want to suggest, is theology.

While we have not found any reason to doubt that Romans 9-11 will continue to be at the center of Christian attempts to reconcile "Church and Israel,"[72] we also have seen that this passage cannot be interpreted in isolation from the many theological issues which it raises. We can never let theological assumptions invalidate our historical work, but shifting exegetical paradigms and theological revision have always gone hand in hand. The employment of the "coexistence of Jews and Gentiles" theme as a key to understanding Romans, and as a goal in systematic theology, witnesses to this fact.

The Church has often struggled to understand God's way with "Israel" according to Romans 9-11, and it has *always* had a theology of Israel, albeit a negative one. The present challenge is to bring the exegetical and theological tasks together in an imaginative and courageous way. Stendahl, Barth, and others who have assisted us in "recovering the real Paul" may serve as our guides, but there is still much uncharted territory ahead. The "new Paul" has not yet reached most of the commentaries,[73] and the new view of "Israel" has not yet found a permanent home in systematic theology. At least until these signs appear, the road to reconciliation will still be before us.

NOTES

1. See e.g., Maritain, **A Christian Looks at the Jewish Problem** (New York, 1939); Parkes, **The Conflict Between the Church and the Synagogue** (London, 1934); Peterson, **Die Kirche aus Juden und Heiden** (Salzburg, 1933); Moore, "Christian Writers on Judaism," *Harvard Theological Review* 14 (1921) 197-254.

2. One only need conduct a casual survey of new books to learn that much Christian thought is still being devoted to aspects of Jewish-Christian dialogue, and reinterpretation of the significance of "Israel" for the Church.

3. An important focal point for early "Holocaust theology" was the International Symposium on the Holocaust, held in New York in 1974. The symposium was an interdisciplinary conference at which Christians and Jews met and shared, among other things, insights into a new way of doing theology. See Eva Fleischner, ed., **Auschwitz: Beginning of A New Era? Reflections on the Holocaust** (New York: Ktav, 1977).

4. This, of course, was the approach of G. F. Moore, and is also that of contemporary thinkers like Charlotte Klein, **Anti-Judaism in Christian Theology**, tr. Edward Quinn (Philadelphia: Fortress, 1978), and E. P. Sanders, **Paul and Palestinian Judaism** (London: SCM Press, 1977) 1-12, 33-59.

5. See especially, Rosemary Reuther, **Faith and Fratricide: The Theological Roots of Anti-Semitism** (Minneapolis: Seabury, 1974).

6. **The People of God**, *JfSNTS* 5 (Sheffield: JSOT Press, 1983) 7.

7. For a bibliography of recent research on Jesus' Jewishness, see M. Barth, **The People of God**, 76, n. 12. For some of the recent literature on Paul, see Clark M. Williamson, "The New Testament Reconsidered: Recent Post-Holocaust Scholarship," *Quarterly Review* 4 (1984) 50-51, n. 14; John Fischer, "Paul in His Jewish Context," *The Evangelical Quarterly* 57 (1985); J. D. G. Dunn, "The New Perspective on Paul," *BJRL* 65 (1983) 95-122; and F. Watson, **Paul, Judaism and the Gentiles: A Sociological Approach,** SNTSMS 56 (Cambridge: Cambridge University Press, 1986).

8. Fischer, "Paul in his Jewish Context," 211.

9. In 1977 Sanders could still refer to this as "probably the majority view" (13). For the roots of this view Sanders looks (with Moore) back to Ferdinand Weber's work of 1880, and the Weber/Schürer/Billerbeck/Bousset outline of Palestinian Judaism, whose "principal elements . . . have endured to the present day" (53). Markus Barth paints the picture with broader strokes,

arguing that "since the time of Marcion the latent or patent anti-Semitism which still pervades Church and world claims to find support in Pauline utterances" (18).

10. This is also the case for study of the New Testament in general, as can be confirmed by comparing the number of articles on "Jewish backgrounds" to those on "Greco-Roman" backgrounds in any recent issue of *New Testament Abstracts.* Sanders sees the turning point of the tide in Pauline scholarship in W. D. Davies, **Paul and Rabbinic Judaism** (London: SCM Press, 1970), and to a lesser extent, in H.-J. Schoeps' **Paul: The Theology of the Apostle in the Light of Jewish Religious History** (London, 1961).

11. In addition to Sanders, see H. Hübner, **The Law in Paul's Thought**, tr. J. C. Creig (Edinburgh: T. & T. Clark, 1984); H. Raisanen, **Paul and the Law** (Tübingen: 1983); and P. Stuhlmacher, "Paul's Understanding of the Law in the Letter to the Romans," *Svensk Exegetisk Arsbok,* 87-104; Robert Jewett, "The Law and the Coexistence of Jews and Gentiles in Romans," *Interpretation* 39 (4, 1985) 341-56.

12. All three of these themes come together in the work of Sanders, who compares the "pattern of religion" in Paul and Palestinian Judaism, pays close attention to Paul's understanding of grace and works (arguing) that Paul's view is not opposed to Palestinian Judaism, and argues that the center of Paul's theology is "participationist eschatology."

13. See, e.g., Henry Keane, "The Church and the Jewish People: Another Look at the Problem," *Theologia Evangelica* 15 (1982) 37-47; O. Hofius, "Das Evangelium und Israel: Erwagungen zu Romer 9-11, " *ZTK* 83 (1986), 297-324; H. Hübner, *Gottes Ich und Israel: Zum Schriftgebrauch des Paulus in Romer 9-11* (Göttingen: Vandenhoeck und Ruprecht, 1884).

14. See Krister Stendahl, "The Apostle Paul and the Introspective Conscience of the West," in **Paul Among Jews and Gentiles and other Essays** (Philadelphia: Fortress, 1976) 78-96.

15. Traditional interpretations of Romans have often seen this section of the epistle as a digression or addendum, while theology has viewed these chapters as of interest primarily in connection with the doctrine of predestination.

16. G. W. McRae and G. A. Nickelsburg, eds., **Christians Among Jews and Gentiles: Essays in Honor of Krister Stendahl on His Sixty-Fifth Birthday** (Philadelphia: Fortress, 1986) and J. C. Beker, **Paul the Apostle: The Triumph of God in Life and Thought** (Philadelphia: Fortress, 1980). Lloyd Gaston refers specifically to Stendahl's essay "The Apostle Paul and the Introspective Conscience of the West" as "seminal." ["Paul and the Torah," in Alan T. Davies, ed., **Anti-Semitism and the Foundations of Christianity** (New York: Paulist, 1978) 448-71].

17. Jewett, "Law and Coexistence . . ," 343-44.

18. **Paul and the Salvation of Mankind** (London: SCM Press, 1959).

19. Stendahl, 3. Ernst Käsemann has reacted quite strongly on this point in "Justification and Salvation History in the Epistle to the Romans," **Perspectives on Paul** (London: SCM Press, 1971) 60-78.

20. For a discussion of theologies of "continuity" between Judaism and Christianity, see Michael McGarry, **Christology After Auschwitz** (New York: Paulist, 1977). For a negative appraisal of the "hermeneutic of continuity" and its relation to Paul and Israel, see Craig A. Evans, "Paul and the Hermeneutics of True Prophecy: A Study of Romans 9-11," *Biblica* 65 (4, 1984) 560-70.

21. **Paul Among Jews and Gentiles,** 35.

22. For an elaboration of this relationship, and of that between "biblical theology," the "descriptive" task and the "religionsgeschichtliche Schule," see Stendahl," Biblical Theology, Contemporary," **The Interpreter's Dictionary of the Bible**, I, (Nashville: Abingdon, 1962) 418-32.

23. See Edgar A. McKnight, **The Bible and the Reader: An Introduction to Literary Criticism** (Philadelphia: Fortress, 1985); Terrence J. Keegan, **Interpreting the Bible: A Popular Introduction to Biblical Hermeneutics** (New York: Paulist, 1985) for introductions to this problem. For a description of an interpretive method which combines historical and literary elements, see Meir Sternberg, **The Poetics of Biblical Narrative** (New York: Crossroad,

1984), ch. 1.

24. Examples of this approach may nevertheless be found in: James W. Aegeson, "Scripture and Structure in the Development of the Argument in Romans 9-11,"*CBQ* 48 (2, 1986), 265-89; W. R. Stegner, "Romans 9:6-29--A Midrash,"*JSNT t*22 (1984), 36-52; F. Siegert, **Argumentation Bei Paulus Gezeigt an Rom 9-11** (Tübingen: Mohr-Siebeck, 1985); F. Watson, **Paul, Judaism and the Gentiles,** where the author discusses the social function of Romans 9-11.

25. Robert Jewett refers to the concern for ecumenical dialogue as one of three "impulses" in the recent study of Romans ("Major Impulses in the Theological Interpretation of Romans since Barth," *Interpretation* 34 [1, 1980] 17-31). Jewett identifies Paul Minear's **The Obedience of Faith (1971)** and Ulrich Wilkens' **Der Brief an die Römer (Röm 1-5)** (1978) as well as the aforementioned work of W. D. Davies, H.-J. Schoeps and E. P. Sanders, as embodying this "ecumenical impulse."

26. Sanders represents a grand exception to this generalization. Not only does he depart from Stendahl's method in his claim that "what Paul thought cannot be directly appropriated by Christians today" (**Judaism**, 522), he also claims that Paul seems to ignore . . . the grace of God toward Israel as evidenced by the election and the covenant. . . .Paul in fact explicitly denies that the Jewish covenant can be effective for salvation. . . ." (551).

27. Jewett, "Major Impulses. . ." 18.

28. This is the term used by Eugene Borowitz, **Contemporary Christologies: A Jewish Response** (New York: Paulist, 1980). In relation to Barth, I am using the term in the sense in which Borowitz employs it.

29. For example, see my "Presbyterians and Jews: A Theological Exploration of the Book of Confessions," *Perspectives in Religious Studies* 15 (3, 1988).

30. See Edward Flannery, **The Anguish of the Jews: Twenty-Three Centuries of Anti-Semitism** (New York: Paulist, 1985) 54 *et passim,* for a discussion of the "witness people" doctrine.

31. See especially III, 3 where Barth implies that the history of "Israel" ended in A.D. 70.

32. See Michael Wyschogrod, "A Jewish Perspective on Karl Barth," where the author cites a letter from Barth to F.-W. Marquardt dated September 7, 1967. in Donald McKim, ed., **How Karl Barth Changed My Mind,** (Grand Rapids: Eerdmans, 1987).

33. A. T. Davies, **Anti-Semitism,** 124.

34. See Robert Badenas, **Christ the End of the Law: Romans 10:4 in Pauline Perspective,** JSNTS, 10 (Sheffield: JSOT Press, 1985), 29.

35. See, e.g., M. Barth, **The People of God.**

36. For an example of emphasis on continuity in the areas of worship and mission in a broadly Barthian context, see **A Theological Understanding of the Relationship Between Christians and Jews** (New York and Atlanta: Office of the General Assembly of the Presbyterian Church U.S.A., 1987), affirmations nos. 1, 3, and 7.

37. This is precisely Stendahl's criticism of Barth in "Biblical Theology, Contemporary," 420.

38. See, e.g., John Pawlikowski, "Theology to an Urgent Task," (review of Paul van Buren's **Discerning the Way)** *National Catholic Reporter* 17 (Oct., 1980); and Peter von der Osten-Sacken, **Christian-Jewish Dialogue: Theological Foundations,** tr. Margaret Kohl (Philadelphia: Fortress, 1986). Both writers express regrets about the state of Christian systematic theology in relation to "Israel."

39. **A Theology of the Jewish-Christian Reality, Part 2, A Christian Theology of the People Israel** (San Francisco: Harper and Row, 1983, 8. See also 4-9, 28-9.

40. Ibid., 8.

41. Van Buren, now in semi-retirement, is a frequent guest lecturer at the University of Heidelberg, most recently on Barth's theology of "Israel."

42. Cranfield, "Light From St. Paul on Christian-Jewish Relations," in David W. Torrance, ed., **The Witness of the Jews to God** (Edinburgh: The Handsel Press, 1982) 22.

43. **Church Dogmatics,** II: 2, (Edinburgh: T. & T. Clark, 1957) 199.

44. C. E. B. Cranfield and J.A. Emerton, eds., **The International Critical Commen-**

tary, Epistle to the Romans, II (Edinburgh: T. & T. Clark, 1978) 448-9. Cranfield's assertion that the "key-word" of Romans 9-11 is "mercy" is in keeping with his "Barthian" approach.

45. Badenas, **Christ the End of the Law**, 33. Another Protestant New Testament scholar whose debt to Barth is significant is Markus Barth. In the footnotes to his **The People of God**, M. Barth repays his debt to his father for his radical and seminal understanding of Israel as the "people of God."

46. "The influence of Karl Barth on Catholic Theology," *Gregorianum* 67 (4, 1986) 664.

47. **Tractate on the Jews: The Significance of Judaism for Christian Faith**, tr. Leonard Swidler (Philadelphia: Fortress, 1984) 130, 132.

48. Mussner refers to these chapters no less than 170 times, according to the book's index.

49. **A Christian Theology of Judaism**, trans. Helga Croner (New York: Paulist, 1980).

50. See Paul S. Minear, "Barth's Commentary on the Romans, 1922-1972; or Karl Barth vs. the Exegetes," in Martin Rumscheidt, ed., **Footnotes to a Theology: the Karl Barth Colloquium of 1972** (The Corporation for the Publication of Academic Studies in Religion, 1974).

51. Ibid., 8.

52. **Christian-Jewish Dialogue**, *Theological Foundations*, 162.

53. For differing views on this question, see P. Sigal, "Aspects of Dual Covenant Theology: Salvation," *Horizons in Biblical Theology* 5 (2, 1983) 1-48; and C. David Harley, "The Church and the Jewish People: A Theological Perspective," *International Bulletin of Missionary Research* (July, 1987) 117-120.

54. Jack Rogers suggests that the *Second Helvetic Confession* explicates the concept of "covenant" as an essential tenet of the Reformed faith, and concludes that "for Reformed Christians there is just one covenant in the Bible." (**Presbyterian Creeds: A Guide to the Book of Confessions** [Philadelphia: Westminster, 1985] 129). Indeed, the *Second Helvetic Confession* does speak of "one testament or covenant," but the Westminster standards muddy the waters considerably by referring to a "covenant of works" and a "covenant of grace."

55. For recent critiques of the traditional models used by the Church to understand its relationship with "Israel," see M. Barth, **The People of God**, 22-26; F. Mussner, **Tractate on the Jews**, 41-2; Jurgen Moltmann, "Church and Israel: A Common Way of Hope?" in **On Human Dignity**, tr. M. Douglas Meeks (Philadelphia: Fortress, 1984) 194-202; and Paul van Buren, **A Christian Theology** , 10, 28-30.

56. For example, during debates over the document "A Theological Understanding of the Relationship Between Christians and Jews" at the 199th General Assembly of the Presbyterian Church (U.S.A.) in June, 1987. Alice Eckardt has described this issue as the one which most frequently divides the authors of contemporary statements on Judaism and Christianity. (in Helga Croner, ed., **More Stepping Stones to Jewish-Christian Relations: An Unabridged Collection of Christian Documents**, 1975-1983 [New York: Paulist, 1985] 21).

57. See Arthur F. Glasser, "Christian Ministry to the Jews," *The Presbyterian Communique* 11 (1988) 6-7.

58. See James I. Cook, "The Christian Witness to the Jews: A Biblical Perspective for the Church Today," *SJT* 36 (2, 1983) 145-61. See also Martin Cohen and Helga Croner, eds., **Christian Mission-Jewish Mission** (New York: Paulist, 1982).

59. **Paul Among Jews and Gentiles**, 4.

60. See R. Badenas, **Christ the End of the Law**, 34-37. We are leaving out, of course, the "polysemous" option, which interprets *telos* as containing some or all of the senses indicated by the other three.

61. Ibid., 30.

62. Ibid., 36.

63. Ibid. Cf. the connection between Cranfield's teleological interpretation of this verse and his statement that "for Paul, the law is not abrogated in Christ." (**Commentary on Romans**, II, 852).

64. See, e.g., Dan O. Via, Jr.'s foreword to Daniel Patte, **What is Structural Exegesis?** (Philadelphia: Fortress, 1976).

65. Patte, **What is Structural Exegesis?**, 7.

66. Cf. Sanders' relatively neutral statement that "the catch-word righteousness by faith must be given up as the clue to Paul's thought," with his contention that the main proponents of the view of Rabbinic Judaism he seeks to "destroy" are German Lutherans. (**Paul and Palestinian Judaism**, 438, 55).

67. Ibid., 57.

68. "Exegese nach Auschwitz?" in "Theologie nach Holocaust?, " *Kerygma und Dogma* 27 (3, 1981) 163.

69. E. Käsemann, "Justification and Salvation History ," 64.

70. See, e.g., Hans Hübner, "Der 'Messias Israel' und der Christus Neuen Testaments" in "Theologie Nach Holocaust?" 207-240; and C. David Harley, "The Church and the Jewish People."

71. **A Christian Theology of the People Israel**, 283.

72. Despite Davies' claim in 1969 that an emphasis on Romans 9-11 is a sign of "kerygmatic" thinking which dictates narrow confines for dialogue (**Anti-Semitism and the Christian Mind**, 161f.), there is no sign that Christians are turning away from this passage or Scripture in general in their struggle to understand their relationship with "Israel."

73. Cf. Ziesler, "Recent Work. . ." 100.

"Do Not Live In Fear, Little Flock!" The Interpretation Of Romans 9-11 Of Georg Eichholz

H. MARTIN RUMSCHEIDT

I

It may be odd to cite words of Jesus (Luke 12:32) as the title under which to consider an interpretation of Paul's classic passage on Israel and the Church. The verse, however, acts as a hermeneutic device to guide the determination of how several exegetically indispensable questions relating to Paul's text may be answered. Some such questions are: To whom was this text written? What occasioned the Apostle to compose this material on Israel and the Church and place it in the middle of the Letter? In what state of mind or faith does Paul see the recipients of the Letter to be, resulting in this kind of pastoral response?

It is my view that were those words of Jesus transposed into the mouth of Paul and taken to be addressed to the church in Rome, to its several house-churches which formed the "body of Christ" in the Empire's capital at the time when *pax romana* was crumbling, they would illumine why those three chapters were written and, consequently, how they might be interpreted. What I call "my view" arises out of the experience which Georg Eichholz, whose interpretation of Romans 9-11 will be presented, and I shared, albeit in different ways, of the Church in Germany during the times of National Socialism and in the post-war years. That experience has given rise to a hermeneutical proviso that has become inescapable to a number, albeit a still far too small number, of theological scholars. The proviso is the Jewish holocaust. To interpret a text, especially one as clear as this one about Israel and the Church, as if the Jewish holocaust had not happened, or as if it were of no significance for the scholarly interpretation of texts, is now impossible for me as a scholar and believer. Theodor Adorno's confession, that no poetry could be written after Auschwitz means, by extrapolation, that those who as Christians seek to understand others' poetic, doxological and confessional writings may not set Shoah aside, morally and hermeneutically.

In his exegetical and theological exploration of Romans 9-11, Georg Eichholz touched upon one of the contributive factors of the Nazis' "final solution," namely, fear! I take *fear* to be one of the crucial reasons why Paul wrote with such passion about Israel to the Christian in Rome in the later fifties of the first century A.D.

II

Georg Eichholz (1909-1973) was well into his study of theology at Tübingen and Bonn when the brown-shirted movement took power through legitimate elections. His own sense of what that event and the movement which roamed through the hearts of so many of his compatriots meant was reinforced by his studies with Karl Barth and the subsequent decision to work within the Confessing Church, itself a movement in opposition to the movement as it manifested itself particularly in the churches. ("Movement" is not brought to this description of events from the outside. The so-called German Christians spoke of themselves as a movement, *die Glaubensbewegung Deutsche Christen*, the "faith-movement German Christians.")

Eichholz was born in Essen, the city where not only the Krupp factories produced the weapons for and the profits from war but where also a characteristic expression of Protestant piety gave foundation to a "courage to be," a steadfastness of witness to Christ which shaped a significant group of lay-people who manifested a fierce loyalty to democracy and who found their way into the Confessing Church. Eichholz' father had been a pastor. From him Georg learned the theory and practice of this defiant piety.

After his ordination, Eichholz quickly became a marked man. The Nazis watched him carefully and, as it became routine regarding people of the Confessing Church, eventually forbade him to make speeches or travel beyond a restricted area. The relations existing between church and state prevented the prohibition of preaching or writing theological works related to preaching. Beginning in 1939, upon being asked by the Confessing Church, he wrote or edited and circulated exegetical aids for preachers on the Church's lectionary readings. The publication was known as *Herr, tue mir meine Lippen auf*, (Lord, open Thou my lips), among its contributors was Dietrich Bonhoeffer. The series carried on for years even after the War.

It was not until after 1945, however, that Eichholz shaped his approach to the Bible in which his studies of Romans 9-11, *inter alia*, developed. Two significant events in the life of German Protestantism, both carried mainly by people who had been associated with the Confessing Church even prior to the War, put an imprint on his hermeneutics and exegesis. The first was the **Stuttgart Declaration of Guilt**, published on October 19, 1945. It contained the deeply moving confession: "We accuse ourselves of not having confessed more courageously, prayed more faithfully, believed more joyfully and loved more fervently" at the time when "through us unspeakable suffering came upon many people and places."[1] The second was *A Word of the Fraternal Council of the Evangelical Church in Germany Concerning the Political Way of our People*, also known as the **Darmstadt Statement**, published on August 8, 1947. Karl Barth, Martin Niemöller and Hans Joachim Iwand were among the drafters of this statement.[2]

By this time, Eichholz had begun his career as a theological teacher. In 1945 he had been appointed Professor of New Testament and Systematic Theology at Wuppertal School of Theology, the very city were eleven years earlier, in one of its subdivisions, his teacher Barth had joined with others to promulgate the theological declaration known as the Barmen Confession. Many of the people who had gathered for the special synod brought with them that defiant piety into which Eichholz had been born. In a way, he had come "home" when he accepted the teaching position at Wuppertal, for now he worked in an institution in which a particular action and reflection set its imprint on the curriculum, one in which the praxis of faith established "theological existence today."

At the core of such existence there stands, for me, the hermeneutical proviso referred to above. It is a proviso which recognizes *metanoia* as a, if not THE, *conditio sine qua non* for the scholarly work of theology. If repentance for the unspeakable suffering of many peoples and places has been declared, if a particular recognition in that repentance includes the "final solution of the Jewish problem," then hermeneutics and exegesis, like all scholarly activity in theology, will no longer proceed without further ado. Genuine re-beginning of the theological enterprise, and with it ecclesial life in all its dimension, stands under the imperative: Remember! Do not forget! For to forget is the first step in handing Hitler a posthumous victory.[3]

Eicholz' discussion of Romans 9-11 reflects the "two natures" of his appointment at Wuppertal: it was exegetical and theological. The work in which his understanding of the "Israel and the Church" passage is developed is his **Die Theologie des Paulus im Umriss (An Outline of Paul's Theology)** which, based on his lecture on Paul, was published in 1972.[4] The concluding chapter is entitled "Kirche und Israel," Church and Israel.

III

It was not Eichholz' concern to depict Paul's concept of Church or his understanding of Israel. The chapter focuses rather on the relation of one to the other at the time of Paul's writing of Romans. It was Eichholz' thesis that the Church is indissolubly tied to Israel and that, in Paul's thinking, one has to be understood in the light of the other. "The Church is Israel, in a way yet to be explained, and can be Church only when it sees itself in the mirror of Israel's history. The origin of the Church can be none other than that of Israel of old. Israel is, in other words, a *question to the Church* " (284).

(a) The first matter to be explored, given that concern, is what place those three chapters occupy in the entire Letter. However "comparatively independent" a unit they appear to be (so Karl Barth),[5] the chapters are not an isolated passage, "unconnected with what preceded it."[6] Instead, Eichholz demonstrates that it is Paul's theology of justification, developed at length and impressively in the preceding eight chapters, which holds the Israel and the Church discussion within the message of the entire Letter. The details of that demonstration have to be left out here; the theological interconnectedness is shown through the linkages in vocabulary in the various parts of the Letter. On the basis of such a demonstration Eichholz claims that chapters 9-11 speak the language of justification (287).

In an earlier chapter on justification and faith Eichholz had used Romans 9-11 to show how they actually clinch Paul's argument of the justification of sinners. By means of those arguments he points out that there are three subsections in the Israel and the Church passage: (1) 9:1-29, which comes to a climax in the statement of 9:11b-12a: in order that it should be God's choice which prevailed, not human merit, but God's call; (2) 9:30-10:21, in which the guilt of Israel is described (9:32a) and (3) 11:1-36, since justification is by grace, it cannot now be by good actions, or grace would not be grace at all (287).[7]

What Eichholz develops here is the claim that Paul approaches the mystery of Israel's history from insights gained in the understanding of justification by divine grace. "The same mystery which Paul refers to with awe and veneration in his theology of justification is the one with which he approaches the history of Israel" (287). God's action towards Israel and the whole world is the action of the Merciful One; Israel and the whole world is the action of the Merciful One; Israel and the world have their hope alone in the justification of sinners (288). Both are found in a final and mysterious solidarity. The struggle of chapters 9-11 is that this solidarity become concrete reality. For what exists in actuality is distance between the Church and Israel. Neither can exist apart from God's free mercy. "Just as Israel can find its origin and its existence only in God's attentiveness to it, so the Church, too, can understand its own origin and existence in the same attentiveness only. Israel's actual, quite illusionary attempt to exist in actions rather than in faith has for its direct analogy the Church's attempt to distance itself from Israel, an attempt in which God's free grace is obscured" (288).

What is so surprising, in the light of the place occupied by the three chapters in the whole Letter is that Israel's way cannot be separated from that of the gentile nations, that, instead, the two are so strongly coordinated one to the other. It is Paul's theology of justification which at first presents and then also explains the surprise.

(b) To whom were those chapters addressed? This is the second matter of inquiry. "The decision about the addressee determines the decision about the exegesis of this text" (289). The problem is not easy. Does Paul make a critique of Israel, of the past, the present and the future of God's history with this people, or are these chapters, from beginning to end, written for the young church in Rome, which seems to see itself as being a church of *all* nations? The demographic evidence seems, indeed, to suggest that the church had experienced a noticeable shift in structure from a majority of Jewish Christians to one in which that group had become not only a minority but also one whose right to exist, as a *Jewish* Christian group, had become a matter of debate. "Was Romans 9-11 written by Paul against the *hybris* of a Church of all nations, given that such a view of the Church is an inadmissible *abstraction*? For the Church, from its origin onward, is the one ecclesia of both Israel and the Gentiles, (called not only from out of the Jews but also the Gentiles [9:24]. [It is] never a Church of Gentiles only, however limited and temporary the presence of Israel in the Church may be" (289). For Paul, it would seem, there can be no real argument in favor of a special Church either of Gentiles or of Jewish Christians.

In this context Eichholz rejects the dialectical distinction of some exegetes, among whom he names especially Erich Dinkler, between "empirical and eschatological Jews" (p. 290). The understanding of Israel, as held by Paul, cannot be split in such a fashion because that distinction is functionally ciritical of *Israel* and that forecloses the investigation as to whether Romans 9-11 is critical of Israel or the Church.

Is Paul critical of Israel? Rom 9:1-5, the opening motif of the entire three chapter composition, is a solemn "Yes" to Israel. This "Yes" is uttered with a surprising emphasis in that Paul's first words are like an oath: "This is the truth and I am speaking in Christ, without pretence." One has to assume that Paul somehow expects the envisaged solidarity with Israel will run into skepticism. In 9:45 he carefully lists Israel's privileges, the signs of God's electing attentiveness to this people; they are all titles of honor; in fact, the very name "Israel" is such a sign and title. "Finally, one of Israel's privileges is that Jesus is a *born Jew*, for which reason Christ is *primarily the Christ of Israel*. The ranking of Jesus Christ himself in the list of Israel's privileges signifies that Christ is *God's 'Yes' to Israel*, that God, in an incomprehensible faithfulness *confirms* all promises to his people. Paul's own 'Yes' to Israel merely repeats that of God" (291).

Rom 9:6a makes one wonder who had asked or stated that God's electing attentiveness, God's promises had ceased to be in effect. *To whom* does Paul recite the uncancelled privileges of Israel? To Israel? "Quite apart from the fact that the Letter to the

Romans is not addressed to the Jewish population of the city of Rome [one might add here that that population had been expelled from the city some six to seven years before Paul wrote this Letter] but to the young church of that city, what sense is there in seeing Romans 9-11 as having been written to Jews? Only one answer remains: the only thinkable addressee is the young church of Rome whom Paul sees in danger of writing Israel off, of no longer regarding Israel's election as valid: at one time Israel's privileges had validity, but now no longer and, so, Israel is without significance in the present" (291, brackets mine).

It is this young church which urgently needs information about Israel's history. But the truly elementary matter is much more than historical reminiscences. Romans 9-11 does not have the style of historical rumination. The urgency, passion and decisiveness of Paul's assertions make this a text of high actuality. "That church *must* know the truth about Israel because it would not longer know the truth about itself [were it to remain ignorant about Israel's truth.] Thus Paul's admonition: I want you to be quite certain, brothers, of this mystery (11:6). This has to be taken literally. The church which is no longer turned toward Israel, which no longer knows what to do with Israel's history (that is, with God's history with Israel) no longer knows about its own origin and misreads its own grace-founded existence which it is led to discern in the history of Israel. We may say that in such a neglectful misjudgment anti-semitism is born. . . .[The church] will see that its own origin lies in God's pure grace only when it is *attentive* to Israel itself" (292, brackets mine).

In Romans 9-11 information about Israel is, at one and the same time, indispensable information about the Church. Whether the Church knows what it is *as Church* is to be learned from how it relates itself to Israel.

(c) The crux of the entire "misinformation" on the part of the young church concerning Israel and, in consequence, concerning its own faith, is the apparent rejection of faith in Christ on the part of Israel. It is as if Paul were faced with an incipient substitutionary theory in which the young church embracing the gospel of the crucified and risen Christ with enthusiasm, takes that apparent refusal of the gospel as a sure sign of God's abandonment of Israel and its own, ever so genuine embrace of it as an equally sure sign of a *new* covenant of God with the Church.

Eichholz, in his suggestion that the young church in the "eternal" city is in fact the addressee of those chapters, implies that such a perception was the actual cause of the distancing on the part of gentile Christians from Jewish Christians, from the synagogue. Paul's pastoral response to the church has several accents, culminating in the metaphor of the olive-tree and its natural and wild branches.

His pastoral response begins with the declaration of Paul's solidarity with Israel--"*Er bekennt sich zu Israel*" (292)--and the affirmation of Israel's privileges as still fully valid. God's affirmation stands as before. "Rom 9:6-13 is not motivated primarily by a critique of Israel. In these verses Paul wants, instead, to show that God holds on to Israel" (p. 293). The examples Paul cites show not only God's gracious actions but that this grace is free and humanly unfathomable grace. "That which according to 9:6-13 triumphs in God's history with Israel is solely God's *free choice*, God's sovereign action which is not conditioned in any way by what humans can and will do" (293). God's action is the mercy which showers attentiveness on Israel; the text of 9:6-13 is primarily about God's grace as directed to Israel. It is critical of Israel in so far as Paul tolerates no self-praise on Israel's part, no understanding of the privileges which are born out of grace as a claim on God's election. God will show mercy on whomever God chooses.

Then comes an interlude in the text, as if Paul were responding to a question:"What about those whom God does not choose?" It begins, axiom-like, with the assertion that "it is not a matter what any person does, but only of God having mercy" (9:16). Once again, here is the either/or of Paul's theology of justification: either people live in the world of God's attentiveness or they live by what they can do and establish on their own, which is the life of illusion. Pharaoh is cast into the role of God's antagonist, illustrating the illusionary dimension, for he, too, serves God's purpose. Eichholz suggests, intriguingly in my view, that to read Pharaoh as the analogue to the Synagogue, so often depicted in Christian art as blind and obstinate, is to fail in grasping what Paul is concerned with, namely, God's grace and the danger, present *always and everywhere,* of falsely understanding God's grace. The Pharaoh interlude has to be read in relation to what preceded it, namely God's merciful action toward Israel. And, as 9:19-21 repeat, that action of mercy and grace is not to be interpreted as depicting God's grace *in the abstract* but in the concreteness of seeking, as ever, Israel, the Synagogue.

It is the miracle of freedom and grace, worthy of all praise, that God's people is now composed--entirely by grace!--of Jews and Gentiles (9:24). "The ecclesia takes part in God's electing mercy, the mercy in which Israel partook from its beginning. The mystery of Israel is also the mystery of the Church: God, this God, is to be seen solely in terms of gracious action" (296).

"The young church of Rome needs information about Israel. That is why Rom 9:9-21 is to be understood primarily not as a critique of Israel but as a critique of the Church. The young church of Rome (like every other church) has to learn from Israel's history, as Paul depicts it, where Israel stands [in God's economy]. And what does the position of Israel there signify? Israel becomes a *challenge, a question to the Church.* The Church has to learn a very difficult lesson: it has to understand what grace is, for it no longer understand grace as its hybris toward Israel would indicate " (296, brackets mine).

The next step in the pastoral response is Paul's attempt to set out what Israel's guilt is. The section comprises 9:30-10:21. "In short, Israel's guilt is its illusionary attempt to exist out of itself, an attempt in which it passes by God's action in Christ" (297). The attempt, instead, to live by "the law" is an "anachronism" (297), as Eichholz puts it, since Christ has fulfilled it. While God does everything imaginable for Israel, which is what God's gracious action in Christ represents, Israel rebels against Christ. Eichholz warns against seeing this situation of guilt from the perspective of tragedy. Israel *can* indeed, embrace faith, according to Paul, no fate prevents it from embracing Christ. It is, nonetheless, *God's* doing when there is faith, not some human possibility which swings into action; the gospel makes faith a gift to Israel. "Israel's guilt, in the final analysis, consist in that it does *not yet believe*" (297).

The climax of Paul's pastoral response comes in chapter 11 which begins with the anguished enquiry. "Has God abandoned Israel?" only to be answered with the emphatic and sure: "Out of the question!" Paul has to take up the problem of Israel as it exists in the young church of Rome once again in the last of these three chapters.

In 11:1-10 he asserts that Israel is the Church in a sign-like (*zeichenhaft*) *way* even now. "Paul himself is the great paradigm: he, the born Jew, still bound up with Israel and obligated to it, is the apostle to the gentile world. In Romans 9-11 he spoke as the apostle to the Gentiles, not as a Jewish nationalist. And that is why he speaks for all Christians in a way which binds them. The call to be the missionary to the Gentiles confirms, as a call to a Jew, also God's "Yes" to "Israel" (297-298).

And then the clincher, the metaphor of the olive-tree and the two kinds of branches. The question which it answers was: What of Israel that *has still not found* its way to Christ? Romans 11:13 spells out whose question that was and to whom the answer is addressed: "Let me say then to you Gentiles. . . ." God's election of Israel, out of sheer grace and for no merit of that people, is like an olive tree which, not making room for other branches, causes the good gardener to use the opportunity of that refusal to ingraft those other branches. Israel's "No" results in God showing mercy to the Gentiles.

What a turn of events! "Their fall has proved a great gain to the world, their loss has proved a great gain to the Gentiles" (11:12). "If *that* is the consequence of Israel's *guilt,* what is the Christian who is not a Jew by birth, what is the young church of Rome to say to that? I dare ask: 'Can the reply be anything other than *gratitude,* unbreakable *solidarity* in the relation of the Church to Israel?'. . . In the metaphor of the olive-tree, Christians are depicted as being haughty and superior toward Jews, declaring that 'branches were broken off on purpose for us to be grafted in'" (298). Paul's ironic "that is so" in 11:20 is the link to the idea of Israel becoming envious because its guilt was the cause for the nations receiving salvation. "In fulfilling his mission to the Gentiles, Paul has no intention of forgetting Israel. . . . May I put it like this? On the detour via his call to be the apostle to the Gentiles Paul remains fully attentive to Jews. Paul can legitimately reject the accusation that in courting Israel he remained passive toward Israel as a missionary. On the contrary, he interprets his labours as a missionary, which have taken him onto all the roads of the world, as his courting of Israel" (299). What is the young church of Rome to make of this argument? It is to realize that wherever Paul found himself he had Israel in mind and was actively searching it out.

But why this insitence? Eichholz sees a sharp portrait of the hybris found in the young gentile Church, a portrait of its own guilt, in 11:16-24. Paul now *warns* that church. Being ingrafted, she must now give up the hybris (or fear, as I shall suggest later) and understand itself as just another example of God's pure grace. Hybris and, paradoxically, fear arise from a sense of security but "*securitas*" for the Church is something unthinkable" (299). It is God who in utter freedom breaks off branches and re-ingrafts them and who, in similar freedom, ingrafts wild branches, can *so much more* re-ingraft genuine branches in the one true olive-tree, so that the Church must be wary of every sort of security; its shelter or foundation is found only in God's free grace the witness of which the Church should, indeed, be in the world" (300). Triumphant superiority over the Synagogue is a bad and, what is worse, self-inflicted danger to the Church.

"God has not written off Israel, however much the young church of Rome has written it off; in doing so the church has run the danger of losing itself, *of writing itself off*. In this way, Romans 9-11 is a comprehensive information about Israel for the young church of Rome which gave a permanent significance to something which for Paul could have only limited and temporary validity, namely that Israel has not yet come to faith in Christ" (300).

Paul searched for clues to God's plan in everything that happened. In relation to the history of Israel, which depicted in allegory and metaphor, and in relation to the history of the Gentiles, he asked what their foundation was. He concluded that God alone triumphs in mercy, "that to Jews but also to the gentile peoples but also to Jews God has become the merciful one who lifts both out of their lostness so that they may be won for the praise of God's mercy and, in that praise, open both one to the other" (301).

Hence the conclusion of 11:33-36, a hymn of praise to God's mercy and wisdom, a mercy and wisdom in which God is attentiive to Israel still, a wisdom and mercy the

Church *cannot* claim for itself in separation from Israel.

The young church in Rome was caught in a deep hybris, according to Eichholz' reading and because of that it needed this vital information about Israel. He specifies the hybris to have led to a distancing of the Church from the Synagogue. In that distancing is something which, if unchecked, will lead to the loss of the Church's substance *as Church.*

In this concluding section an attempt is made to extrapolate from the experience of the Confessing Church, to which Eichholz belonged, what may have caused that hybris in the Roman church. The answer to be given is not Eichholz', but it is my hope that no injustice will be done to him and his exegesis in the following superimposition of one historical context on another.

The substance of the answer appears in the title to this article: fear. The young church of Rome manifested a general and a specific fear in its belief that God had abandoned the Synagogue.

The general fear is related to the expulsion of Jews by Claudius.[8] However negligible their numbers may have been in relative terms (it is estimated that 2% of the population of the city of Rome was Jewish at this time),[9] there expulsion was significant to the small groups of Christians since it affected their numbers, their "membership" as we would say today, by including the Jewish Christians as well as the *theologically* most significant opposition to the church at this stage. In an atmosphere of *ideological* divergence from a common basis the *political* branding of one of the divergent groups by the authorities generally tends to provide the other group with a sense of rightness about itself, of a superiority in its position vis-a-vis the others. What a theological/philosophical argument often fails to settle, the imposed removal or stigmatisation of an opponent quickly accomplishes with a concomitant sense of vindication of the "victor." The experience of the National Socialists' Aryan legislation and what followed it provided the concerned reader of the Scriptures at that time with an immediate analogue to the situation in Rome to which Paul responded, particularly since in both instances the stigmatised group was the same.

The general fear of which I speak is the fear which creates scapegoats. A decline in the welfare of the community and the vague, yet real worries about its survivability is often used as a vehicle to deflect critical attention away from those who hold power, real and perceived, in that community. The deflected attention is then focused on a visible minority of alleged "aliens." The *pax romana* was crumbling and with it the welfare of Rome[10] which had been built on so much violence throughout the Empire. The politically instigated scapegoating of the Jews by Claudius paralleled, but did not by far equal, that of Hitler; whether Romans or Germans had *in fact* anything to fear from Jews is beside the point. The general stigma and the unfocused fear associated with it fused readily with the specific fear which resided in the community of gentile Christians in Rome during the later fifties of the first and in the thirties in the twentieth centuries A.D.

Eichholz identifies the*locus* of the specific fear I have in mind when he speaks of security. When what scholars now call "the family quarrel"[11] between Jews and Christians had turned into a full-fledged parting of the ways and public opposition with growing hostility, the struggle turned into an "either we or they" situation. The fear that the other might prevail, even in arguments, produces theories and practices of the others' invalidation and isolation which, if successful--even by the quite unrelated fiat of the rulers' decrees--provide those theories and practices with a validity which amounts to what Eichholz had called security. The hybris of such certainty and its gift of security is the conviction of being right and being legitimated in that conviction. If Paul responds to the view that either God has abandoned the Jews and their election or our faith in Christ is false, as Eichholz suggests, then a specific fear for the Church is at issue. The fear for the Church's validity and the fear of Israel with the concomitant distancing of the former from the latter on the basis of theological arguments is the birthplace of anti-Judaism, Eichholz has said (292). The anti-Judaism reflection of Jews, including Jewish Christians, on the part of German Christians, even in the milder forms of their silence before the Nazis' policies, rested in the conviction of the rightness of the Church or, as I would put it, rested in the fear that if God is, indeed, the God faithful to Jews then the utter certainty of German-Christian faith in Jesus Christ is in vain. And Germans wanted no part of that. It is of that utter certainty of which the two post-World-War II declarations of the Confessing Church speak in repentance. The sentence of the **Stuttgart Declaration of Guilt** cited above reflects the fear which thwarted a more courageous, faithful, joyful and fervent witness. The **Darmstadt Declaration** shows that the certainty--*securitas* in Eichholz' terminology--led the Church astray.

"We went astray when we began to dream the dream of a unique German mission, as if the world could be healed by means of Germany's nature. That opened the way to an unrestrained use of political force and put our nation on the throne of God... .We went astray when we began to establish a 'Christian front' against the reorientation of social life which had become so necessary. The alliance of the Church with the powers that preserved the old and the traditional has wreaked havoc among us. . . . We went astray when we felt that a front had to be set up in the political sphere of the good against the evil, of the light against the dark and of the just against the unjust, and that this front, this battleline, had to be set up by political means. In so doing we corrupted God's free gift of grace. . . . The cry cannot be 'Christianity and the culture of the West' but, rather, 'Return to God and the neighbor in the power of Jesus Christ's death and resurrection'. . . . Long ago we confessed and confess again today: In Jesus Christ there comes to us the joyful liberation from all the godless linkages of this world, the liberation for grateful service to God's creation. [The reference is to the second article of the **Barmen Declaration**.] That is why we pray you not let fear become your master, for Christ is our Lord."[12] The Declaration ends with a call to the Christians of the German churches to exercise responsibility for justice, the welfare of people, peace and reconciliation. If Romans 16 is, indeed, a postscript to the Letter, and chapter 15 the real ending, it is remarkable how much the **Darmstadt Declaration** parallels Paul's call to the Christians of the church in Rome to exercise responsibility for mutual sensitivity, perseverance, encouragement, hope, acceptance one of the other and, especially, oneness among Christians and Jews. It is as if he were saying: "Do not live in fear, little flock, the fear of the Emperor and those whom he made into his scapegoats, the fear of your illusionary security, the fear of 'the others.' For if love be among you then there is no room for fear."

NOTES

1. Martin Greschat, ed., **Im Zeichen der Schuld. 40 Jahre Stuttgarter Schuldbekenntnis** (Neukirchen-Vluyn: Neukirchener Verlag, 1985) 45-46. (Cited as **Zeichen**).

2. Ibid., 85.

3. Emil Fackenheim, with whom I had a personal association while being a pastor in Toronto in the late sixties, not only taught me that "new commandment" but also clarified its methodological significance.

4. Georg Eichholz, **Die Theologie des Paulus im Umriss** (Neukirchen-Vluyn: Neukirchener Verlag, 1972). (Citations from this work will not be footnoted but indicated in the body of the article with the requisite page number. All translations are mine.

5. K. Barth, **A Shorter Commentary on Romans**, tr. D. H. van Daalen (London: SCM Press, 1963) 110.

6. C. H. Dodd, **The Epistle of Paul to the Romans** (London: Hodder and Stoughton Ltd., 1954) 131

7. The quotations from Scripture are from the **New Jerusalem Bible** (Garden City, NY: Doubleday, 1985)

8. Cf. Acts 18:2.

9. K. D. Schmidt, **Grundriss der Kirchengeschichte** Göttingen: Vandenhoeck und Ruprecht, 1960), 42.

10. Cf. the excellent new study by K. Wengst, **Pax Romana and the Peace of Jesus**, trans. J. Bowden (Philadelphia: Fortress Press, 1987).

11. Cf. e.g. Rosemary Ruether, **Faith and Fratricide** (New York: Seabury, 1974).

12. **Zeichen**, 85-86, brackets mine.

Can Romans 9-11 Be Used In The Pulpit?

DONALD G. MILLER

How do you *preach* on Romans 9-11? One of many ways of answering this question is to examine what preachers have done with it through the ages. The first answer suggested by a search through the library resources available to me is: "You don't!" As far as I can tell, there has been a paucity of homiletical use of this section of Scripture. Alexander Maclaren is typical. In his multi-volumed **Expositions of Holy Scripture**, he goes from Romans 8 to Romans 12, with no mention that 9-11 even exists. Ten volumes of John Donne's sermons are silent on this passage. Spurgeon's fifty volumes of sermons are almost as lacking in dealing with this area of Scripture, as are the many volumes of Alexander Whyte and Joseph Parker's **People's Bible**, which consisted of six years of sermons from Genesis to Revelation with but one sermon on this section entitled "Paul on the Heart" (Rom 10:11) in which he mentions the Jews to illustrate "zeal without knowledge."

Occasional sermons are to be found on specific texts applied to situations other than that to which Paul was speaking. For example, "zeal for God" that is not "enlightened" (10:2); of confessing with one's "lips that Jesus is Lord" and believing in one's "heart that God raised him from the dead" as the means of salvation (10:9); or the necessity of proclaiming the gospel since man cannot "hear without a preacher" (10:14); or the fact that "grace would no longer be grace" if election were based on "works" (11:6)--these and more have been put to pulpit use with no mention whatsoever that they are part of Paul's wrestling with the subject of the Jewish rejection of their Messiah, and the problem which that poses for the Christian faith. Occasionally, however, published sermons have touched upon aspects of this general theme, and it is an analysis of these which claims our interest here. (See paper in this volume on Calvin as a representative of the Reformers.)

I. JOHN CHRYSOSTOM

The Homilies of John Chrysostom include the earliest homiletical use of Romans 9-11 that I have been able to unearth. In one homily he begins with an interesting turn of thought concerning Paul's wishing that he himself were "accursed and cut off from Christ for the sake of [his] brethren, [his] kinsmen by race" (Rom 9:3). Rather than seeing in this the unusual interpretation that Paul was wishing to offer "his life for his people,"[1] to trade his salvation for theirs, to forfeit eternal life "for the sake of [his] brothers" (Moffatt), or for the benefit" of his brothers (Knox), he rather wished himself accursed solely for Christ's sake. He wanted, according to Chrysostom, to lift the burden of Jewish criticism which fell upon his Lord because of his gospel. If, he argued, it were for "others he was willing to be accursed, he ought also to have wished for this in the Gentiles behalf." But it is for Christ's glory that he is concerned.

The Jews were arguing that if Paul's gospel were true, God had failed, had been unjust. They were saying: If Paul is right, God has played favorites. After "being counted worthy of the name of sons, and receiving the law, and knowing him beyond all men, and enjoying such great glory, and receiving him beyond the whole world and receiving the promises, and being from fathers who were his friends, and what was the greatest thing of all, having been forefathers of Christ himself . . . they were now cast out and disgraced; and in their place are introduced men who had never known him, of the Gentiles." This, said Chrysostom, "cut [Paul] to the heart." He did not want to hear the Jews saying that "it has all been for stage-effect; [God] promises to one, and gives to another. [Messiah] was sprung from one race, he saved another. It was to the forefathers of the Jews that he made the promises and yet he has deserted their descendants, and put men, who never at any time knew him, into their good things. They labored in the practice of the Law, and reading the Prophets, while men have come but yesterday from heathen altars and images have been set up above them."

Pauls reaction to this, says Chrysostom, was similar to that of Moses pleading for Israel, basing his appeal solely on "God's glory" before the Egyptians (Exod 32:32). "Now that these things may no longer be said of my Master, even if they are said unjustly, Paul meant, 'I would willingly lose even the kingdom and the glory unutterable, and any sufferings would I undergo, as considering it the greatest consolation possible no longer to hear him whom I so long for, so blasphemed."[2]

Could Chrysostom have been right in this? One's judgment must rest largely on three things: (1) the meaning that Chrysostom gives to the preposition (*huper*); (2) the context; and (3) Chrysostom's motivation in holding this view. Although *huper* usually in the New Testament means "in behalf of" or "for the sake of," there are instances in Paul where it means simply "about" or "concerning," where it is practically "equivalent to *peri*."[3] In Rom 9:27 Paul writes: "And Isaiah cries out concerning Israel," where it obviously means more "about" Israel rather than "in behalf of" Israel. In 2 Cor 1:18 Paul writes that he does not want them "to be ignorant . . . of the afflictions we experienced in Asia," where obviuosly *huper* means simply "about" the affliction. The same Letter assures the Corinthians that Paul has great pride "in" them, or "about" them, or "concerning" them (7:4 and 7:14), and he boasts "about" them (9:2)--hardly "in their behalf," or "for their sake." In Phil 1:7 Paul expressed his feelings "about" them.

These usages suggest the *possibility* that Chrysostom was gramatically right in his interpretation here, although a concordance shows that the predominance of *huper* meaning "in behalf of" or "for the sake of" is about 30:1 in the New Testament. Certainly Chrysostom knew his Greek better than most of us, since that was his field of expertise, and in the light of the second consideration, namely, that the context immediately after speaks of the Jewish charge that "the word of God had failed" (9:6), we may grant him the grammatical possibility that Paul here was expressing a willingness to suffer reprobation to stop this charge rather than to exchange his eternal state with his Jewish brethren. In his view, then, the expression becomes just an extreme rhetorical statement: "This blasphemy is so appalling that I would be willing to risk my eternal welfare to have it stopped!" The major difficulty with this is that there seems to be no clue as to how Paul's reprobation could accomplish the end he had in view. Chrysostom recognizes this, inasmuch as he continues: Since this is impossible, "he next attempts to go into a defence against the charges," trying to show "why they who had received the promise fell short of it, while those who had even never heard of it were saved before them."[4]

It may be that Chrysostom's general attitude toward the Jews motivated him in his view here, as in many other instances. He seems generally to have championed the view that the Old Testament covenant had been "abrogated" rather than "fulfilled," since the Jews had "rejected God's blessings and now God has rejected Israel."[5] In fact, one contemporary scholar, R. L. Wilken, has dubbed Chrysostom "the notorious Jew-hater,"[6] and another, Friedrich Heer, has assigned him weighty significance in stimulating subsequent anti-Judaism down to the present day.[7] These judgments, to me, seem as extreme and subjectively motivated as Chrysostom's remarks may have been; and also seem to be totally dissociated with the context in which Chrysostom spoke--that of a Christian pastor, many of whose demi-Christian parishioners were facing a threat to their Christian faith by the influence of the strong community of Jews in Antioch.

Chrysostom stressed the fact that neither Paul nor God are enemies of the Jews. Paul, he points out, calls them "kinsmen" and "brothers." He indicates how God willed their salvation through all the past privileges that had been theirs. Yet he insists, by quoting their own prophets, that their current rejection is "their own fault," inasmuch as those on whom God shows no mercy, even Pharaoh, had been the recipients of his favor just as those who will not have it. . . ."[8] By so doing, Chrysostom avoids the trap of "double predestination," agreeing with an expression of a later churchman, "not even the wicked perish because they have been unable to be good, but because they have been unwilling to be good."[9]

Chrysostom warns his gentile audience against vainglory in their own acceptance by God, and closes his sermon with a long three and a half page exhortation to show their gratitude by embodying it in their behavior toward their children and the poor, and by freeing their slaves. By this means he was following Paul's suggestion in Rom 11:11 that the Gentiles should make the Jews "jealous" of their faith by a profound embodiment of it in their living.

He is silent on the problem raised by Paul's hope of the final ingathering of all the Jews by making no comment on it whatsoever. He may have done this because he saw no hope of it ever taking place and felt that Paul had overweighted this hope because of his kinship with them. On the other hand, he may have done it because of a conviction expressed in another place that we should not be too eager to pry into the strange providence of God. In his **Discourse Against Judaizing Christians**, he said: "Paul did not search and pry into God's very essence, but only into his providence; I should say rather that he looked only on the small portion of divine providence which God had made manifest when he called the Gentiles. And Paul saw this small part as a vast and incomprehensible sea when he explained: 'O the depth of the riches and of the wisdom and of the knowledge of God! How uncomprehensible are his judgments, and how unsearchable his ways.'"[10] Chrysostom was persuaded that in likening us to clay in the hands of the potter, Paul was not "depriving us of our freedom, heaven forbid, . . . nor destroying our power to choose," but was rather rebuking "those who seek to inquire out of curiosity into God's management of affairs."[11]

In my judgment, Chrysostom, in his preaching on Romans 9-11, was not as anti-

Jewish as his critics allege, but was making an honest effort to interpret certain aspects of its meaning in the light of the pastoral situation he was facing. In circumstances somewhat similar to those faced by Paul when he wrote Galatians, he was seeking to keep some of his congregation from Judaizing Christianity to a point where it would be vitiated. He also had the problem with others of his flock which the writer to the Hebrews faced, of keeping them from abandoning the faith for Judaism. With these pastoral concerns uppermost, he did, however, miss other emphases of Romans 9-11, such as the possibility of Israel being re-ingrafted into the faith, and the deep indebtedness that Christians have to their Jewish spiritual forebears

II. AUGUSTINE

Saint Augustine dealt with the Jewish-Christian question rather too frequently in his writings. This was occasioned not only by his study of the Scriptures, where the question cannot be avoided, but by the presence of a large number of Jewish residents both in Hippo and in Carthage, whose objections to Christian understandings had to be answered in Augustine's solicitude for his Christian flock.[12]

He had a beautiful conception of what the relation between Jews and Christians in the faith should be. In one of his sermons, speaking of the Magi and the shepherds at Jesus' birth, he said: "The shepherds were Israelites; the Magi, Gentiles. The one group came from nearby; the other, from afar. Both, however, were united in [Christ] the cornerstone. For, as the Apostle says: . . . 'Of the two he has created in himself one new man, making peace, and he has reconciled both in one body to God, having slain the enmity in himself.'"[13] In another sermon he says: "Both groups, as if they were the beginnings of two walls coming from different directions, that is, of circumcision and of uncircumcision, hurried on to the cornerstone so that He might be their peace, making both one."[14] In yet another sermon, he sees, along with Paul, "how much more" the "full inclusion" of all the Jews in the one Church of Christ would mean. "How wonderful it would have been," he says, "if these leaders of the Jews, when they heard from the Magi that under the guidance of the star they had come desiring to adore him, had associated themselves with the searchers for Christ, had led them to Bethlehem, which pointed out from the sacred books, and had seen, understood, and adored him along with them?"[15] But they did not. And Augustine realizes the poignancy of that fact. He says: "Instead, after directing others to the fountain of life, they preferred to die of thirst. They became, as it were, milestones to these strangers; they indicated the path to the travelers but they remained motionless and immovable. The Jews . . . having pointed out Bethlehem, withdrew . . . happier for the ignorance of the babes whom Herod in his terror persecuted than the knowledge of those whom he in his anxiety consulted. Children not yet capable of confessing Christ could suffer for him; they who could point out the city of his birth did not follow the truth enunciated by him as a teacher."[16]

Augustine seems to differ from Chrysostom in that he does not lump all Jews together. Chrysotom tended to apply all the condemnatory words of the prophets spoken against Israel and Judah to the Jews of his day as a class--to *all* Jews. Augustine, conversely, says: "These prophecies have not been made, however, about all the Jews; only about those to whom the predictions apply. These indictments do not concern those who believed in Christ at that time because of these very prophecies, nor those who have believed in Christ up the the present or who, henceforth, up to the end of the world, will believe in Christ, that is, the true Israel who will see the Lord face to face."[17] He bases this on Rom 9:6-8: "But they are not all Israelites who are sprung from Israel; nor because they are the descendants of Abraham, are they all of his children; but: 'Through Isaac shall thy posterity bear thy name.' This is to say, they are not the sons of God who are children of the flesh, but it is the children of promise who are reckoned as a posterity."[18]

Augustine, in his preaching, also insisted that God's covenant with his ancient people had not been abrogated. Although "the wild olive tree" has been "engrafted in place of the branches which had been broken off . . . yet, on that account is the Lord not King of the Jews. For, the trunk of the tree bears the engrafted wild olive; not the wild olive, the trunk. And, even though the branches were broken off because of infidelity, the Lord *did not*, for that reason, *cast off His people whom He foreknew* . . . And, although the sons of the kingdom who did not wish the Son of God to rule over them go into exterior darkness, nevertheless, 'many will come from the east and from the west and will feast,' not with Plato and Cicero, but 'with Abraham and Isaac and Jacob in the kingdom of heaven.' Pilate definitely wrote 'King of the Jews,' not 'King of the Greeks' or 'King of the Latins,' even though the Lord was destined to rule over the Gentiles. . . . All the Gentiles believe in the King of the Jews; he rules over all the Gentiles; but still he is King of the Jews. The trunk is strong enough to change the engrafted wild olive into itself, but the wild olive cannot take away the name of the olive tree."[19]

In another sermon Augustine, in referring to Israel as a vineyard brought out of Egypt, says: "Christ did not plant another; by his coming he changed that into a better vineyard. Accordingly, we find in the Gospel: 'He will utterly destroy those evil men, and will let out the vineyard to other vinedressers.' The Gospel does not say: 'He will uproot, and will plant another,' but, 'this same vineyard he will let out to other vinedressers.'" The fact that "unfruitful" branches had been "broken away" and "the wild olive of the Gentiles was ingrafted" did not mean "that the root of the patriarchs and prophets died."[20] Although to Augustine, all of this was "a great and wondrous mystery,"[21] it is clear that he felt that the Jews were still, in some profound sense, the elect people of God; and that, since "the gifts and the call of God are irrevocable" (Rom 11:29), "as regards election they are beloved for the sake of their forefathers," and "they also may receive mercy" just as the formerly disobedient Gentiles "have received mercy because of [the Jews'] disobedience" (Rom 11:28, 30-31). In fact, he says in another sermon, "Even after losing their temple, their sacrifice, their priesthood, and their kingdom, they hold on to their name and race in a few ancient rites, lest, mixed indiscriminately with the Gentiles, they perish and lose the testimony of the truth. Like Cain, who in envy and pride killed his just brother, they have been marked with a sign so that no one may kill them."[22]

Although it is quite likely that Augustine did not have many, if any, unconverted Jews in his congregation when preaching, he more than once pled with them to accept the gospel, perhaps doing so to stimulate his Christian hearers to seek to evangelize the unbelieving Jews. In one sermon he directly addressed the Jews from the prophet Isaiah

> The law and the Word of God [are] going to proceed from Sion and Jerusalem to all nations, not from Mount Sinai to one nation. This we see most evidently fulfilled in Christ and the Christians. A little later, the Prophet says: 'O house of Jacob, come ye, and let us walk in the light of the Lord'. . . but listen a moment to what follows. . . . The Prophet continued: 'For he has cast off his people, the house of Israel.' Here say: 'We are the house

> of Israel'; here acknowledge yourselves and forgive us for reminding you of these facts . . . . Behold, not I, but the Prophet whom you read--through whom you cannot deny God has spoken, to whom you cannot deny the authority of the sacred Scriptures--at the Lord's command vehemently cries out and lifts up his voice like a trumpet and, rebuking you, says: 'O house of Jacob, come ye, and let us walk in the light of the Lord.' . . . For a long time you have not believed in Him and you have opposed Him, but you are not yet lost, because you are still alive; you have time now for repentance; only come now. You should have come long ago, of course, but come now, your days are not yet ended; the last day is still to come.[23]

In another sermon, he said to his Christian hearers: the Jews "do not listen to what we say because they do not understand what they read. Certainly, if they understood what the prophet, whom they read, is foretelling: 'I have given thee to be the light of the Gentiles, that thou mayest be my salvation even to the farthest part of the earth' they would not be so blind . . . . Consequently, testimonies are to be selected from sacred Scripture, which has great authority among the Jews, and if they do not want to be cured by means of this advantage offered them, they can at least be convicted by its evident truth."[24]

These passages suggest that Augustine felt a strong Christian responsibility to seek to persuade Jews of the truth of the Christian faith.

I found no direct affirmation in Augustine's sermons of Paul's hope that some day "all Israel will be saved" (Rom 11:26a). We may infer, however, that he shared some form of this hope from the fact that he held the Jews still to be the special concern of God; he believed in the convertability of the Jews, "If they do not continue in unbelief, will be grafted in; for God is able to graft them back."[25] A recent translator of Augustine's **Answer to the Jews**, which though longer than an ordinary sermon "bears all the characteristics of the sermon in form, style, and diction,"[26] says that the "persuasive firmness and kindness of the bishop, so evident in this sermon, might almost be construed as an invitation to the Jews to come into the Church,"[27] as though he were seeking a way to make Paul's hope a reality.

The unique contribution of Augustine to the discussion of Jewish-Christian questions, both in his City of God and his sermons, consists of his view that both the preservation and the dispersion of the Jews throughout the world served as a providential witness to the truth about Christ to all nations. There was a two-fold aspect to this. First, their dissemination of the Old Testament Scriptures served as a witness of Christ, the meaning of whom was foreshadowed there. The Jews, he claims, "who are scattered over the whole earth wherever the Church is expanding and who possess and preserve these books, are living witnesses, however reluctant, to the truth of our position."[28] He was firmly convinced that the Old Testament witness to Christ was so clear that any unprejudiced mind would see foregleams of him there. The knowledge which the pagans received from the Jews, therefore, was a providential preparation for the dissemination of the gospel.

The second aspect of this was apologetic. There were some apocryphal Sybilline prophecies of the Messiah floating around in Augustine's world which led the pagans to propose that any writings antecedent to Christ which bore witness to him were merely Christian forgeries. But the Scripture of the Old Testament pointed to Christ, and there could be no question that they far antedated the Christians and were genuine documents of those who had no interest in Christ. Commenting on the gentile Magi inquiring where Christ was to be born, Augustine said that "the Jews were interrogated to show that they were preserving the divine records" for the sake of "the Gentiles. For this reason, the Jews were expelled from their own kingdom and scattered throughout the earth so that, in all places, they might be forced to become witnesses to the faith which they hated."[29] He also referred to this in his City of God: "The only cogent way that is left for refuting any non-Christians who may argue this point (and for converting them, if they will do some straight thinking)--is to produce the divinely inspired prophecies of Christ which are contained in the books of the Jews--the people who were torn away from their ancestral home and scattered over the whole earth and have thus furnished a witness to help the Church in its universal expansion."[30]

Although Augustine has been accused of anti-Judaism, I found no evidence of it in his sermons, unless the yearning judgments of Israel's own prophets and the words of her weeping Messiah, that tragedy awaited her because she "did not know the time of [her] visitation" (Luke 19:41-44), are anti-Jewish. A real anti-Jewish sentiment would hardly have stressed, as Augustine did, the admonition of Paul in Rom 11:18a that the engrafted wild olive branches "not boast over the branches." This is illustrated in the rather moving conclusion of one his sermons: "Dearly beloved, whether the Jews receive these divine testimonies with joy or with indignation, nevertheless, when we can, let us proclaim them with great love for the Jews. Let us not proudly glory against the broken branches; let us rather reflect by whose grace it is, and by much mercy, and to what root, we have been ingrafted. Then, not savoring of pride, but with a deep sense of humility, not insulting with presumption, but rejoicing with trembling, let us say: 'Come ye and let us walk in the light of the Lord,' because His 'name is great among the Gentiles.' If they hear Him and obey Him, they will be among them to whom Scripture says: 'Come ye to him and be enlightened; and your faces shall not be confounded.' If, however, they hear and do not obey, if they see and are jealous, they are among them of whom the Psalm says: 'The wicked shall see, and shall be angry, he shall gnash with his teeth and pine away.' 'But I,' the Church says to Christ, 'as a fruitful olive tree in the house of God, have hoped in the mercy of God for ever, yea for ever and ever.'"[31]

III. AN UNKNOWN NINTH CENTURY PREACHER

I unearthed in a French publication of ancient Christian sources a homily by an unknown author from North Italy in the ninth century. This is not based directly on a text from Romans 9-11, but touches on the Jewish-Christian question raised there. It indicates that there were Christian preachers at that time who, in interpreting Paul, were not anti-Jewish in their outlook and who judged Christians by the same standards they applied to the Jews, warning them as "wild olive shoots" not to boast over "the branches" which were "broken off."

In closing a sermon on John 8, where we are told that the Jews "took up stones to throw at him" (9:59a), the preacher said: "Take care, brother, that you do not stone Jesus by your works or evil thoughts. . . . Perhaps you say: The Jews who wished to stone and crucify Jesus did evil. Know and stedfastly believe that Christians today by their evil lives are doing what the Jews did in persecuting Christ. Who, in realty, is Jesus, if not truth, peace and justice? Thus one who bypasses truth by cheating, who lacerates and despises peace by envy, who conceals justice for some sort of gain, does nothing other than stone, crucify and kill Christ . . . . O how few there are in the immense crowd of Chrisrians who do not persecute, stone and kill Jesus"[32]

This preacher was guided by Paul's word in Rom 11:21 and 32: "For if God did not spare the natural branches, neither will he spare you. . . . For God has consigned all men to disobedience, that he may have mercy upon all." There is no distinction--Christian and Jew stand on common ground before the judgment and grace of God.

IV. JOHN WESLEY

The question of Jewish-Christian relations does not seem to have loomed large in Wesley's Protestant England. From the beginning of the Crusades at the very end of the eleventh century until the revolutionary movements near the end of the eighteenth century, the Jews were a persecuted minority pushed from pillar to post in most parts of the Christian world. In 1290 they were totally driven out of England, and not many had returned by Wesley's day. It was well over a half century following his death that Jews were permitted to hold municipal offices in England, and nearly a century before they could be admitted to the universities or hold office in the House of Commons or House of Lords.[33] Religious commerce between Christians and Jews in Wesley's England was, therefore, at a minimum. For that reason, he did not deal with the Jewish-Christian problem in terms in which it confronts us today. Wesley did, however, in his preaching on occasion touch upon certain passages in Romans 9-11.

He shared the view that the Jews had missed the way in rejecting Jesus as their Messiah, and were in need of faith in Christ to give their religious faith authenticity; but in contrast to his denunciation of much of Protestant and Roman Catholic Christianity in his day, he avoided denunciatory treatment of the Jews. In a sermon "On Faith," in describing various sorts of faith, such as that of the heathen, the Muslims, and the Deists, he spoke of the Jewish faith. He rated the faith of the "serious and sincere" Jew who "lived between the giving of the law and the coming of Christ" above that of "a heathen or Mohamedan." They believed that in the fulness of time the Messiah would appear "to finish the transgression, to make an end of sin, and bring in everlasting righteousness." He then passes to "the faith of our modern Jews" on whom, he said, it is "not easy to pass any judgment." They were still hard hearted and blind-eyed, and exemplified what the Scripture had said of their forefathers. "Yet," he added, "it is not our part to pass sentence upon them, but to leave them to their own Master."[34]

In another sermon, he used Rom 10:3 to illustrate his own view of the difference between "outward" and "inward" righteousness. He interpreted Paul to mean that the unbelieving Jews were ignorant "not only of the righteousness of Christ, imputed to every believer, whereby all his sins are blotted out, and he is reconciled to the favour of God; but (which seems here to be more immediately understood) they were ignorant of that inward righteousness, of that holiness of heart, which is with the utmost propriety termed 'God's righteousness' . . . . And because they were ignorant of this they 'went about to establish their own righteousness.' They laboured to establish that outside righteousness which might very properly be termed 'their own'; for neither was it wrought by the Spirit of God nor was it owned or accepted of him. They might work this themselves, by their own natural strength; and when they had done, it was a stink in his nostrils."[35]

Wesley also made brief mention of Rom 11:18-22 in one of his sermons as a warning against pride. "Does not the preaching of salvation by faith, and faith alone lead men into pride?" he asks. He answers that "accidentally it may. Therefore ought every believer to be earnestly cautioned (in the words of the great Apostle): 'Because of unbelief the first branches were broken off, and thou standest by faith. Be not high-minded, but fear. If God spared not the natural branches, take heed lest he spare not thee.' "[36] There was no mention of the fact that the "natural branches" were the Jews, but he likely presumed that his hearers were familiar enough with the passage to know that.

Wesley makes an interesting use of Rom 9:16-21, interpreting it in line with his strong distaste for the doctrine of predestinating grace. He grants that it "does not become poor, guilty, sinful worms, who receive whatsoever blessings they enjoy . . . of grace, of mere favour, and not of debt, to ask of God the reasons of his conduct. It is not meet for us to call him in question 'who giveth account to none of his ways': . . . 'But he limits the application of this to God's decision to offer salvation solely by faith. Who are those on whom God "will have mercy"?--"those who believe on the Son of his love." Who will God "harden"?--"those who believe not, 'he hardeneth'--leaves at last to the hardness of their hearts."[37] Wesley here applies the passage to individual salvation, of which it is doubtful that Paul was speaking in this passage, since he is speaking of the function of electing grace in God's choice of Israel as his instrument in history. Wesley also avoids the knotty question of why some have faith and others do not. He insists that "it is not of him that willeth, nor of him that runneth,' *to choose the condition* on which he shall find acceptance" (bold mine); but this implies that whether one *accepts* the condition or not is solely *his own decision*. It is doubtful that this fully explains the "mystery" of election of which Paul is speaking in Romans 9-11.

The possibility that one day "all Israel will be saved" (Rom 11:26a) was, in Wesley's views, not so much a fulfillment of God's special covenant with Israel as the natural result of the spread of the gospel throughout the world. This view is stated near the conclusion of a sermon on "The General Spread of the Gospel," where he paints in broad strokes his optimistic hope of the gospel's triumph over the whole world. He first paints a vivid picture of the plight of the religious life of the world before his day. Nineteen out of thirty in the world were heathen, six in thirty Mohammedan, and only 5 in 30 nominally Christian. But most of these latter lived in a deplorable spiritual state. Many Christians of the Eastern churches, under Turkish dominion, lived, he said, in a state of "total, stupid, barbarian irreligion." The Church of Rome was corrupt, and Protestantism was in a deplorable state.

Basing his judgment, however, on the thesis that "As God is one," we may "conceive how he *will* work on the souls of men in times to come by considering how he *does* work now," he concludes that God can "convert whole nations, or the whole world. And it is as easy for him to convert a world as one individual soul." He then describes his own movement, begun at Oxford between fifty and sixty years before, as "a sign of hope and a model of God's final design for the spread of the gospel." It spread throughout Britain and Ireland, then to America, Newfoundland and Nova Scotia. "Is it not then highly probable," he asks, "that God will carry on his work in the same manner as he begun? That he *will* carry it on I cannot doubt; however Luther may affirm that a revival of religion never lasts above a generation, that is, thirty years (whereas the present revival has already continued above fifty): . . . No: I trust this is only the beginning of a far greater work--the dawn of 'latter day glories.' "

He then pictures the movement spreading to Holland, then to the Protestants in France, Germany, Sweden, Denmark, Russia, "and all other Protestant nations in Europe" Then it will capture Roman Catholicism in all countries where Roman Catholics and Protestants live together. Then purely Romanist countries, such as Italy, Spain and Portugal will be won. Finally, the remotest parts of Europe, Asia, Africa, and America will be included. The rich, the noble, the rulers and kings of the earth will be converted; and finally, "all the wise and learned, the men of genius, the philosophers, will be convinced that they are fools; will 'be converted and become as little children, and enter into the kingdom of God.' " The "holy lives of the Christians will be an argument" that no one will know how to resist, so that the East Indies, the Tartars, Russia, Norway, Finland and Lapland, and the countries with which the Christians trade, such as the interior parts of Africa, China and Japan and adjoining countries will be Christianized. Finally, when the "fullness of the Gentiles" is complete, all Israel shall be saved, her blindness will be overcome, and the "Deliverer that cometh out of Zion shall turn away iniquity from Jacob." He concludes that all "unprejudiced persons may see with their own eyes, that he is already renewing the face of the eath. And we have strong reasons to hope that the work he hath begun he will carry on unto the day of his Lord Jesus . . . until he hath put a period to sin and misery, and infirmity, and death; and reestablished universal holiness, and happiness, and caused *all* the inhabitants of the earth to sing together, 'Hallelujah! the Lord God omnipotent reigneth!' "[38]

In another sermon he tells us what he thinks the earth will be like when "the fullness of the Gentiles be come in" and "all Israel shall be saved."

> . . . What a prospect is this! All is "peace, quietness, and assurance forever." Here is no din of arms, no "confused noise," no "garments rolled in blood." "Destructions are come to a perpetual end;" wars are ceased from the earth. Neither is there any intestine jar remaining: no brother rising up against brother; no country or city divided against itself, and tearing out its own bowels. Civil discord is at an end for evermore, and none is left either to destroy or hurt his neighbor. Here is no oppressor to "make (even) the wise man mad"; no extortion to "grind the face of the poor"; no robbery or wrong; no rapine or injustice; for all are "content with such things as they possess." . . . And with righteousness or justice, mercy is also found. The earth is no longer "full of cruel habitations." "The Lord hath destroyed both the bloodthirsty" and malicious, the envious and revengeful man. Were there any provocation, there is none that now knoweth to "return evil for evil": but indeed there is none doth evil, no not one; for all are "harmless as doves"; and being "filled with peace and joy in believing," and united in one body, by one Spirit, they all "love as brethren"; they are all "of one heart, and of one soul, neither saith any of them that ought of the things which he possesseth is his own." There is none among them that lacketh; for every man loveth his neighbour as himself. And all walk by one rule: "Whatever ye would that men should do unto you, even so do unto them."
>
> It follows that no unkind word can ever be heard among them--no "strife of tongues," no contention of any kind, no railing, or evil speaking--but everyone "opens his mouth with wisdom, and in his tongue there is the law of kindness." Equally incapable are they of fraud or guile: their "love is without dissimulation": their words are always the just expression of their thoughts, opening a window into their breast, that whosoever desires may look into their hearts and see that only love and God are there.[39]

I have quoted this at length because I have seldom, if ever, read a more eloquent or beautiful picture of--heaven! But, on earth? One marvels that one as astute and as practical as Wesley could have imagined a world like this in history, and hoped for it before long! In my judgment, he failed to take the measure of the enemy, and thus had a truncated doctrine of sin. He forgot for the moment, an old adage: The surest way to the dislike of other men is to behave well where they behave poorly. He seemed to forget that rather than "admiring" the life of the One who embodied all this, and being led to "consider and embrace" his doctrine, the men of Jesus' time put him on a cross. He seemed also to forget that, with all the uplifting wonder of his gospel, he and his own most intimate brother, Charles, differed and often had hot words for one another; that he himself caused Whitefield great pain in his dealings with him; that his brother once referred to his great fellow-Christian, John Calvin, as the "firstborn son of the devil";[40] and that he himself was either unable or indifferent to making peace with his own wife, saying, when she left him: "I have not left her; I have not sent her away; I will not recall her."[41] Given these, and other facts, in his own life and religious movement, empirical observation would seem to have suggested that his picture of the possibilities of grace in historic human nature are somewhat limited.

What he would say now, two hundred years later, in a century when perhaps more human blood has been shed by fellow human beings than in any century in history; and world unrest and hatred are uncontrollably rampant; and bitterness is so intense that men will stone trains carrying relief to earthquake victims; and the churches through whom all this historic process was supposed to take place have pretty largely lost their own sense of mission and are perhaps less effective in molding public life than in any day since Wesley's time, I do not know. Perhaps he was wrong only in his timing. Perhaps in future centuries his dream will be realized. I suspect, however, that righteousness will have to do battle with evil to the very end of time; that Christ's victory over cosmic evil will remain a "hidden" victory, seen only by faith, as long as the centuries endure; and that history will have to await the eschaton to see "every knee" bow and "ever tongue" confess the Lordship of Christ "to the glory of God the Father."

V. JONATHAN EDWARDS

Jonathan Edwards, born in the same year as Wesley, but of a wholly different persuasion, used Romans 9-11 for exactly the opposite reason. He, like Wesley, bypassed the profound problem of Jewish-Christian relations posed by Paul. It is as though the lack of a Jewish population in America in his time made this an indifferent question to him. Using Rom 9:18 as his text--"So then he has mercy upon whomever he wills, and he hardens the heart of whomever he will," he develops the theme that "God exercises His sovereignty in the eternal salvation of men." He first *interprets* God's sovereignty as action "without constraint," without "the will of another, " and without "any proper obligation." It is "absolute and independent." The *implications* of God's sovereignty are that he "can save any sinner consistently with the glory of His attributes, except men who have committed the unpardonable sin--consistent with His holiness, majesty, justice and truth; all because of what Christ has accomplished." He may likewise "refuse salvation to any sinners consistently with the honor of His attributes." Edwards then turns to the *fact* of God's sovereignth, by illustrating how it has worked in human experience. Some nations have been blessed with the gospel, others bypassed; some have been given the advantages of Christian families and powerful ministries which others lack; the persons called demonstrate this--princes are passed over and cottagers called; the wise are overlooked and those of weak understanding are called; children of pious parents are sometimes outside the pale, while those who grew up in wicked homes are sometimes called; some who seek are quickly converted, while others seek long and do not obtain. The reasons for God's sovereignty in salvation are that it is agreeable to his design in creation, and glorifies his sovereignty. He concludes, however, by holding out hope to all: "Let your case be what it may--if you have not committed the sin against the Holy Spirit, God can bestow mercy upon you. God can, if He pleases, greatly glorify Himself in your salvation."[42]

Despite Edwards' great mind and spiritual insight, he ignored totally the larger context of the passage on which he was preaching. He applied it wholly to personal salvation, whereas Paul was speaking of the great mystery of God having elected Israel as the instrument of his purpose--as demonstrated in their long history culminating in the coming of Christ; then seemingly being bypassed for the sake of the Gentiles also becoming the heirs of that purpose--and expressing the hope that in the furture, all Israel would again become the beneficiaries of their own history through God's electing grace.

VI. NINETEENTH AND TWENTIETH CENTURY PREACHERS

After an extensive, but not an exhaustive, survey of published nineteenth and twentieth century sermons, it became evident that Romans 9-11 is seldom chosen for pulpit presentation, and when it is, even more seldom does the preacher deal with the basic problem which Paul was facing.

(a) Charles G. Finney

The great evangelist of the first half of the nineteenth century, Charles G. Finney, preached a sermon on the subject "Religion of the Law and the Gospel," based on Rom 9:30-33. In a long introduction, he did set the passage in its place in the whole sweep of Paul's thought in Romans. Both Gentiles and Jews were in a state of depravity, for "no human being will be justified in his sight by works of the law. . ." (Rom 1:1-3:20). The only solution to the problem, for both Jew and Gentile, is justification by faith (Rom 4:1-5:21). Sanctification, too, is by faith (Romans 6). Romans 8 and 9 introduces the subject of divine sovereignty, and the last part of Romans 9 indicates that the Jews "made the fatal mistake of attempting to become pious by obeying the law, and have always come short, while the Gentiles have obtained true religion by faith in Jesus Christ."

At this point, Finney turns from Paul's larger wrestling with this problem to point out "the true distinction between the religion of the law and the religion of faith." First, he shows in what the distinction *does not* consist: not that under law men were justified by works without faith; not that the gospel has set aside the moral law; not that the gospel is less strict or allows any greater latitude of self-indulgence; not that those who have a legal religion profess to depend on their works. Rather, they have a "false dependence on Christ." In what, then, does the distinction consist? Both produce "good works," but "one is based on the principle of *fear*, the other on *confidence* and *love*." Furthermore, one is justified by faith only if he is also sanctified by faith, responding to God's love rather than merely obeying the voice of conscience. He concludes by bringing forth some illustrations of this, beginning with that of Paul in Romans 7. He sums it up by saying that some religion is all faith without works, whereas some is all works without faith. True Christianity differs from both.[43]

This is an honest effort to set the passage in the broad sweep of Paul's thought in the entire Letter, but finally stops short of the larger problem Paul is wrestling with in Romans 9-11; namely, how does one explain in the purpose of God, how the Jewish people whom God prepared for the redemption by faith in Christ somehow missed the point, whereas the Gentiles, who had had not special preparation for this as did the Jews, found its meaning.

(b) *Charles H. Spurgeon*

A quick survey of Spurgeon's many volumes revealed only one published sermon on a text from Romans 9-11, namely, Rom 10:16: "But they have not heeded the gospel; for Isaiah says, 'Lord, who has believed what he has heard from us?' " Spurgeon simply uses Israel as an example of disobedience, illustrating "the depravity of man's heart that . . . disobeys his God, whether he speaks to him in love or in law." He affirms that the gospel "comes to men with the force of a command," with "a death penalty attached to disobedience." He then lists a fivefold claim of the gospel to obedience: the authority, the motive, the greatness of the gift, the reasonableness, and the earnestness of the author of the gospel. What is "the obedience required by the gospel?" Faith in Christ, renunciation of self-righteousness and confession of guilt; repentance and abandonment of sin; discipleship; and public confession. He closes with a warning that refusal to obey leads to a deeper unbelief and a self-condemnatory exclusion from eternal fellowship with God.[44]

Here, again, is an avoidance of wrestling with the Jewish-Christian problem, and a shift from Paul's dealing with God's purpose in history to an emphasis on individual salvation.

(c) *G. Campbell Morgan*

In his **Searchlights From the Word**, Campbell Morgan deals honestly with the sweep of Paul's thought in Romans 9-11. "Paul's great subject in all this section," he says, "was that of the salvation of the ancient people of God, Israel. He saw 'some of the branches . . . broken off,' whereas the root-purpose of God through them and for them was not destroyed. The breaking-off was very real, and it resulted from their unbelief. Now the Apostle declared that if they continued not in unbelief, they would be grafted in again."

He does not apply this, however, to the Jewish-Christian problem of today. He rather makes a general affirmation of "the grace and power of God " who is "able to graft in again branches that have been broken off," if they "continue not in the unbelief which was the secret to [their] fruitlessness."[45] Morgan also deals with this subject in like manner, but a bit more at length, in his **Analyzed Bible: Matthew to Revelation.**[46] In both cases, he deals with the passage in its setting, and interprets it, in my judgment, truly, but makes such a general application of the truth that specific problems are avoided.[47]

VII. CONCLUSION

This rather sketchy survey indicates that Romans 9-11 has not been a favorite mine of preaching materials. This may be partly due to the ghettoizing of the Jews because of persecution, or their expulsion from many Christian areas, which has isolated

Jews and Christians from one another. If no Jews are present in a worship service, it is pointless to direct a sermon to them. On the other hand, it could be considered pointless to preach to Gentile Christians on this area of Scripture if they have no converse with Jews.

A deeper reason may be, however, that the passage is so difficult of interpretation that it is difficult to know exactly what Paul meant by some of the things he said. Or, if we think that we can finally work our way into what he had in mind, can we make it meaningful to modern hearers? Does he not himself, after wrestling with the problem he poses, confess that it is insoluble when he speaks of "the riches and wisdom and knowedge of God" being so "deep" that his judgments are "unsearchable" and his ways "inscrutable." Here is imponderable mystery. How, than, can one preach on it?

Paul seems to contradict himself in this passage. In fact, one commentator heads his comment on the section: "A Problem With Different Solutions," then lists about eight answers he thinks Paul makes to it, some of which are difficult to reconcile with others.[48] He seems to suggest, for example, that the exclusion of the Jews was purposed by God for the sake of the Gentiles, yet , on the other hand, that it would have been better if the Jews had believed along with the Gentiles. Logic would propose that Paul here thinks that God's purpose could have been improved! But--he would have been the first to deny such an implication, and would reply: "But, who are you, a man, to answer back to God?" It is easier, therefore, to leave the subject untouched and to justify this by its manifest inscrutability. And yet, Romans 9-11 is here, as a part of the Word of God and challenges our pulpit wrestling with it. Kenneth Foreman insists: "these chapters are no parenthesis. For as fond as [Paul] was of parentheses and side remarks, he would not have spent nearly a third of his available space on a parenthesis."[49]

If we can do nothing more with it, we can at least utilize it to keep before Christians the fact that the Christian faith has no place for anti-Judaism, calling for penitence for past Christian failures at this point and seeking grace to overcome it in the future. (This must not be confused with anti-Zionism or criticism of current Jewish political policy. One can differ with the Zionists without being in any sense anti-Jewish.) Beyond this, however, Christians ought to be frequently reminded of their deep debt to the Jews for their faith. Without the Old Testament there would have been no New Testament; and, even if there had, it would have made no sense. Without the Jews there would have been no Christians. Their history is *our* history. They were the first heirs of a promise which we Christians have inherited. They were the ones who, through the long discipline of the years, kept the gospel alive and brought us Christ. In **An Autobiography**, Abba Eban tells of studying the classics in an exclusive British school during the weeks of his early life, from eight to eighteen, but being immersed in the biblical literature and the Talmud by his grandfather every "Friday after school until Sunday night or Monday. . . . It was the weekend, not the weekday world," he says, "that came to excite my deepest sources of feeling . . . . My own sufferings and suspense were of Isaac beneath Abraham's threatening knife. My sense of awe came to life in the 'thunder and lightning and the the trumpets exceeding loud' that accompanied Moses on Mount Sinai. My sense of nationhood was born with the parting of the Red Sea and the Israelites defiance of Egyptian tyranny."[50] As for him, so for us Christians, the history of the Hebrew people should be personalized. It is *our* history too. Our sense of religious awe is born there. And, although we do not share his "sense of nationhood," we find a larger nationhood--the sense of a kingdom as broad as humanity, the universal kingdom of God which shall one day be established over all the kingdoms of the world. It is this Jewish heritage of which we must make our people aware.

But is there here any Christian word for the Jew? Or should we leave the Jews to their own religious faith undisturbed? I cannot believe that Paul would be comfortable with the current view which proposes that Christians and Jews worship the same God, and there are two distinct communities living side by side, equally valid in the purpose and work of God, and continuing on a corresponding footing until the end of the age; for which reason, the Jew is adequately related to God through the old covenant, and does not need the Christian faith. It is significant that no Christian preacher we have surveyed held this view. Paul declares in Rom 1:16 that the gospel "is the power of God for salvation to every one who has faith, *to the Jew first* and also to the Greek." The writer of the Fourth Gospel tells us not that God sent his Son for the Gentiles, but for "the world," *ton kosmos* "all humankind"; or, as it is put in the Martyrdom of Polycarp, "for the salvation of the sum total of those who are saved."[51] This is not the place to do it, but passages of the New Testament to this effect could be multiplied endlessly, not as mere proof texts but as contextually interpreted indications that Christ has "once for all" rent the veil that divides holy God from sinful humanity and opened the one "new and living way" into God's presence for all humanity, having become "the source of eternal salvation to *all* who obey him" (Heb 5:9). As the writer to the Hebrews tells us, "perfection" was not obtainable through "the former commandment." It is now "set aside because of its weakness and uselessness"; it is now "obsolete" and replaced by a "better" covenant, law, temple, priesthood, sacrifice and promises; its mediator "has appeared once for all at the end of the age to put away sin by the sacrifice of himself" (Heb 7:11, 18; 8:13; 9-10:39). This "scandal of particularity" is not something which we in our spiritual pride have invented, but is simply, as D. T. Niles said many years ago, "one beggar telling another beggar where to find food." It is a gospel which has been brought down to us from the apostolic witnesses, which we may accept or reject but are not at liberty to exchange for a "different gospel" which is not "another gospel" but a "perversion" of the gospel of Christ (Gal 1:6, 7). If we surrender this gospel, we have nothing unique to offer the world, and may as well as Thackeray said in another context, "shut up the puppets, for our play is played out."

Is not the final word on this to be found merely by asking two simple questions. Ask Paul, or any modern Jewish Christian, if his Jewish faith was adequate, apart from Jesus Christ. A resounding No would be the reply. Then, ask any religiously serious Jew if "the God of Abraham, Isaac and Jacob" is the same as "the God and Father of our Lord Jesus Christ." Again, one would get a resounding No. It is true that the two are the same in the sense that there is only one God, and in the sense that we have a common point of departure in our religious history. But the God of the Old Testament interpreted by the New Testament differs from the God of the Hebrew Bible interpreted by the rabbis.[52]

Romans 9-11 is a summons to the Jew to faith in Jesus Christ, as is the entire Letter of Romans and Galatians and Hebrews and I Peter--yes, the entire New Testament.

But how is the Jew to be evangelized? This seems to me to be perhaps the most difficult question facing the Christian Church. In the light of historic Christian anti-Judaism, culminating in Hitler's holocaust, the moment the Jew hears the name of Jesus Christ he is not confronted by the true Christ whom we know, but by a picture of a vicious monster who has dogged the Jews with unspeakable persecution throughout the centuries. One could almost say that through centuries of Christian behavior, we have presented the Jew with a Christ whom to reject is commendable. Who of us would believe in the Christ in whose name unconscionable crimes have been perpetrated? It seems to me, therefore, that the first step in bringing the Christian message to Jews is so to relate to them that they are convinced that we are not anti-Jewish. And this is an almost impossible task, in the light of the early struggle between church and synagogue in early Christian history and the history of anti-Judaism in the Christian Church during the centuries since.

It is difficult for a Jew to distinguish between Christian religious claims and anti-Judaism. In fact, it seems to be so even for many Christian scholars who are now equating the New Testament writers with being anti-Jewish. Some Jews themselves are wiser than this, for it is reported that a leading Jewish scholar has remarked that there is nothing said about Jews in the New Testament as severe as the judgments the Jewish prophets spoke against them in the Old Testament--and they were hardly anti-Jewish! Who could outstrip Hosea, the prophet of love, in putting these words into the mouth of God: "you are not my people and I am not your God" (1:9b)?

As to who was responsible for the death of Jesus, the New Testament is clear. Luke tells us in Acts 4:27 that it was "both Herod and Pontius Pilate, with the Gentiles and the peoples of Israel." Both rulers and ruled, both Jews and Gentiles--in other words, everybody, *the human race,* crucified Jesus. And it is hardly anti-Jewish for the New Testament writers, on the basis of the principle of responsibility according to privilege drawn by both the prophets and our Lord, to bring the Jews under special judgment for rejecting Jesus, since their religious privileges were greater than those of the pagans. They were merely expressing the theology of Amos: "*You only* have I known of all the families of the earth; therefore I will punish you . . ." (3:2). Isaiah, as Paul recalls, had called Israel "a disobedient and contrary people" (Rom 10:21), and our Lord himself had said of the Jews: "the Kingdom of God will be taken away from you and given to a nation producing the fruits of it" (Matt 21:43). So, for the New Testament writers to insist that the Jews *ought* to have accepted Jesus as their Messiah is not anti-Jewish, unless the prophets and Jesus were anti-Jewish. And when we rightly interpret that theology now, it is no cause for gloating over the Jews--it is rather applied to the Christian Church: "For the time has come for judgment to begin with the household of God; . . . " (1 Pet 4:7a). It is *we* now of whom it can be said: "You only have I known; therefore . . . ."

It is not anti-Jewish, therefore, to insist with Paul that the gospel "is the power of God for salvation to everyone one who has faith, to the Jew first and also to the Greek" (Rom 1:16b), and that "faith comes from what is heard, and what is heard comes by the preaching of Christ" (Rom 10:17). The Jew, as well as the Gentile, needs the gospel.

But how does one press the Christian claim on the Jews without them seeing in that anti-Judaism? I have often felt that in most cases it cannot be done by a non-Jewish Christian, and that perhaps the burden of Jewish evangelism should fall on the shoulders of Christian Jews. We know, too, that some Christian Jews have accepted that as their burden, such as Frederick Neumann. My Jewish-Christian friends, however, tell me that it is even harder for them to do this than for Gentiles. The Jews say to the non-Christian Jews: "The Gentile may not know any better; but *you*--you who have come out of our tradition--ought to know better. You are traitor to your own people." If anyone can do it, it may be the "Jews for Jesus" who accept Jesus as Messiah but try to remain Jews and do not identify themselves with the Christian Church. They may perchance be able to approach their own people more effectively than either a Gentile Christian or a Jewish convert who has identified himself with the Gentile Christian Church. It may be that God has raised them up for this very purpose. It may be, however, that at this point of history nobody can directly preach the gospel to the Jew and get a hearing.

We may have to await God's time to give the Jews a more receptive mood--that time for which Paul hoped when "the full number of the Gentiles come in, and so all Israel will be saved" (Rom 11:25b, 26a).

In the meantime, Karl Barth may be right that "there can be only one way to fulfil" the church's ministry of witness to the Jews. "To use the expression of Paul in Rom 11:11, 14, it must make the Synagogue jealous . . . It must make clear and desirable and illuminating to it him who it has rejected . . . No particular function can be this call, but only the life of the community as a whole authentically lived before the Jews."[53] Do our individual and corporate embodiments of loyalty to Christ make anybody wish to know the secret?

NOTES

1. Johannes B. Bauer, **Encyclopedia of Biblical Theology**, ed. Johannes B. Bauer (New York: Crossroad, 1981) 85.

2. **Homilies of St. John Chrysostom, Archbishop of Constantinople, on the Epistle of St. Paul the Apostle to the Romans**, trans. J. B. Mannis and W. H. Simcox; revised, with notes, by George H. Stevens, in a **Select Library of the Nicene and Post-Nicene Fathers of the Christian Church**, ed. Philip Schaff (New York: The Christian Literature Company, 1889) XI, 460-61.

3. W. F. Arndt and F. W. Gingrich, **A Greek-English Lexicon of the New Testament** (Chicago: The University of Chicago Press, 1957) 847.

4. **Homilies**, 462.

5. Paul Harkins in John Chrysostom, **Discourses Against Judaizing Christians** in **The Fathers of the Church**, tr. Paul W. Harkins (Washington, D.C.: The Catholic University Press, 1977) LXVIII, 5, n. 20.

6. Quoted by Paul W. Harkins, op. cit.,XXXVIII, n. 74.

7. Ibid., XXXVIII.

8. **Homilies**, 483.

9. Florus the Deacon, quoted by C. Spicq, **Encyclopedia of Biblical Theology**, 699.

10. **The Fathers of the Church**, Vol. 68, 2.

11. **On the Incomprehensible Nature of God**, in **The Fathers of the Church**, LXVIII 85-86.

12. Cf. Mary Sarah Muldowney, Introduction to Augustine's **Sermons on the Liturgical Seasons**, tr. Mary Sarah Muldowney in **The Fathers of the Church**, ed. Roy Joseph Deferrari (New York: Fathers of the Church, Inc., 1959) XXXVIII, xvii

13. Ibid., 71-73.

14. Ibid., 75.

15. Ibid., 60-61.

16. Ibid. 61.

17. **In Answer to the Jews** in **The Fathers of the Church**, tr. Marie Liguori, ed. Roy Joseph Deferrari (New York: Fathers of the Church, Inc., 1955) XXVII, 398.

18. Ibid.

19. **Sermons on the Liturgical Seasons**, 167.

20. **In Answer to the Jews**, 399.

21. **Sermons on the Liturgical Seasons,** 68.

22. Ibid., 70.

23. **In Answer to the Jews,** 407.

24. Ibid., 392-93.

25. Ibid., 392.

26. Blumenkranz, quoted by Marie Liguori, Introduction to **In Answer to the Jews,** 388.

27. **In Answer to the Jews,** 389.

28. **The City of God, The Fathers of the Church,** tr. Gerald G. Walsh (Washington, D.C.: The Catholic University of America, 1953) XXIV, 164.

29. **Sermons on the Liturgical Seasons,** 70.

30. Ibid., 167.

31. **In Answer to the Jews,** 414.

32. **XIV Homélies Du IXe Siècle D'Un Auteur Inconnu De L'Italie Du Nord,** tr. Paul Mercier, in **Sources Chrétiennes,** ed. C. Mondesert (Paris: Les Edition du Cerf, 1970). No. 161, 201. The English translation is my own.

33. See "Jews," **Encyclopedia Britannica** (Chicago: Encyclopedia Britannica, Inc., 1946) 59.

34. **The Works of John Wesley: Sermons,** ed. Albert C. Outler (Nashville: Abingdon Press, 1984) III, 495.

35. Ibid., I, 643.

36. Ibid., 125.

37. Ibid., 197.

38. Ibid., II, 485-87.

39. Ibid., I, 170-72.

40. Arnold A. Dallamore, **A Heart Set Free: The Life of Charles Wesley** (Westchester, Ill.: Crossway Books, 1968) 97.

41. **The Journal of the Rev. John Wesley,** ed. Nehemiah Curnock (London: The Epworth Press, 1914) III, 400.

42. Sheldon B. Quincer, **Jonathan Edwards' Sermon Outlines** (Grand Rapids: Eerdmans, 1958) 123-25

43. Charles G. Finney, **Principles of Victory: Great Themes from Romans,** ed. Louis Gifford Parkhurst, Jr. (Minneapolis: Bethany House Publishers, 1981) 137-39.

44. C. H. Spurgeon, **My Sermon-Notes: A Selection from Outlines of Discourses** (Louisville: Baptist Book Concern, n.d.) 39-41.

45. New York: Fleming H. Revell Company, 1926, 375.

46. New York: Fleming H. Revell Company, 1908, 102-04.

47. He has a separate volume on Romans, in which he may have made more specific applications of the truth, but it was not available to me.

48. Kenneth J. Foreman, **The Letter of Paul to the Romans** in **The Layman's Bible Commentary** (Atlanta: John Knox Press, 1961) 45-47.

49. Ibid.

50. New York: Random House, 1977, 6-7.

51. Arndt and Gingrich, op. cit., 448.

52. I am indebted here to my former colleague, Professor James L. Mays, of Union Theological Seminary in Richmond, Virginia for helping to clarify this in some unpublished notes he shared with me of a private presentation made to a discussion group.

53. **Church Dogmatics,** IV, 3, second half, tr. G. W. Bromiley (Edinburgh: T. & T. Clark, 1962) 878.

ON PREACHING FROM ROMANS 9-11

DAVID G. BUTTRICK

I. "OUR HEARTS HAVE CUT THESE STONES"

How often do we hear sermons drawn from Romans 9-11? How frequently do we hear preachers address the issue of Jewish-Christian relationships. Answer: Seldom, if ever. In the free church tradition where, more often than not, texts are chosen somewhat capriciously, the subject is seldom ventured. In churches that follow prescribed readings from a lectionary, the subject is seldom offered.[1] So, though Jewish-Christian relationships are strained in many of our communities, the subject is infrequently broached. Apparently the topic is not considered central to the gospel as far as most of us clergy-types are concerned.

Of course, anti-Jewish sentiment is still around. Anti-Jewish sentiments haunt most Christian congregations and, unfortunately, seem to be deeply imbedded in the American mind. Perhaps it is on the increase of late. In the past decade we have been shocked by swastikas scrawled on synagogue walls, by the desecration of Jewish cemeteries, and by air-headed remarks from some Christian leaders ("God doesn't hear Jewish prayers"). The rise of a fairly aggressive Evangelical movement may have exacerbated the problem, but anti-Jewish sentiments have been with us since the early days of the American religious enterprise and, obviously, is with us today, expressed either by our obtuseness or by indifference. So, if only for the sanctification of Christian people who may be captive to a cultural anti-Jewish sentiment, we should address the issues.

One of the serious problems we face as Christians is the alleged anti-Jewish statements in the Gospels, Mark, Matthew, Luke and John.[2] The Gospels, all written some time between 60 A.D. and the dawning of the second century, may have been influenced by Jewish-Christian conflict and, of course, by a desire to accommodate to the gentile world. Matthew's Jewish-Christian community was no doubt assailed by a neighboring Jewish synagogue.[3] At least one strand of Johanine material reflects a similar conflict.[4] As a result both Gospels are strident toward "the Jews." And Luke, writing for a gentile audience, clearly blames Jewish leadership for the death of Christ as also does Mark.[5] Now the Gospels have shaped Christian minds for centuries, especially as liturgical readings during annual celebrations of "Holy Week." So naturally, the Gospels have promoted anti-Jewish sentiments in Christian communities. Though we can explain how and why hostility toward the Jews was written into the Gospels, such explanations do not ease the problem; they seldom trickle down to local parishes. In spite of enlightened criticism of the Gospels, scripturally supported anti-Jewish sentiments are still very much a problem. Of late it may be heightened by renewed assertions of

Biblical authority both from neo-fundamentalist groups and from widespread Barthian theology. If the Gospels are the "Word of God," then God appears to lay blame for Christ's death on the Jewish community.

In the second half of the twentieth century, the problem of anti-Jewish sentiment in Christian communities is peculiarly urgent. For now we preach in the shadow of the Jewish holocaust, an event of such appalling calculated cruelty as to call the gospel itself into question. In Arthur Miller's **After the Fall**, the action of the play takes place on a bare multi-leveled stage which represents different levels of memory in the mind of a man named Quentin. But at the back of the stage "rising above--and dominating the stage is the blasted stone tower of a German concentration camp," a symbol of the Jewish holocaust in human memory. Throughout the two-act drama, Quentin speaks of the dark tower; he senses that the tower questions him: "'What do you believe as true as this?' Yes! Believers built this, maybe that's the fright--and I, without belief, stand here disarmed." And later, he admits: "What is the cure? Who can be innocent again on this mountain of skulls? . . . our hearts have cut these stones! And what's the cure?"[6] Christian preachers must stand before the fact of the Jewish holocaust and ask if a faith scribbled down in anti-Jewish Gospels can offer a "cure" or be "as true as this?" Somehow or other we must speak so that congregations may consider the deep issues of what is often termed "Jewish-Christian dialogue," a dialogue that takes place these days in the shadow of the same dark tower.

II. HOMILETIC THEOLOGY: A PROBLEM

Again, let us pose the question: Why do we not preach Romans 9-11? In part, our homiletic traditions may hamper us. Many of us who preach were taught to distill topics from one-verse texts, a procedure that permits an interpreter to expound on "Everyone who calls upon the name of the Lord will be saved" (10:13) without even mentioning the subject of Jewish faith, or to take a single verse such as "They were broken off because of their unbelief, but you stand fast only through faith" (11:20) and turn it into a gloating Christian triumphalism. Even if we have been trained to preach pericopes, it is possible for a preacher to interpret Rom 10:8b-13 (skipping v. 12) as a text for Christians, or to expatiate on the mysteries of God's providence in Rom 11:36-39 without reference to issues of Jew and Gentile.[7] Such preaching may reflect an attitude, namely, that the Jewish community, unresponsive to Jesus, has been relegated to the past tense. For Christians there is no other truth than Jesus the Christ.

Obviously many pastors, singularly those within free church "conversionist" traditions, may tend to regard members of the Jewish community as ripe prospects for Christian evangelism. Such a position seems to be based on a somewhat triumphalist understanding of the finality of Christ and on a relational model of salvation--"a personal relationship to Jesus?" The position is usually buttressed by appeals to texts from Acts, such as "Jesus of Nazareth, whom you crucified, . . . There is salvation in no one else, for there is no name under heaven given among men by which we must be saved" (Acts 4:10-12). In other words, many pastors suppose that the salvation of the Jews will only be posssible through conversion to Christ, Christian baptism, and church affiliation.[8] So our tendency toward what has been termed "Christomonism" seems to consign the Jewish community to the category of unbelief; it is an unbelieving "other religion" to be distinguished from true faith, namely faith in Jesus the Christ alone. They had their chance to respond to Jesus Christ and they blew it; the stone they rejected is God's cornerstone on which our churches have been built.

Such a position can only be maintained by a docetic Christology that is asserted at the expense of the Hebrew Scriptures; it smacks of the Marcionite heresy. To suppose that Jews are unbelievers or, worse, apostate believers can only be pushed by denying the obvious Jewishness of Jesus and the status of the Hebrew Bible in the life of our churches. As is well -known, it is almost impossible to locate any teaching of Jesus that is not in continuity with the Hebrew Scriptures.[9] The somewhat Lutheran shibboleth to the effect that Jesus displays a marked antithesis to the law is difficult to sustain, and may be based on a misreading of the Pauline Letters.[10] Clearly, Jesus was a child of Israel. Moreover, both the narrative structure of our faith and its mythic foundations are an inheritance from Israel, from Israel's story and from the great myths recorded in Genesis 1-11. Likewise, the shape of Christian eschatology is largely a Jewish gift; the book of Revelation's vision of the holy city draws heavily on the prophet Ezekiel. To deny our inheritance, the thought of the Hebrew Scriptures, is to deform Christianity. Authentic Christianity is obviously much more than a Jesus cult dishing up a gnostic salvation from the world.

If we are to preach from Romans 9-11, we will have to brood over Paul's emphatic "All Israel will be saved" (11:26), even if it means rethinking our own Christological assumptions. While we may not wish to end up in a two-path, law and free grace, optional ways to salvation scheme,[11] we will have to reconsider what we mean by "salvation," by "limited atonement," and by "the finality of Christ." Some Christian notions of salvation, formed by an Augustinian Western tradition, may have to be amended in the direction of the Eastern tradition, which seems to work on a narrative line toward a universal eschatological future. As for the finality of Christ, we can affirm that it in no way abrogates the God of Israel or the salvation promised Israel. Revelation in Christ is revelation of the nature of the God of Israel and is assuredly not antithetical to Israel's faith.

III. THE PASSAGE: ROMANS 11: 25-32

Let us suppose that we will preach Rom 11:25-32, a passage which appropriately begins "I don't want you to be ignorant of this mystery, brothers [and sisters], lest you be wised-up in your own eyes." The passage appears to be addressing directly a Christian congregation. My translation of the passage would run as follows:

> 25. I don't want you to be ignorant of this mystery, brothers [and sisters], lest you be wised-up in your own eyes: a hardening has happened to Israel in part until the full complement of Gentiles has come in. 26. Then all Israel will be saved, as it is written:
>
> "The Deliverer will come out of Zion;
> He will turn godlessness away from Jacob.
> 27. And this is my covenant with them:
> (when) I will take away their sins."
>
> 28. On the one hand, in view of the gospel, they are enemies for your sake; but, on the other hand, in view of election, they are loved for the sake of the Fathers. 29. For God's gifts and calling are irrevocable. 30. Just as you, who once disobeyed God, have now received mercy because of their disobedience; 31. so they, though disobedient now because of the

mercy shown you, will also receive mercy. 32. For God locked all in disobedience in order to show mercy to all.

Some exegetical notes may be in order because to translate the somewhat cryptic Greek of the passage is to be confronted with some difficult theological decisions.

Verse 25

The opening phrase, "I don't want you to be ignorant . . . " is a familiar Pauline gambit; see 1 Cor 10:1; 12:1; 2 Cor 1:8; 1 Thes 4:13. The words "this mystery" apparently refer to God's plan of salvation which, now, has been openly revealed in Christ Jesus. Perhaps Paul's opponents may have a somewhat exclusive mystery cult mentality, prompting his use of "mystery." Paul notes a "know-it-all" tendency among them.

The phrase "in part" poses a problem: Does it modify "Israel" or "hardening?" Has only part of Israel refused Jesus Christ or is the "hardening" only partial and, thus, not permament. Though I favor the second reading, my translation retains the ambiguity. The tense of "has happened" probably implies divine action.

In v. 25b, the sentence ends, "until the full complement of Gentiles has come in." The phrase "come in" is almost a technical term, and probably refers to the sphere of salvation under God's rule. I have used the word "complement" which might imply a limited number; it does not. The emphasis is rather clearly on "full." The passage is not counting noses, but rather thinking in terms of the whole gentile world and the whole Jewish world (see "all Israel" in v. 26a).

Verses 26-27

The quotation v. 26b-27 is a composite of LXX texts from Isa 59:20 and Isa 27:9 with almost no alteration, except that Paul changes "to Zion" in Isa 59:20 to "out of Zion" which of course, fits his theological agenda. Paul appears to identify the "Deliverer" as Christ.

Verse 27 might be paraphrased "This will be the fulfilling of my covenant with them: I will take away their sins"--the word "when" from the LXX is somewhat awkward. Does Paul's appeal to Scripture indicate that he is dealing with Jewish-Christians?

Verses 28-29

In v. 28, Paul is contrasting perspectives, ways of looking at the Jewish world. In rejecting the gospel message of Christ, the Jewish world is in enmity with the gentile Christian world. But, in view of the covenant promises given to patriarchs of Israel, they are a people chosen by God.

The real problem is with v. 31. Does the verse imply (1) that Jews will be saved through the agency of the Christian community, or (2) that Jews will receive mercy through forgiveness shown them by Christians, or (3) that the Jews will receive free mercy even as have Christians?[12] The text *per se* cannot answer our questions; a theological judgment is required. Verse 32, however, would seem to support option three: "All are bound in disobedience that God may show mercy to all."

IV. MOVING TOWARD A SERMON

Elsewhere I have written that we do *not* actually preach from Bible passages. Instead, as we study a passage, an analogous pattern of *contemporary* understanding will form in consciousness. We preach from a contemporary structure of understanding.[13] So let us examine the structure of understanding we have achieved:

(1) Prologue: We are addressed because we could be ignorant "know-it-alls" blindly anti-Jewish.

(2) Statement: "All Israel will be saved." Their temporary "hardening" has permitted the gentile mission which brought the gospel to us.

(3) Scripture: Our Savior, Jesus Christ, has come "out of Zion." We recollect the Jewishness of Jesus.

(4) Discussion:
- (a) God loves Israel and will keep covenant promises with Israel even though we may view Israel as opposed to the gospel.
- (b) All have sinned and all will be shown mercy by God. Therefore, even as we have been given free mercy, so also will Israel.

The problem we face is where to enter the structural understanding that we have in consciousness. We could, of course, begin where the passage begins with a diagnosis of our ignorance and arrogance, but wise preachers do not commence a sermon with diatribe. Probably we will want to begin by hearing Paul's bold, flat-out assertion, "All Israel will be saved," because it will raise the issues nicely. Instead of a finished sermon, examine the following semi-developed "sketch" for a sermon:

V. A SERMON SKETCH

Introduction: There's an old story about a man who shows up at the gate of heaven. The man smiles confidently and shouts out, "Well, I'm here!" To which a great voice from heaven replies: "And where are all the others?" The story jars us; it shakes all our well-worn notions of personal salvation, the idea that we stand before God one by one. But suppose the story were rewritten a little so that, when the man shouts, "I'm here!," the voice from heaven replies,"Where are all your Jewish brothers and sisters?" We would be doubly shocked. We imagine God's kingdom filled with well-scrubbed Christian souls, but the Bible does not. "All Israel will be saved," shouts Paul, "All Israel will be saved."

(1) *The claim is absolute: "All Israel will be saved!"* St. Paul is emphatic. His words come as a slap to our over-confident Christianity. We're saved, we say, and regard our Jewish neighbors as being in deep trouble with God. After all, once upon a time we stood up in church and declared ourselves: "I believe in Jesus Christ," we said. They haven't. We've been baptized in the name of the Lord Jesus. They haven't. So how on earth can they expect to be saved? What's more if you try to collar them and talk about Jesus all you are apt to get is a hurt look or a deaf ear: they just won't listen. The blunt truth is:

We believe in Jesus and they don't; they're unbelievers. And yet, when we flip the pages of our New Testament what do we get? "All Israel will be saved," says Paul. His words are emphatic.

(2) *Of course, maybe Paul is trying to change our minds.* "I don't want you to be ignorant," he says addressing us Christians. I don't want you to think you are know-it-alls when you're not. Well, maybe he's got our number. We've certainly been smug, haven't we? We've treated our Jewish neighbors as if they were unbelievers or, worse, enemies of God, or still worse, Jesus killers! We seldom see our anti-Jewishness, but it's there. So the shadow of the Holocaust falls on our lives; six million Jews and many millions of non-Jews slaughtered in concentration camps. Could the carnage have happened without the compliance of Christians? (Describe Arthur Miller scene: "Who can be innocent? . . . Our hearts have cut these stones.") Maybe that's what Paul is trying to cure; our anti-Jewish feelings. "I write so you will not be ignorant," says Paul. He speaks to us now.

(3) Do you begin to see what we've done? *Though there is only one God, we've tried to build a two-God world*--there's the Jewish God and then there's our God who is Jesus Christ. Isn't there an old story that explains why camels seem to walk around with a supercilious smirk: there are a hundred names for God but, according to the story, the camel alone knows the right one. Well we have been supercilious. We know God's name, Jesus Christ, and everyone else in the world is pagan, including the Jews. Remember it was a Christian leader a few years ago who stated baldly, "God doesn't hear Jewish prayers!" But how can we get away with it: our Lord Jesus was a Jew and his God was the God of Abraham and Sarah, of Isaac and Jacob. We try to split the Bible in two, but it can't be done. There is only one God., the God of Israel, and by grace we have been let in on God's glory.

(4) *Well, the one God's name is Mercy!* After all isn't that what we see at the cross? Faithful mercy. For on the cross Christ was crucified by the whole human world--a Jewish and a gentile world! Before the cross of Christ we share a common guilt, a guilt that runs through our politics, our military, our religious institutions. Yes, there was Jewish stiff-necked pride, but there was also anti-Jewishness on the part of Rome's gentile leaders. Yet what was it Christ said, "Father, forgive them. They don't know what they're doing!" (Illustration: Church in western state with a mural of the crowd around the cross--Roman soldiers, Jewish crowds, frightened disciples scurrying for their lives. But members of the congregation posed for all of the faces in the picture.) So on the cross you can see clearly, exactly what Paul says, "*All* have been fixed in guilt that all may be forgiven. Take a long look at the cross and see: the judgment, yes, and the great absolution given by God. Our God's name is mercy."

(5) *So guess what? We can count on God. God's mercy will never fail.* Yes, we have been forgiven in the name of Jesus Christ, but so have all our Jewish brothers and sisters--all alike forgiven. And it isn't really a question of whether we respond or not; can our little decisions determine God's love? No, God is ever faithful. For God has created us, God has called us to be a special people. God will not turn away from love. Did not God promise Israel a great salvation? God will not go back on promises. As Paul says, All will be saved! And God has promised in Christ Jesus to be our God, God will not waver. God is constant. (Illustration: Poster showing all the people of earth, from every race and nation, all gathered together. The caption: "Promises, Promises.") Promises, promises but only one God, the God of Abraham and Sarah and Isaac and yes, of course , the God disclosed in Jesus Christ. We can count on the faithfulness of God, the one God. "All," says Paul, "all have been forgiven. All will be saved."

Conclusion: So where are we? We're in a world where millions of Jews and non-Jews perished in concentration camps and wars: we Christians were there. We are in a world where Jesus was strung up to die; we were all there, Jews, Gentiles, Christians. But thank God we are in a world overruled by the faithfulness of God. The name of the God is mercy. We live in mercy, all of us, all the many different children of God.

Please notice that the sermon sketch has embodied the structural features of the passage. Verse 26 shows up in the first move and vv. 25 and 28a in the second (where they are placed in the shadow of the Holocaust). The third move picks up the one God theme from vv. 26b-27. Verse 32 figures in move four. Whereas vv. 28b-29 are woven into the final move. So though the sermon doesn't talk *about* the scriptural passage or quote from the text extensively, nevertheless the passage forms in the sermon sketch. Biblical preaching need not talk about biblical texts, but rather, can "play" within the structures of meaning that texts form in our contemporary understanding.

Let us analyze the pattern of the sermon in more detail.

The Introduction attempts to address the tacit "theology" of many American protestant congregations, namely, personal salvation as getting into heaven. While a doubled story is not normally a good idea within an Introduction, here it is deliberately used, first to counter the personal paradigm, and second to introduce Paul's contention, "All Israel will be saved." Should a congregation giggle over the man's brashness, the giggle will help to discard the position being represented.

In the first move we articulate Christian shock at the very notion that Jews will be saved. The move is deliberately written to *imitate* reactions to hearing Paul's words. Thus the move has a specific "point of view." We do not talk about our churchly reactions, we do them.

The second move incorporates much more self-awareness; we realize and, indeed, acknowledge our ignorance--"We've certainly been smug, haven't we?" On top of the admission, we begin to see our implicit anti-Jewishness and do so, what's more, in the shadow of the Holocaust. Invoking the images of the Holocaust will not be easy; Americans cling tenaciously to the illusion of national innocence. Here the vivid scene from Arthur Miller will give graphic representation to lurking cultural memory.

In the third move we sense more deeply our theological error. Discussions of Marcion might not grip an average congregation, but the issues are represented through the two-God *though there is only one* theme.The deliberate use of the camel citation tends to make our arrogance absurd and, therefore, easier to discard. Thereafter we appeal to the Jewishness of Jesus who is "*out of* Zion." So, in a sense, we are reduplicating the strategy that may live behind Paul's use of the quotations from the Septuagint.

The fourth move is tricky. Here we appeal to the revelation in Jesus Christ crucified which is often the point of division between Christians and Jews. But in the move the cross is used to establish a common guilt--of both Jew and Gentile--and yet, at the same time, a common mercy. So, in the move, we are preaching the declarative statement in v. 32. "All are bound in disobedience that all may receive mercy." The illustration locates Christians in the crowd around the cross. Because this is a familiar rhetorical strategy that Christians have heard before in sermons, it should function nicely.

The final move works from vv. 28-29. Here we correct the heavenly image from the Introduction and depict God's salvation as reconciliation, a reconciliation of all people with each other and with God (see the "poster" illustration). We have all received eschatological promises, both Christians and Jews; we affirm that God's promises will be. The images in the move not only pick up the idea of God's faithfulness to promises, but serve to counter the getting to heaven image with which we began the sermon.

In the Conclusion we gather images--the concentration camp and the cross are deliberately drawn together but, in the mercy of God, are replaced by a picture of a new, redeemed humanity, the "children of God."

Notice that the sermon does not follow the sequence of the Romans passage. Though all facets of the passage form within the sermon, the sequence from Romans has been replotted.[14] We do not attempt to dissuade a congregation by formal logic. Instead the plot of our sermon is a journey from Christian prejudice toward a wider vision of salvation. The logic of the sermon is a rhetorical logic of realization through images.[15] Notice the use of images: the man at heaven's gate, the concentration camp, the camel, the mural of the crowd at the cross, the poster of a reconciled humanity. People nowadays think things through in relation to formed symbols and images in consciousness. Thus, preaching must often be *through* images.

VI. THE PROBLEM OF UNIVERSALISM

For some Christians, the big problem with preaching on Romans 9-11 is that old bug-a-boo "universalism." If, as Paul says, "All are bound in disobedience so that God may show mercy to all," isn't Paul treading on the thin, dangerous edge of universalism? While we may admit grudgingly that God wants to save all us human sinners, what about our repentance and what about believing--do they count for nothing?

The question of universalism is a question peculiarly connected with what might be termed "vertical" models of salvation, models connected with our status before God and the possibility of a future life after some sort of personal "judgment day." Rather clearly, Paul's images appear to be somewhat more "horizontal" and are associated with God's anticipated new aeon which, in view of the resurrection of Jesus Christ, is imminent. While Paul does not use the term "Kingdom of God," he obviously expects a new order; his thought is apocalyptic.[16] In other words, in Paul's thought, salvation is a social vision.

Of course, the image of the kingdom, an image of social salvation, can be traced from the early "promised land" expectations, to the time of the monarchy, through the crisis of exile and the hopes of restoration, all the way to the final impressionistic depiction of the "Holy City" that fills the final pages of Revelation.[17] Such an image clearly animates the preaching of Jesus as well as the hope of early Christian communities; the Kingdom, God's new aeon, was at hand.

Now, it can be argued that Jesus seems to have altered the image of the Kingdom in two ways: he rejects its exclusive character and he disconnects it from the strands of Jewish triumphalism.[18] Certainly Jesus seems to have populated the Kingdom with all kinds of social rejects. Not only did he "eat and drink with sinners," thus proleptically celebrating a very different sort of messianic banquet, but many of his parables contend against exclusive definitions of the Kingdom, as for example the parables of the Great Feast and of the Leaven.[19] As for the idea that the Kingdom would be realized through the triumph of Israel, in the parable of the Mustard Seed he replaces the symbol of Israel's greatness, the towering Lebanese cedar (Ezek 17:22-24), with a lowly often rejected weed.[20] Nevertheless, Jesus' gospel was a promise of God's new order, an eschatological vision of social salvation.

Obviously, when Romans 9-11 anticipates the salvation of both the Jewish and the gentile worlds, Paul is articulating a similar social vision. He is looking to God's future purposes; a quite inclusive new order of reconciled humanity. Though indeed all have been disobedient, as the cross demonstrates, God has mercy for all, as the cross also demonstrates--"While we were yet sinners Christ died for us" (Rom 5:8). Thus in the wide largess of God's good mercy, Paul can say "all" emphatically, three times in a scant seven verses!

Of course, Paul may also reject the incipient triumphalism of both Jewish and Christian communities. The world will be saved neither by the triumph of Israel nor of the Church--"Let who would boast, boast of the Lord" (1 Cor 1:31). Salvation is God's promise and God's achievement. No wonder that immediately following Romans 11:25-32, Paul all but sings out a final doxology: "O the depth of the riches and wisdom and knowledge of God! How unsearchable are God's judgments and how inscrutable God's ways! . . . To God be glory for ever. Amen."[21]

NOTES

1. Actually, passages from Romans 9-11 are listed as Sunday readings four times in the Catholic lectionary and a similar four times in the new "Common Lectionary." The passages listed, however, include Rom 9:1-5; 10:8-13; 11:13-15, 29-32; and the concluding doxology from 11:33-36. Because 10:8-13 and the doxology can be preached without reference to the issue of Jewish-Christian relations, out of a total listing of around five hundred lections the subject will arise only twice.

2. See general discussion by Samuel Sandmel in the **Interpreter's Dictionary of the Bible**, Supplementary Volume. (Nashville: Abingdon, 1976), 477-478. Also see R. Reuther, **Faith and Fratricide: The Theological Roots of Anti-Semitism** (NY: Seabury, 1974) with an introductory essay by Gregory Baum.

3. Douglas R. A. Hare, **The Theme of Jewish Persecution in the Gospel according to St. Matthew** (Cambridge: Cambridge University Press, 1967).

4. J. Louis Martyn, **History and Theology in the Fourth Gospel** (Nashville, TN: Abingdon, 1968) Part I.

5. See discussion in G. S. Sloyan, **Jesus on Trial** (Philadelphia: Fortress, 1973), particularly notice his candor in a final concluding chapter.

6. Arthur Miller, **After the Fall** (New York: Bantam Books, 1965) 1, 21, 162.

7. Unfortunately, I have done so; see "Cast and Plot," *Pulpit Digest*, LXI (1981) 53-56.

8. Oddly enough the same position shows up in a great commentary on Romans; see W. Sanday and A. C. Headlam, **The Epistle to the Romans** (Edinburgh: T. & T. Clark, 1964 [1895]) 336: "So the words of St. Paul mean simply this. The people of Israel as a nation . . . shall be united with the Christian Church."

9. See discussion in my **Preaching Jesus Christ** (Philadelphia: Fortress Press, 1988). Chapter 3.

10. See the developed argument by E. P. Sanders in **Jesus and Judaism** (Philadelphia: Fortress, 1985) particularly in his Introduction and in Chapter 9 on The Law.

11. K. Stendahl seems to approach such a position in his **Paul Among Jews and Gentiles and other essays** (Philadelphia: Fortress, 1976) as does Paul M. van Buren in his remarkable **A Theology of the Jewish-Christian Reality**, Parts 1 and 2 (San Francisco: Harper & Row, 1980, 1983). See articles in this issue for various interpretations of this question.

12. Readers may wish to compare different translations of the text. The KJ reads "that through your mercy they may also receive mercy," a reading which would seem to support either option (1) or (2). The RSV has "that by the mercy shown to you they may also receive mercy," a somewhat ambigious translation. Most recent translations--Jerusalem, NAB, NIV, NEB--would clearly support option (3). For careful discussion of grammatical issues, see C. E. B. Cranfield, **The Epistle to the Romans,** II (Edinburgh: T. & T. Clark, 1981) 582-588.

13. See my **Homiletic** (Philadelphia: Fortress Press, 1987) Chapter 19.

14. See the discussion of plotting in **Homiletic,** 285-93.

15. Rational philosophical argumentation simply will not function in sermons these days, if it ever did. Instead we set up a kind of transformational "logic." For discussion of such rhetorical logic, see the remarkable study by Ch. Perelman and L. Olbrechts-Tyteca, **The New Rhetoric: A Treatise on Argumentation** (Notre Dame, IN: Notre Dame University Press, 1969).

16. I concur here with J. Christiaan Beker, **Paul the Apostle** (Philadelphia: Fortress Press, 1980), see chapters 15 and 16 in particular.

17. A splendid book by Donald E. Gowan, **Eschatology in the Old Testament** (Philadelphia: Fortress Press, 1986) not only traces the gradual formation of the Bible's eschatological vision but discusses its primary features -- the transformation of society, human nature, and nature.

18. While John Bright's **The Kingdom of God** (Nashville: Abingdon-Cokesbury, 1953) traced the forming of the content of the Kingdom, he seems to suggest that the Kingdom image is given a personal twist by Jesus, a position which I do not suppose can be substantiated.

19. See Robert W. Funk, **Language, Hermeneutic, and Word of God** (New York: Harper & Row, 1966), Chapters 6 and 7 on the Great Feast, and his **Jesus as Precursor** (Missoula, MT: Scholars Press, 1975) 51-72 on the Parable of the Leaven.

20. Robert W. Funk, "The Looking-Glass Tree for the Birds," *Interpretation* 27 (1973) 3-9; see also John Riches, **Jesus and the Transformation of Judaism** (New York: Seabury Press, 1982), Chapter 5 "Jesus' Preaching of the Kingdom."

21. Text from **An Inclusive Language Lectionary. Readings for Year A** Copyright 1983 Division of Education and Ministry, National Council of Churches in the U.S.A.

THE CONTRIBUTORS

MARKUS BARTH	University of Basel, Basel, Switzerland
DAVID G. BUTTRICK	The Divinity School, Vanderbilt University, Nashville, Tennessee
BRUCE CHILTON	Bard College, Annendale-on-Hudson, New York
SCOTT HAFEMANN	Gordon-Conwell Theological Seminary, South Hamilton, Massachusetts
STEPHEN R. HAYNES	University of Durham, Durham, England
I. JOHN HESSELINK	Western Theological Seminary, Holland, Michigan
BEN F. MEYER	McMaster University, Hamilton, Ontario, Canada
DONALD G. MILLER	Gaithersburg, Maryland
H.-MARTIN RUMSCHEIDT	Atlantic School of Theology, Halifax, Nova Scotia, Canada